Managing Continuing Professional Development in Schools

edited by

Harry Tomlinson

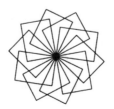

British Educational Management & Administration Society

P·C·P
Paul Chapman
Publishing Ltd

Copyright © 1997 BEMAS (British Educational Management and Administration Society)

Paul Chapman Publishing Ltd
144 Liverpool Road
London N1 1LA

British Library Cataloguing in Publication Data
Managing continuous professional development in schools. –
    (BEMAS series in education management)
    1. Teachers – In-service training – Great Britain 2. Career
    development
    I. Tomlinson, Harry, 1939–

371.1'2'0941

ISBN 1 85396 345 3

Typeset by Dorwyn Ltd, Rowlands Castle, Hants
Printed and bound in Great Britain

A B C D E F G H   9 8 7

Contents

Notes on Contributors   ix

Preface   xiii

1   Building on the Past: New Opportunities for the Profession   1
Diane Gaunt

2   Continuing Professional Development in the Professions   13
Harry Tomlinson

3   Teaching as a Profession: The Role of Professional Development   27
Viv Garrett with Colin Bowles

4   Values and Ethical Issues in the Effective Management of Continuing Professional Development   40
Pauline Smith

5   Privatising Policies and Marketising Relationships: Continuing Professional Development in Schools, LEAs and Higher Education   52
Sue Law

6   Initial Teacher Training: Providing a Foundation for a Career   66
David Turner

7   The Early Years of the Teacher's Career: Induction into the Profession   79
Ken Jones and Peter Stammers

8   Energising Middle Management   91
Jeff Jones and Fergus O'Sullivan

9   The Introduction of the National Professional Qualification for Headship   108
Terry Creissen

10   HEADLAMP – A Local Experience in Partnership   120
Hugh Busher and Liz Paxton

11   Continuing Professional Development for School Leaders: the   135
     UK and North American Experience
     Gary Holmes and Austin Harding

12   Continuing Professional Development: the European Experience   147
     Joanna Le Métais

13   Building on Success: Professional Development in the Future   161
     Brian Fidler

Bibliography   176

Index   189

For Berry and Kate

Notes on Contributors

Colin Bowles is a senior manager at Rawlins Community College in Leicestershire (14–18 years). His responsibilities cover most aspects of staffing, appointments, contracts, staff development, appraisal and job descriptions. The case study of Rawlins started life as part of his MA (Professional Studies) at the University of Leicester, which will be completed during the next year.

Hugh Busher is a lecturer in the Division of Education, University of Sheffield. After teaching in comprehensive schools he went to the University of Leeds from 1985 to 1987. He then moved to Loughborough University where he focused much of his work on leadership, management and policy making in schools as organisations, and coordinated a Headteacher Management Training Programme in partnership with Leicestershire LEA. He is Series Editor for BEMAS books and coordinator of the British Educational Research Association's Special Interest Group on Leading and Managing Schools and Colleges. His most recent co-edited publications have been *Managing Educational Institutions: Reviewing Development and Learning* and *Managing Teachers as Professionals in Schools.*

Terry Creissen is Principal of The Colne Community School, a large grant maintained comprehensive school outside Colchester, Essex. He is a Board Member of the Teacher Training Agency and former Chair of its Continuing Development Committee. In this capacity he has been on the advisory group for the new National Professional Qualification for Headteachers. He began his career as a music teacher in Cornwall, Slough and Luton before moving into senior management roles in Harlow and Brightlingsea, Essex. He has recently completed an MBA with Leeds Metropolitan University and has researched this topic for his dissertation.

Brian Fidler teaches and researches at the University of Reading where he is senior lecturer and course leader for the MSc Managing School Improvement. He was editor with Myra McCulloch of *Improving Initial Teacher Training? New roles for teachers, schools and higher education* and his most recent BEMAS book is *Strategic Planning for School Improvement* (1996). He is editor of *School Leadership and Management*, the international journal of leadership and school improvement. He has chaired the BEMAS Improving

School Management Initiative working party which examined ways of improving school management to improve education in schools.

Viv Garrett is a lecturer in Education Management at Sheffield Hallam University. She entered the world of higher education in 1990 after working in the schools sector for over 20 years, most recently as a deputy head in a large comprehensive school. She currently coordinates Sheffield Hallam's award-bearing programmes in Education Management, and, with her colleagues in the Centre for Education Management and Administration (CEMA), is involved in the design and delivery of management development programmes for schools and colleges. She was co-author of Sheffield Hallam University's distance learning packs: *Managing Staff Development in Schools*, and its sister volume, *Managing Staff Development in Colleges*. Viv is Secretary of BEMAS.

Diane Gaunt is Principal Lecturer in Continuing Professional Development at Oxford Brookes University. She has contributed to books on education for the professions and partnership in teacher education. Currently she chairs the In-Service and Professional Development Association (IPDA).

Austin Harding (BA, MEd, University of Leeds) taught in primary and secondary schools before becoming Senior Lecturer in Education at Leeds Metropolitan University. Now retired, he is a freelance consultant and educational researcher.

Gary Holmes is Head of the School of Professional Education and Development at Leeds Metropolitan University. He was formerly Head of the Oxford Centre for Education Management at Oxford Brookes and is Visiting Professor in Educational Administration at the University of Victoria (British Columbia). He has written extensively on school leadership and publications include *Essential School Leadership* (1993), Kogan Page.

Jeff Jones is currently Inspector for Professional Development and Head of Governor Services for Hereford and Worcester LEA. Formerly a secondary school teacher and middle manager, Dr Jones has held the posts of Director of In-Service Training for teachers and advisory teachers, and Inspector for Assessment and Appraisal, before taking up his present post in 1995. He has written extensively in the areas of professional development, appraisal, assessment and on a range of management issues. His doctoral thesis centred on the management of staff development in schools. He is currently Visiting Professor in Education Management at the University of Wolverhampton. He is trainer and consultant for schools in the UK and abroad.

Ken Jones is Principal Lecturer and In-Service Coordinator at Swansea Institute of Higher Education. He has published, with others, two books: *Staff Development in Secondary Schools*, and *Staff Development in Primary Schools*, and has for a number of years worked closely with schools on the management of continuing professional development. He has led the evaluation of a number of educational initiatives and has been involved in research projects including the induction of qualified teachers, teacher appraisal and effective school management. He is coordinator of the Institute's MEd programme. He is a member of the Editorial Board of the British Journal of In-service Education and on the committee of IPDA.

Sue Law is Professor of Education and Head of the Department of Secondary and Tertiary Education at Nottingham Trent University. Until recently, as Director of In-service Education at Keele University, she was responsible for continuing professional development, taught higher degrees and INSET. She has been Chair of the In-service Professional Development Association (IPDA) and researches into teacher development, education management and INSET education policy. She is currently directing nationally-focused research (the Effective Educators Project) into the impact of school-managed INSET and CPD on school improvement and pupil learning.

Joanna Le Métais is Deputy Director of Information at the NFER and Head of the Education Policy Information Centre for Europe, which includes the EURYDICE national unit for England, Wales and Northern Ireland. She undertakes comparative research across a range of education policy areas and is the author of numerous publications on education policy in the UK and elsewhere in Europe. She is currently conducting an international review of curriculum and assessment frameworks in 15 countries.

Fergus O'Sullivan has been an LEA education officer, senior county inspector, county INSET coordinator and deputy headteacher in a large city comprehensive school. He has taught in schools and colleges for twenty years and has been active in curriculum and staff development at a local and national level. His interests are management development, particularly competency development for middle managers, research into the 'learning organisation' approach to organisational development in times of rapid change, and the use of information technology and the Internet in supported distance learning for continuing professional development. He is currently Vice Chairman of IPDA.

Liz Paxton is an Education Officer with Leicestershire LEA. Following over seven years of headship she joined the local authority in 1991 as Adviser for Management Development, a responsibility which she has retained and developed since then. A particular focus for her work has been the development of a comprehensive framework for headteacher support and development. Implementing this framework has involved working in partnership with a range of organisations including the Headlamp partnership with Loughborough University. Liz contributes occasional articles to BEMAS and other journals.

Pauline Smith is Head of Continuing Professional Development at Crewe School of Education, Manchester Metropolitan University, which has successfully developed collaborative links with neighbouring local education authorities, particularly in relation to mentor NQT developments and management training initiatives, including HEADLAMP. She has recently evaluated the implementation of appraisal in Oldham and Manchester schools, and is a registered OFSTED Inspector. She is co-editor of 'Mentoring in the Effective School' and is Chair of BEMAS Management Development Committee and a member of the IPDA Committee.

Peter Stammers taught in inner city primary schools in London and set up the first Teachers' Centre in Lewisham in 1972. From 1973 he ran the induction programmes for primary and secondary teachers in Lewisham and set up the 'mentoring' professional tutors and their professional support programme. Now Head of INSET at Kingston University, Peter Stammers has developed the tutors' professional support programme that was born in the crucible of the inner city into a course accredited at Master's level.

Harry Tomlinson is Principal Lecturer in Education Management at Leeds Metropolitan University where he is course tutor for the MBA in Education Management. He has been a headteacher and principal for 18 years in Manchester and Stockport. He has edited three books: *Performance Related Pay in Education*, *The Search for Standards*, and *Education and Training 14–19*. He was Treasurer of the Secondary Heads Association for four years. At present he is Chair of BEMAS and an NPQH Training and Development Centre Manager.

David Turner is Assistant Director (ITE) in the School of Education at Sheffield Hallam University. He has developed and runs a radical 3 year secondary ITT programme which incorporates six secondary routes to QTS in twelve subject areas. He is also responsible for the new primary ITT programmes. He is Vice-Chair of the NUT's Advisory Committee on Teacher Education and worked with the TTA developing the career entry profiles for NQTs. He has written extensively on a variety of topics in the education field including a chapter on The Rise and Fall of the Sheffield LEA 1970–1990.

Preface

This book is particularly well timed in that it provides an opportunity to consider the most significant issue in education management at a major turning point in policy making. A new model of the teacher's career and associated continuing professional development emerged in 1997. The process of further exploration of the implications and implementation will be a challenge until well into the next century.

The Teacher Training Agency (TTA) began the process of consulting on new Qualified Teacher Status (QTS) standards early in 1997. These set out the knowledge, understanding, skills and abilities which teachers must demonstrate before they can be awarded qualified teacher status. Essentially this is a National Professional Qualification for Teaching.

Following this there were consultations on standards for expert teachers. This is a particularly contentious element. Only time will show how this relates to the other, more clearly recognisable standards and career roles. In the TTA Chief Executive's Annual Address in October 1996, Anthea Millet suggested that 'in the future we shall want to examine closely the possibility of a qualification for expert classroom teachers'. The significance of expert teachers' standards is considered in this book. It also addresses what might be described as the missing aspect of the whole TTA model – induction into the profession.

The consultation on standards for Special Educational Needs Co-ordinators (SENCOs) takes place in the summer of 1997.

Consultation on the National Professional Qualification for Subject Leaders (NPQSL) took place between November 1996 and February 1997. This will be particularly significant for the profession. It could be argued that this qualification will be appropriate for the majority of teachers. Most teachers in primary schools exercise a subject leadership role, including deputy heads. In secondary schools the subject leaders are heads of departments. Others who exercise a leadership role at middle management level, both pastoral and cross-curricular responsibilities, will need to be aware of this strong focus on subject leadership in the TTA model for CPD. It represents a clear commitment to focus on improving learning in the classrooms.

The National Professional Qualification for Headship, for aspirant head-teachers, was piloted from January 1997 and is fully operational from September 1997. The consultation on training for serving headteachers, building on the NPQH development work, occurred between November 1996 and February 1997. How this might relate to HEADLAMP funding is still being considered. The implication appears to be that this formal training might be somewhat later in the headship. The language used, expert headteacher, is particularly significant in its implications for the requirement for continuing improvement of performance for headteachers.

What is clearly happening is the establishment of a model of professional lifelong learning, a radically new framework for the continuing professional development of teachers. The Summary of Evidence for the Review of Head-teacher and Teacher Appraisal (1996) of the TTA and OFSTED noted a number of weaknesses in the appraisal system which these new national qualification and standards seek to address. The failure to secure the role of *line manager* as the appraiser has weakened the impact of appraisal on the quality of teaching. *Target setting* for teachers has often failed to focus sharply on improving teacher effectiveness in the classroom. The relationship of appraisal and mentoring to continuing professional development is a theme throughout this book. Appraisal and mentoring are explored in a number of chapters.

The standards for all these roles and qualifications comprise the core purpose, the key areas for development and assessment, professional knowledge and understanding, and skills and abilities. These considerations are embedded in all the chapters of this book, as is the insistent emphasis on school improvement.

Managing Continuing Professional Development in Schools opens with a chapter putting CPD in its historical context, and concludes with a chapter which explores all those developments in terms of their implications for the future of the profession. Throughout there is a commitment to a recognition that the learning of children is central to the personal and professional development of teachers, and that the values underpinning the self-respect that teachers have through their professionalism are serving society extremely well. There is a shared pride in belonging to the teaching profession.

1

Building on the Past: New Opportunities for the Profession

DIANE GAUNT

Changes in the continuing professional development (CPD) of teachers reflect changes taking place in the education system as a whole. A shift in the balance of power is the result of radical changes in philosophy of those controlling funding. Whereas once the professional development needs of individual teachers were seen as paramount, these are now seen as secondary to the needs of schools and the system as a whole which is itself subject to political manipulation. The mid-1980s saw fundamental changes in emphasis in education which were accompanied by alterations in the way that resources for in-service education and training (INSET) were allocated with a move towards short narrowly-focused, curriculum-led training activities. On the positive side more teachers now take part in INSET than was previously possible, but the need to respond to educational innovation has resulted in school-focused activities taking priority. This chapter will chart the increasing government intervention in teachers' professional development and examine the opportunities for the profession likely to result from the emergent policies of the Teacher Training Agency (TTA).

THE INSET POOL

Until the mid-1970s few teachers undertook any courses of study beyond their initial training. In-service education and training was limited to supplementary courses for non-graduate teachers who had completed one or two year initial training courses, advanced courses to enable other teachers to improve their professional qualifications and short courses organised by the local education authorities (LEAs) and Her Majesty's Inspectors (HMI). In the ten years following the 1944 Education Act funding for individual teachers to take long supplementary and advanced courses was restricted to grants up to maximum of £300 (Henderson, 1978), but in 1955 new opportunities were created when a system was introduced to allow LEAs to pool some of the costs of sending teachers on courses lasting one term or a year. Under the scheme LEAs could recoup the full salaries of their seconded teachers and other associated costs. The pool was made up of a contribution from the Ministry of Education, later the Department of Education and Science (DES), and each LEA put in an amount according to a formula which did not take into account how many secondments it had. The pool was not capped in any way and so as the number of secondments rose the cost to central government and to a lesser extent local government rose (Goddard, 1989). There was a distinct binomial distribution of secondees: at one end of the scale there were high-flyers who needed a qualification in order to gain promotion and at the other end were teachers seconded to solve overstaffing problems and those who needed a break from their school and their school from them.

THE JAMES REPORT

The publication of the James Report, *Teacher Education and Training* (DES, 1972a) brought about an enormous expansion of INSET provision. A recommendation was made for the reform of the system of education and training which evidence suggested had been rendered inadequate by an overdependence on initial training and a disregard for continuing professional development. The James Committee described the education and training of teachers as falling into three cycles: the first, personal education; the second, preservice training and induction; the third in-service education and training. They urged that the highest priority be given to the third cycle and pointed out that effective and successful teachers with a high degree of satisfaction with their work tended to be those who had had the benefit of in-service opportunities. They recommended a large expansion of third cycle provision to give every teacher an entitlement to regular in-service education and training equivalent to one term every seven years and eventually every five years in addition to shorter duration activities. This recommendation stemmed from evidence from the teachers' organisations, the colleges and departments of education who would have to provide the courses and the local education authorities (LEAs) who would, in large measure, have to meet the cost. INSET would be managed by a partnership of these major agencies. Expansion of third cycle activities was considered to be 'the quickest, most effective and most economical way of improving the quality of education in the schools and colleges and of raising standards, morale and status of the teaching profession' (DES, 1972a).

The White Paper *Education: A Framework for Expansion* published later in the same year called for a general reorganisation of teacher education. As initial training numbers were to be reduced, establishments were charged with the task of expanding their in-service commitment (DES, 1972b).

Following a recommendation of the James Committee, the Advisory Committee on the Supply and Training of Teachers (ACSTT) was established and in 1974 produced a paper *In-service Education and Training: some considerations* which put forward a career profile illustrating the likely staff development needs of individual teachers at key stages in their professional lives. *Making INSET Work* (ACSTT, 1978) drew attention to the role of the school. It pointed out that INSET should address not only the needs of individual teachers, but also the needs of functional groups in the school and indeed the school as a whole.

Spending through the uncapped in-service pool grew substantially in the immediate post-James years which gave cause for concern at central government level such that secondment funded through the pool was restricted to priority areas: management training for heads and senior teachers, mathematics teaching, special educational needs in ordinary schools, prevocational education and craft, design and technology (DES, 1983 and 1984). The Advisory Committee on the Supply and Education of Teachers which replaced ACSTT emphasised local and national needs in its report *The In-service Education, Training and Professional Development of School Teachers* (ACSET, 1984). As far as funding was concerned, it was recommended that LEAs' budgets for INSET should be based on a target equivalent to about five per cent of their expenditure on teachers' salaries. Shortly after the publication of its 1984 document the Secretary of State, Sir Keith Joseph, announced that ACSET was to be dissolved reportedly in part due to its advice on an increase in resources for INSET being unpalatable (Santinelli, 1985). Whilst a new national body was established for initial teacher education no new organisation was set up for teacher education in general or INSET in particular.

THE LOCAL EDUCATION AUTHORITY TRAINING GRANTS SCHEME (LEATGS)

The draining of the in-service pool was heralded in the White Paper *Better Schools* published in March 1985 which reported that the £100m expenditure by LEAs on INSET was not being used to best advantage. The system was criticised for favouring relatively long courses, notwithstanding that shorter, less traditional activities may be more effective for many purposes (DES, 1985). Training in selected national priority areas had been stimulated by the training grants scheme introduced in 1983–4. The White Paper announced the intention of the DES to introduce a specific new grant to be paid in two parts: one part would be used for national priority areas and the other for locally assessed priorities. Each LEA would continue to be responsible for much in-service training, 'but within a framework which would lead to more effective planning and management of training' (DES, 1985, para 176).

Another Government department became interested in teacher development at the same time as the DES was proposing changes. The Manpower Services Commission had earned a reputation for implementing its initiatives rapidly then monitoring and evaluating them closely and systematically. One month after the publication of *Better Schools* it invited LEAs to submit proposals for support under the TVEI Related Training Grants Scheme (TRIST) which followed the Further Education Unit's (1982) model of curriculum-led staff development and did much to prepare the way for the implementation of the Local Education Authority Training Grants Scheme announced in DES circular 6/86. This circular stated that the main purposes of the new scheme were to:

- promote the professional development of teachers;
- promote more systematic and purposeful planning of INSET;
- encourage more effective management of the teacher force;
- encourage training in national priority areas.

Despite some initial disappointments concerning the level of funding, each LEA set about formulating policy and appointing a designated advisor/inspector or officer for INSET. An HMI report on the first year of the scheme, whilst acknowledging that management of the scheme was still developing and there were some weaknesses, noted that:

> The introduction of the LEATGS has resulted in more systematic approaches to the planning, organisation and delivery of INSET. . . . In general terms INSET is more healthy than it has been at at any time previously. . . . The LEA systems being put into place and gradually refined make them well placed to accommodate the challenge of providing the training necessary to help teachers and lecturers introduce the various changes required by the Education Reform Act.
>
> (DES/HMI, 1989, 3)

In addition to the LEATGS, resources for INSET were provided by Education Support Grants which had come into operation in 1984 for the purchase of materials and equipment, for the training of support staff and governors and for the employment of advisory teachers who acted as agents for change by planning, coordinating, implementing and evaluating INSET. Secondments as advisory teachers offered superb opportunities for first rate teachers to pass on their skills and knowledge to others whilst at the same time exploring a new area of work such that at the end of the secondment, instead of returning to their schools, a substantial proportion obtained new posts in teacher education.

The introduction of the LEATGS overlapped with the implementation of the Teachers' Pay and Conditions Act, 1987 which provided for five non-teaching days annually and certain hours of 'directed time' outside the normal timetable, both of which could be used for INSET.

More teachers than ever were benefiting from continuing professional development opportunities. Under Local Management of Schools (LMS) LEAs devolved a proportion of INSET funds to schools where they were meant to be ring-fenced and not open to virement. Thus the LEATGS led a move towards school-focused training, INSET no longer had to mean going on a course. To a large extent schools and teachers could identify and prioritise their training needs and choose for themselves how best these needs might be met. The events might be for a few hours or a day or more. Teachers provided some of their own INSET, giving recognition to their own expertise, or training might be from the LEA, from higher education or from a growing number of private trainers. A variety of venues were used: schools, teachers' centres, higher education institutions and hotels, largely with catering provided. Many teachers saw this standard of provision as giving them well-deserved parity with other professions whilst others deplored the expenditure on hospitality and would have liked to have diverted the funds to resources for their classrooms.

Reaction to the new INSET arrangements varied. Jones, O'Sullivan and Reid (1987) applauded the involvement of more staff than was previously possible and welcomed the move away from educational theory towards classroom practice and pupil outcomes; they viewed the involvement of teachers as peer educators as 'more egalitarian'. Harland (1987), strongly critical of curriculum-led staff development, took the opposite view and regarded the restriction of funding to categories identified by the DES and LEAs as undermining the professionalism of teachers.

GRANTS FOR EDUCATION SUPPORT AND TRAINING (GEST)

A DES scrutiny of ESGs and LEATGS was undertaken (Glickman and Dale, 1990) and found that both were broadly meeting their declared objectives and were responding to the imperatives of the Education Reform Act 1988 in contributing to the implementation of school government, local financial management and the National Curriculum: however it was reported that this short term emphasis in ERA initiatives had disappointed some teachers by not fulfilling the promise of promoting their professional development. Other criticisms included the fact that the expertise of higher education institutions was not being used to best effect and that the administration of LEATGS was excessively bureaucratic. The authors pointed to the essential complementarity of the two schemes with training provided by the LEATGS and equipment, materials and advisory teachers provided by the ESGs. They recommended that the two be combined within a unitary grant in order to take a broader view of activities and to promote efficiency and economy of operation. By linking and combining activities the overall number of programmes was to be be kept to a minimum, however the authors recommended that 20 per cent of expenditure should be reserved for locally determined priorities. A multiphase rolling programme of projects was recommended to replace the annual review of priorities which had prevented LEAs from planning provision efficiently. The new unitary system came into operation in 1991 under the title of Grants for Education Support and Training (GEST). The local priority element was soon phased out in favour of national priority areas announced in an annual circular. Whilst a large proportion of the funding is devolved to schools the LEAs retain control of funds for designated courses. At first these were all of 20 days duration but many have since been reduced to 10 or 5 days. The overall GEST budget has been reduced since 1991–2 because it no longer provides for further education colleges and grant-maintained schools, but it remains the principal source of funding for CPD and continues to meet with the approval of the Department for Education and Employment (DFEE) and the Treasury in that funds can be targeted by the Secretary of State and their use closely audited.

LOCAL EDUCATION AUTHORITY ADVISORY SERVICES

Each LEA established a framework of support to meet the needs of its teaching staff in response to the introduction of the LEATGS. Teams of advisory teachers worked with advisers whose work was coordinated by a chief adviser or an education officer. Thus there was a whole network of support available from staff with a knowledge and understanding of the region and its schools. The Education Reform Act introduced Local Management of Schools under which INSET moneys were divided between a central fund held by the LEA and budgets delegated to schools. In many parts of the country the introduction of the National Curriculum changed the role of the adviser to one of inspector with a remit to monitor the implementation of the new curriculum and as schools were given more responsibilities for running their own affairs so headteachers became reluctant to second staff as advisory teachers and the effectiveness of the service was further reduced.

With increasing devolution of funds, the role of the LEA in INSET has changed. On the one hand it acts as a broker matching supply and demand, but on the other hand it has to compete with other providers offering activities which schools may or may not wish to purchase. Despite their weakened position the LEAs still retain overall responsibility for the monitoring and evaluation of provision within schools. The creation of unitary authorities will reduce the impact of some advisory services even further, to the extent that their viability may be brought into question.

THE CHANGING ROLE OF HIGHER EDUCATION

The new funding arrangements had a profound effect on higher education. Staff found themselves trading in an INSET market and, if they were to survive, needed to develop new working relationships with LEAs, schools and teachers based on concepts such as partnership, product design and customer care (Gaunt, 1995). Award-bearing courses were redesigned to offer greater flexibility and accessibility to appeal to teachers studying in their own time and often at their own expense. This challenging process involved changing course structures, content, modes of delivery and assessment whilst maintaining academic rigour. Most providers have changed from linear to modular schemes which offer greater scope for individualised programmes of study, flexibility in pace and modes of attendance, a variety of entry and exit points, recognition of prior and parallel learning and credit accumulation and transfer schemes (CATS). Many course elements are assessed through assignments which encourage teachers to research and evaluate their own practice. There is a growing demand from teachers and their employers for the accreditation of short courses and school-based development activities that count towards certificates, diplomas and degrees.

The majority of INSET partnerships grew out of partnerships for initial teacher training (ITT). Schools which provided school experience placements were often repaid with vouchers to attend INSET modules or with a tailored programme of training or consultancy. Experienced teachers who act as mentors for student teachers have generally welcomed their new role and seen their responsibility as a new professional opportunity. The training provided is normally accredited by the higher education partner and can lead to a further qualification bringing the concept of the master teacher advocated by Warnock (1979) closer to reality.

THE TEACHER TRAINING AGENCY

Established by Act of Parliament in September 1994 the Teacher Training Agency (TTA) included among its statutory objectives a contribution to raising the standards of teaching. At first it concerned itself largely with initial teacher training but in March 1995 the Secretary of State discussed with the TTA its involvement in the development of more targeted and effective continuing professional development Three main areas formed the thrust of its preliminary investigation:

- to survey the nature and cost of existing provision;
- to determine national training priorities;
- to consider strategic approaches to managing and focusing CPD.

A MORI survey was commissioned to examine current CPD activity. Three lengthy questionnaires were developed and circulated to teachers, headteachers/INSET coordinators and INSET providers. There appeared to be substantial difference in the perceptions of teachers and their headteachers or INSET coordinators on the extent and usefulness of provision but overall the researchers concluded that 'CPD currently taking place in most schools appears to operate on an *ad hoc* basis with no real linkage across school development planning, personal development planning and teachers' appraisals' (MORI, 1995). This finding once again brings into question the balance between the needs of the school and the needs of the individual. A teacher's appraisal targets may be disregarded if they do not fit neatly into the school development plan. It might then be argued that teacher appraisal and school development planning should be harmonised to facilitate more systematic use of CPD resources, but that would run counter to any notion of an individual teachers' rights to give priority to their own short-term and long-term professional imperatives. The shortcomings of appraisal identified in the survey prompted the Secretary of State to ask the TTA and the Office for Standards in Education (OFSTED) to undertake a review. Morris (1995) cited appraisal as an example of an initiative which had slowed down and lost its way and expected the review to lead to its resuscitation.

In addition to the MORI survey the TTA undertook an extensive consultation with schools, professional and subject associations, higher education institutions, OFSTED and other interested parties on identifying priorities and strategies for targeting funds and formulating longer term strategic approaches to CPD. The initial advice to the Secretary of State submitted in July 1995 was informed by the results of the consultation. The following areas were proposed as national priorities:

- leadership and management of schools;
- heads of department in secondary schools;
- subject coordinators in the primary phase;
- subject knowledge of Key Stage 2 teachers;
- effective teaching in the 14–19 phase;
- the use of IT to improve pupils' achievements;
- effective teaching for early years children;
- special educational needs coordinators.

The first four were identified as the most urgent. The TTA found that although some of these areas were already covered by GEST there was evidence that provision is not always targeted at the right teachers nor are those teachers always given the most appropriate training by the best teachers (TTA, 1995a).

Turning to strategic direction for CPD the consultation identified weaknesses and variation in CPD particularly as resources were not being used to best effect, activities were not sufficiently targeted to meet needs and there was inadequate planning, evaluation and follow-up to ensure a direct impact on teaching and learning. It must be acknowledged that measuring outcomes of professional development in terms of the improved effectiveness is far from straightforward, Burgess *et al.* (1993) cautioned that 'whilst impact in the classroom is said to be the acid test of INSET, the paradox is that it can be very difficult to identify' (p. 170) and went on to point out that 'the literature emphasizes the unreliability of self reports by teachers of changed practice' (p. 172).

The TTA's initial advice concluded with a set of proposals. The first was the setting of national standards of excellence for teachers in key roles in order to provide a more coherent approach to improving teaching quality. It seems unlikely that standards for CPD will be defined in the same way as those for ITT and at present there is little possibility of any involvement with National Vocational Qualifications (NVQs). The key roles were identified as:

- newly qualified teachers;
- expert teachers;
- experts in subject leadership and management;
- experts in school leadership and management.

The concept of a ladder of opportunities is not new. ACSTT (1974) put forward a career profile with a similar structure though with significant differences which reflected an expectation of higher levels of investment including periods of secondment. The proposed framework offered opportunities to teachers at different stages of their careers:

- year 1: induction;
- years 2–5: consolidation;

- years 5–8: orientation;
- years 9–15: advanced studies for new responsibilities;
- mid-career: preparation for top management for a few and 'refreshment' for others.

More recently Day (1993) suggested targeting programmes at 'landmark' stages of intellectual, career and role development and Brighouse (1995) put forward a model which included opportunities for a sabbatical term as a consultant practitioner and provision for teachers entering retirement.

The standards proposed by the TTA are to be developed with groups of practitioners. The new National Professional Qualification for Headteachers will be based on the standards for headship. The standards for expert teacher and subject expert are likely to lead to a revision and standardisation of the content of master's degrees.

The notion of the expert teacher is worthy of comparison with expert practitioners in other professions. Eraut (1994) in a discussion of theories of professional expertise explored the Dreyfus (1979) model of skill acquisition with its five levels: novice, advanced beginner, competent, proficient and expert; each level marked by decreasing reliance on rule-guided learning and an increasing use of intuition based on experience. Benner (1984) applied the model to the professional development of nurses and suggested that competence is the level normally reached after a nurse has been in practice for two to three years. Coincidentally Brighouse (1995), describing the route from beginning teacher to established expert, envisaged teachers accomplishing a master's degree and expert status after five or six years. This would certainly be an ideal situation, newly qualified teachers would bring with them career entry profiles which could be extended to each of the Dreyfus levels but, whilst it is to be hoped that the majority would reach expert status in five years, there will be some who will take a lot longer.

As well as developing national standards the TTA's advice included the recommendation that teachers should take responsibility for developing their knowledge, understanding and skills.

In her reply to this initial advice the Secretary of State, Gillian Shephard, (1995) praised the TTA's clear vision, endorsed the proposed framework for CPD and declared since professional development is at the heart of school development, it is the responsibility of schools to train and develop their whole staff as well as to educate their pupils. The Secretary of State estimated that £400 million was being invested annually in teachers' professional development. The most recent statistics (DFEE, 1996) gave a provisional estimate of almost 400,000 full-time equivalent (FTE) teachers employed in the maintained nursery, primary and secondary school sectors in England. By simple arithmetic this means that approximately £1,000 should be available annually for each full-time teacher. Whilst the TTA has made it clear that there will be a shift towards teachers contributing to the cost of their own development there have been no statements concerning entitlement either to funding beyond the induction phase or to study leave. Barber (1995) has argued for a minimum involvement in professional development over a five year period supported by a system of professional development vouchers.

In the 1996–7 academic year the TTA will take over funding for long award-bearing courses for school teachers from the Higher Education Funding Council for England (HEFCE). The funding had been used by the HEFCE to support all education courses other than initial teacher training including the bulk of award-bearing CPD courses for teachers from all sectors. Many higher education institutions provide for a student body which includes a high proportion of teachers from further, higher and adult education as well as teachers from the health service and HM Forces. Modular programmes include generic modules which attract both school teachers and those from post-compulsory education. There will inevitably be some funding transferred to the TTA which will be used to support teachers from other sectors attending courses designed primarily for school teachers but that will be offset by HEFCE funding used to support school teachers who are studying elsewhere in the university or college in order to enhance their subject knowledge. Some higher education departments and schools of education welcome the transfer of funding to the TTA as resources will be earmarked for education and not subject to virement to other parts of the institution.

RESEARCH

The TTA has reopened the debate about teaching as a research-based profession with a particular emphasis on classroom practice (TTA, 1996k). A quarter of a century ago the James Committee (DES, 1972a) highlighted the importance of wider opportunities for research by practising teachers and advocated that 'research' should be interpreted in its widest sense to include an evaluation of school activities. The idea of 'teacher as researcher' was developed by Stenhouse (1975) who saw professional development as a research process and argued that teachers should have opportunities to research their own practice. Recently Hargreaves (1996), in a TTA lecture, compared teaching, where very little published research is carried out by practising teachers, with medicine where research is firmly rooted in doctors' day-to-day professional practice. He pointed out that although an estimated £50–60m is spent on educational research each year there is next to no influence on the quality of education provided in schools and deplored the absence of an evidence-based body of knowledge about what goes in classrooms. To this end the TTA has developed a pilot scheme of research grants to provide opportunities for teachers to investigate pedagogy and for their findings to be disseminated to the wider teaching community. Increasing numbers of teachers are taking higher degrees and carrying out research in their own professional settings yet few of their findings ever reach a wider audience. Some courses conclude with a module on dissemination in order to encourage teachers to publish an article in a journal or in the educational press. But then there is the problem of communication identified by Hargeaves; whereas in medicine there are journals such as the Lancet and the British Medical Journal the only publication which reaches most teachers is the Times Educational Supplement which gives little coverage to research. Every teacher should have access to high quality research and development and should see themselves as able to contribute to, as well as benefit from, research about practice.

A GENERAL TEACHING COUNCIL

Giving greater prominence to research would, almost certainly, raise the status and morale of the profession. Another initiative which would advance the standing of teachers and teaching is the establishment of a General Teaching Council (GTC). The concept gains prominence from time to time and inevitably comparisons are drawn with organisations such as the General Medical Council and the Law Society. A recent comprehensive review by Tomlinson (1995) sets the argument for a GTC within a historical and political context and assigns it three major functions:

1. To maintain a register of those qualified to teach.
2. To control professional discipline.
3. To advise on standards of entry to the profession and for continuing professional development.

(Tomlinson, 1995)

The Council already exists in an embryonic form as the General Teaching Council for England and Wales which was set up in the mid-1980s and is widely supported by professional associations as it works towards a fully established statutory Council. Papers produced for the GTC by Williams (1993) and Bolam (1993) on CPD identified the shift in emphasis towards national priorities and reasserted the importance of the professional development of individuals. Barber (1995) called for a General Teaching Council which would be committed to the priority of the long term development of the profession and Tomlinson (1995) suggested that, notwithstanding the TTA's role in education and training, a GTC which maintained a register of teachers, assumed responsibility for professional conduct and formed a focus for the profession might be envisaged.

CONCLUSION

The entry of the Teacher Training Agency on to the CPD stage has to be greeted with cautious optimism. Cordial, collegial and consultative relationships have been established with the profession notwithstanding that the Agency is a quango with an arms-length arrangement with the DFEE whose policies it is required to follow. A career structure with an associated framework of opportunities for professional development is to be welcomed. This will necessarily be linked to school development plans, action plans arising from inspection and national priorities. These different needs must be reconciled within a coherent system which satisfies the demand for short skills-based training and at the same time provides opportunities for education, the reflective scholarly activity essential for long-term professional development.

Questions for discussion

How do you interpret the changing role of government in the last 25 years?

What do you see as the role of the Teacher Training Agency?

How would a General Teaching Council add value?

2

Continuing Professional Development in the Professions

HARRY TOMLINSON

This chapter is based on a research project carried out for the Teacher Training Agency, *Continuing Professional Development in Five Professions* (Tomlinson and Holmes, 1996). It has been structured to explore similarities between the five professions, architects, doctors, engineers, nurses and solicitors, and the teaching profession.

There are, it is suggested, four groups of strategies for career development for professionals over the next decade (Watkins and Drury, 1994, p. 66).

·developing a new mind set;
learning to promote and market one's skills, networking and cultivating relationships;
developing self-insight and taking personal charge;
developing a range of competencies.

Madden and Mitchell (1993, p. 8) define a profession as 'A discrete body of individuals applying advanced learning or scientific knowledge and expertise to provide a service to clients and bound together by a membership of a professional body which assumes responsibility for monitoring professional standards and which confers benefits and may impose sanctions on members.' Teachers have not recognised this new career environment and nor do they have such a professional body.

Other professional bodies are imposing intense pressure on their own members to improve standards and quality of service. There is an insistence on the maintenance of high level professional competence, and that members become more flexible in their working practices and in the services offered. In a world of intense competition, professional privilege which is not overtly of benefit to clients is being eroded.

With a lack of job security and a hostile environment with increased competition for members, professional bodies are developing strategic planning techniques and redefining their missions, goals, objectives, and criteria for success as well as seeking additional sources of funding. There is a positive and strong response to the need to survive. The teacher associations have not yet done this.

Most professions devolve the provision of the initial qualification to higher education, but impose clear quality assurance procedures. The development of higher level continuing professional development skills is occurring in a context where there is considerable scepticism about the value of NVQs for professionals.

The professional bodies are very clear about the effects of rapid change on standards that underpin professional values. Hence the recognition of the potentially massive significance and impact of CPD. As new employment practices shift responsibility for ensuring continuing competence to the individual the role of the professional bodies has to change. The maintenance of high standards and quality, and exemplary good practice require clear effective disciplinary and complaints procedures. Any individual weakness undermines the credibility of the whole profession. However members also expect strong support. In professional bodies there are pressures for collaboration and full merger and counter pressures towards fragmentation.

CONTINUING PROFESSIONAL DEVELOPMENT IN FIVE PROFESSIONS

Architects

Architects have a duty to complete CPD though The Royal Institute of British Architects (RIBA) does not yet monitor compliance. In 1992 the RIBA Council agreed to make CPD obligatory and introduced a bylaw which came into effect from January 1 1993, affecting all Corporate Members. Some architects are now demanding a more formal and structured approach to CPD including monitoring; essentially a mandatory scheme. A commitment to CPD is now a prerequisite for inclusion in the RIBA Directory of Practices and the RIBA Register of Planning Supervisors.

Much of the work of architects can be done by others. In 1995 there was a successful resistance to proposals to allow those not chartered to describe themselves as architects. Since only 20 per cent of construction projects are managed by architects, they need to demonstrate the distinctiveness of their professionalism to survive. The initial training – three years of higher education, one year in practice, two years of higher education, one year in practice – provides control of entry and a rigorous foundation. This skill level is now to be sustained by CPD post chartered status.

Architects work in very large practices, with very sophisticated appraisal and performance management systems, and as sole practitioners. The onus is on the individual to determine appropriate CPD. RIBA recommends that there should be concentration on learning outcomes. CPD related to recent legislation is often a requirement. Since every architect researches for each new brief, RIBA is concerned to ensure that this learning process is recorded to produce evidence of reflection. RIBA also wants to stimulate greater development in new areas of knowledge and to encourage practices to become learning organisations.

Career planning is not easy in a profession which has been particularly hard hit by the recession. It is arguably therefore more necessary. Architects have to be concerned with the public image of the architect since the distinctiveness is in the title. They need to demonstrate, however, that they also have the skills of project managers, and of planning supervisors.

RIBA is writing a Guide for Practices which is intended to reduce the possible tension between CPD for individual career development and that which progresses the needs of the organisation. As a professional institution RIBA has to try and encourage members to be aware that CPD is the individual's responsibility, and that the organisation should support that individual whilst expecting her/him to carry out work-specific CPD within reason. RIBA has established the CPD Providers Network to assess the quality of CPD provision and itself delivers very comprehensive programmes regionally.

Architects – policy statements

From *The Guide to Continuing Professional Development*

CPD is the activity which maintains, enhances or increases the knowledge and skills of the member to the benefit of his or her capabilities as an architect.

The CPD Duty
A commitment to CPD is expected of all RIBA corporate members from 1 January 1993. Only members who are fully retired from practice are exempt.
CPD is an individual responsibility designed to ensure sound professional development.
Do not be deterred by CPD. On-the-job learning is already part of your professional life as an architect. Searching out information from technical literature, reading the construction industry press, discussions with colleagues, attending conferences and courses are all CPD activities.
To meet the annual CPD target of thirty-five hours you can either complete thirty-five hours each year or choose to spread the hours over three years. This allows you to average out of 105 hours according to your own needs and diary. A further thirty-five hours CPD each year is seen as desirable.
You are recommended to prepare a Personal Development Plan (PDP) which offers the opportunity to plan and record your achievements, and identify areas for individual action taking into account your own workload and the experience already on hand in the practice. Building new areas of interest can bring you even greater benefits.
The Personal Development Plan (PDP) is an important aid to achieving work-related development in a systematic way. The PDP will help you plan, guide, record and review activity . . . When drawing up your PDP, think about:

- Your own particular interests and objectives, long-term aims, experience since qualification, job description, the nature of your workload and degree of specialisation.
- Your aims and targets for the future. Consult a colleague or fellow member if you can.
- Timescale. Do you want to participate in immediate, on-going or long-term activities?
- Decide what level of achievement you are aiming for. This might be an awareness

of a subject or skill, competence to operate at normal professional standards, or expertise to be able to advise or work as a specialist in a particular area.

- Your CPD needs may sometimes alter – allow for unexpected but necessary changes.
- Decide on the most convenient and interesting learning formats – seminars, reading, open learning, etc. Choose methods you find most appropriate and accessible.
- Record what you do, how you do it and the number of CPD hours achieved on your PDP.
- Keep an eye on your progress, and make sure you experience the benefits of your CPD activities in your professional life.

General practitioners

The Royal College of General Practitioners (RCGP) has approximately 60 per cent of general practitioners (GPs) in membership. It has two complementary working parties. Higher Professional Education covers the early professional development of young GPs. Continuing Medical Education concentrates on the further professional development of GPs throughout their careers.

In 1990 a new contract incorporating a postgraduate education allowance changed the continuing professional development system for GPs. Until 1990 they attended free courses and received expenses. Seniority allowances were part of the formal payment system. In 1990 some money was removed from these allowances. GPs now receive this back when they demonstrate that they have attended 5 days of approved medical education. The programmes are in three broad areas: Health Promotion and Prevention, Disease Management and Service Management. The concern of the Royal College is that this structure and practice is not professional learning.

The Higher Professional Education Committee has been established recently to ensure that young principals receive a stronger induction into the profession. This is because there has only been one year of specific GP training, perhaps like PGCE entrants to teaching. The very security of the GP within a practice creates a problem for young principals for whom there is no obvious career promotion. The independent contractor status of doctors within a practice also has implications for CPD. A recent report *Portfolio Based Learning in General Medical Practice* (1993) suggests support for developmental work with mentors. The appointment of GP tutors to organise postgraduate education is a recent development. From 1997 there will be compulsory assessment at the end of training as part of the quality assurance process. A priority for the Higher Medical Education Committee is to appoint a coordinator to research what education young principals are now receiving and to evaluate its effectiveness. Another is the accreditation of the more substantial courses to encourage more focused education.

The Continuing Medical Education Committee is considering improvements for more experienced doctors. The development of modular masters' degrees with the universities is proposed to build in academic rigour for those seeking higher qualifications. Recertification will almost certainly be required every five to seven years.

The requirement of the health commission/authorities to improve standards of health, means new initiatives for developing practices. The Medical Audit quality assurance process encourages practices to set targets, establish performance indicators, and monitor the process of achieving these standards. The measurable is perceived as easy, the more qualitative indicators are more complex. Those who went for fundholding early may have been the more enterprising. They have had significantly greater opportunity to invest in career development.

The Royal College membership includes the vast majority of young doctors. Some of the older are concerned that the college is insisting on continually raising standards. The support of the College for preventative medicine at the expense of traditional areas of practice, and the subsequent emphasis on health promotion in the new contract was a further cause of disaffection.

The College is determined to enhance the professionalism of general practitioners. This includes a thorough understanding of current research. The activities of these two committees are a reassertion of that commitment despite the desperately low morale within the profession. Individual ownership of CPD is seen as crucial. In view of the problems within general practice, the energetic insistence by the college on continuously raising standards is impressive.

General practitioners' policy statements

From *Education and Training for General Practice*

Higher Professional Education

3.4 Vocational training provides broadly based experience that is needed for all general practitioners. It equates largely with the period of general professional training that is characteristic of other medical training programmes. In its Educational Strategy the College described the purpose of higher professional education for general practice and outlined its content. This included

- clinical aspects
- the development of techniques that will enable doctors to relate their continued learning to their work within the practice setting through peer and performance review, and audit
- activities designed to promote more efficient practice management and the development of teamwork and a greater understanding of the responsibilities of individual members of the team
- preparation for undergraduate teaching and vocational training
- experience and research in general practice as a way of increasing the body of knowledge of the discipline and enhancing the doctor's own professional development.

Continuing Medical Education

4.1 In a rapidly developing profession such as medicine, doctors need to learn about changes in the practice of their profession throughout their lives. In this way, their professional development is sustained so that they are able to provide high quality patient care at all stages of their careers. Through continuing medical education doctors must be able to incorporate validated scientific research findings into their practices, to adapt management and organizational principles for the more efficient delivery of their services, and through the audit of their practices, to become better able to ensure the effective delivery of care.

4.4 The content of continuing medical education must be relevant to the needs of doctors and to the services they provide. It must take account of clinical developments, changes in health service organization and changes in patients' expectations. For general practice this means maintaining a doctor's ability to provide acute and emergency care and to manage chronic disease. Through continuing medical education, management and organizational skills, including those needed for quality assurance, will have to be sustained so that they can be effectively deployed within the practice. Other essential elements will include the refinement of consulting and interpersonal skills, the development of skills in assessing the needs of practice populations, in strategic management and in the purchasing and commissioning of secondary care. Programmes will need to address the multiprofessional approach to primary care with particular emphasis on team building and team working. Opportunities will have to be created for the development of skills in audit and their application in quality assurance, as well as in research and in the incorporation of research findings into daily practice.

ENGINEERS

The Engineering Council acts in a coordinating and leadership role with the thirty nine professional engineering institutions. There are 300,000 registered engineers. The Engineering Council expects a minimum of 35 hours of CPD. The Institution of Mechanical Engineers (IMechE) is an institute within the Council which has 60,000 members. For chartered engineers IMechE is recommending a target of 50 hours CPD. The Engineering Council is strongly committed to CPD, not as a prescription by the professional body to maintain registration, but as a commitment to lifelong learning. CPD for engineers is about performance and employability not regulations or government requirements or consumer pressure.

There is a clear need to satisfy employers for the engineering profession. The vision is of a broad engineering profession with specialist areas, with the Engineering Council setting standards exercising a regulatory function. This involves establishing broadly quality assurance expectations. A second function is assisting in the implementation of those standards through the institutions. These institutions are only just developing staffing support for CPD. The Institution of Civil Engineers with approaching 70,000 members had (1995) one part-time person for CPD.

There have been two major changes in the last ten years. One is the increased accountability of the professional bodies generally for the competence of their members throughout their working lives. The other is that, because of changes in companies and employment, the centre of gravity for learning has moved strongly towards the individual. The Engineering Council would ideally want a model where, after registration, the first few years have fairly clearly prescribed development activities to bring professionals to a high level of competence. Thereafter there is a continuing requirement to demonstrate competence.

Quality assurance within the engineering profession is controlled. The Institutions have to register every five years with the Engineering Council. From May 1995 CPD was part of that quality assurance system. The Institutions must provide their policy statement, show that they are promoting CPD, what requirements are laid down, and how they help their members with guidance and advice. The role of the Engineering Council allows it to provide the ultimate accolade of Chartered Engineer status. This is particularly important in an international context since engineers abroad frequently have many more years of higher education. The Chartered Engineer essentially has a three plus two plus two years model. Like the architects and doctors there is a more substantial professional foundation than for teachers, particularly those with the one year PGCE.

Lifelong learning and continuous improvement is essential if engineers are to retain employment. Hence the emphasis on business performance. *Competence and Commitment (1995)* aspires to see engineers as members of multidisciplinary learning teams in learning organisations with an emphasis on outcomes. The commitment is to maintaining competence, and being ethical and professional. This professional obligation is not yet mandatory.

Half the engineers have some form of appraisal. Much more important is the focus of the learning culture within organisations, matching individual aspirations with organisational needs, particularly as shown by Investors in People. Career planning requires a continuous adaptation to market needs, and planning for a future in which business engineers market themselves because of their engineering excellence. Over the last 10 years the average length of employment has dropped from eight years to five and a half. For the Engineering Council the learned engineering institutes should become learning organisations.

Institution of Mechanical Engineers

The Institution, a non-statutory body, has control only over its 60,000 members. CPD is becoming progressively mandatory and has virtually reached that stage in the IMechE. However to practise as an engineer it is not necessary to be a member of the Institution. Standards are being driven up for Chartered Engineers. Though the Institution has carried out what is now called CPD for 150 years there is a distinctive renewed sense of purpose. The formal CPD policy, which talks about a professional obligation, was only developed very recently.

The Institution is working with higher education institutions to provide high quality appropriate CPD. Distance learning using the Internet is being developed. CPD is about learning outcomes not just the 50 hours annually which have to be recorded. Though self-authentication is accepted, members are advised to seek authentication from their employer or events organisers. Large companies which employ engineers will have their own CPD schemes. IMechE members have to establish CPD which is acceptable to their employers and the Institution. The Chartered Engineer is someone who can respond creatively to tomorrow's problems. There is a concern that NVQs based on competence may not be capable of reaching out to the skills to solve entirely new problems which require the pushing forward of the frontiers of technology.

Engineers' policy statements

Engineering Council
From *Continuing Professional Development: The Practical Guide to Good Practice*

The Engineering Council's Vision
Among our key beliefs about Continuing Professional Development;
- Effective CPD leads to quality products and services.
- CPD is an investment for both individuals and their employers.
- CPD can be implemented largely through learning structured around the job itself.
- There is a need for commitment by everyone to continuous self improvement.
- Individuals and companies must commit TIME as well as money to CPD.
- Effective CPD requires a systematic approach and attention to detail.
- There increasingly needs to be a European and an International dimension.

Institution of Mechanical Engineers
From *Continuing Professional Development: A Guide for Mechanical Engineers*

Why CPD
Your first degree was one stage in a lifetime of learning experience in both your business and non-business life. Before you could practise as an engineer you had to complement your degree with industrial training and experience. That process will continue throughout your career.
It has to

- since engineering is changing at an ever-increasing rate and what you learned in your degree rapidly starts to date;
- if you are able to respond to new legislation and new social pressures which will affect your work;
- if you are to compete with your continental colleagues and compete with them against international competition;
- if you are to realise your full potential as an engineer;
- if you want to be in a position to take advantage of career opportunities;
- if you want to remain marketable and maximise your contribution (and thus your return) to present and future employers.

A *disciplined* approach to CPD will enable you to become a more competent engineer in your current position and better equipped for whatever changes of direction your career takes, be those changes planned or fortuitous.
Remember that this is *your* life and you alone must, in the end, set and achieve your own aims and objectives. OWNership of CPD is yours and you should commit time and resources to this activity, so that it can be carried out systematically and in the detail required.
YOU ARE RESPONSIBLE FOR YOUR OWN CAREER DEVELOPMENT AND SELF-IMPROVEMENT.

NURSES

The PREP Report

The United Kingdom Central Council for Nursing, Midwifery and Health Visiting (UKCC) produced a report *The Future of Professional Practice – the*

Council's Standards for Education and Practice following Registration in March 1994. PREP (Post Registration Education and Practice) is a new obligation for nurses developed as a result of this report. *PREP and You* was circulated to all nurses in March 1995. They are now required to undertake a minimum of the equivalent of 5 days of study for their professional development every three years to renew and maintain registration. Until the mid-1980s registration had been for life.

There is a new requirement to maintain a personal professional profile throughout the career. Profiling is seen as a continuous process of reviewing experience to date, self-appraisal, and setting goals and action plans. This is seen as contributing to professional development by helping nurses to recognise, understand and value their abilities, strengths, achievements and expertise, as well as a source to be drawn on for compiling standards for the UKCC.

Individual practitioners are responsible for ensuring they fulfil their professional obligations and renew their registration. This process is through self-verification. After 31 March 2001 all practitioners will have completed three years in the new system. There will then be a formal audit system to monitor the effectiveness of PREP policies and to evaluate the ways in which the requirements are being met.

The UKCC is committed to the development of the concept of Advanced Nursing Practice. This is concerned with the validation of autonomous expert practice. These advanced level practitioners are perceived to be practising at Master's degree level. This is a particularly interesting concept, with some parallels to the Master Teacher concept.

Project 2000, the new preparation for nurses in training in the United Kingdom is now well under way. PREP may in principle make very limited demands. The self-verification of appropriate CPD requiring five days of study or the equivalent is arguably limited. The Royal College of Nursing (RCN) which represents approximately 300,000 of the 640,000 potential nurses, intends to build quality into the provision it makes for its members to support the intended learning outcomes, a critique of the learning undertaken and reflection on learning.

The RCN is attempting to create a learning culture within the profession by ensuring high quality training. Course organisers are required to send the College the results of a clearly structured evaluation. There is a concern about some providers who may take advantage of PREP requirements. It is clear that some of the Trusts and independent nursing chains will make provision which is directed to corporate gain as well as the professional and personal gain of nurses.

The RCN is in a unique position in terms of CPD in that it is a higher education institution able to award degrees, has a Royal Charter, is a professional organisation and a trade union. The stewards in the union are recognised as a particularly useful conduit for ideas for new CPD developments because of their thorough understanding of the issues in the health service. This provides a very rich organisation.

Nurses' policy statements

From PREP and You.

PLANNING YOUR PROFESSIONAL DEVELOPMENT

When planning your professional development, you may find it helpful to work through the following stages:

Review your competence

Identify your strengths and weaknesses and areas in which you want to develop.

Set your learning objectives

Identify what you want to achieve to enable you to develop

Develop an action plan

Select appropriate learning activities to meet your needs. These could include: a literature search, seminar, course, visit to another unit or centre of excellence/ specialist expertise relevant to your practice.

Implement your action plan

Discuss your plans with an appropriate person such as your manager, clinical supervisor, supervisor of midwives or a tutor to ensure the plans are feasible, particularly in terms of finance and resources. Negotiate with your manager for study time and, if necessary, assistance with funding.

Evaluation

Having carried out your action plan, think what happened and what you actually learned. Consider, for example:

- The strengths and weaknesses of the activity, event or visit
- Whether it enabled you to meet your objectives
- The value of what you learned for your patients, clients and colleagues
- How you will share the knowledge you have acquired.

You may find it helpful periodically to reflect on the experience and its continuing effect on your development and practice.

What is advanced nursing practice?

Advanced nursing practice is concerned with:

- Adjusting the boundaries for the development of future practice
- Pioneering and developing new roles which are responsive to changing needs
- Advancing clinical practice, research and education to enrich nursing practice as a whole
- Contributing to health policy and management and the determination of health needs
- Continuing the development of the professions in the interests of patients, clients and health services.

Advancing nursing practice in this way will lead to

- Innovations in practice
- An increase in nursing research and research-based practice
- The provision of expert professionals who will have a consultancy role
- High level professional leadership
- Increased political and professional influence in respect of nursing and health services
- Expert resources for, for example, education, supervision, management.

SOLICITORS

The Law Society

There are approximately 60,000 solicitors, the vast majority in private practice. Solicitors are required to carry out 16 hours per year of CPD of which at least 25 per cent must involve participation in courses by providers authorised by the Law Society; up to 25 per cent may be undertaken by writing, for example articles for legal journals or legal research; and up to 50 per cent for undertaking distance learning courses, though this can increase to 100 per cent if the course requires an examination and/or dissertation.

Solicitors practise either in partnership, as sole practitioners, or as employed solicitors, either within private practice or commerce, industry and local government. The larger the practice the more likely it is that the partnership will be organised on corporate lines. Practices range from the small high street self-employed sole practitioner to the very large operating in the global environment with offices worldwide and only corporate clients. Though the nature of the work that people do varies considerably, the CPD requirements are the same and therefore the need for flexibility.

The process of phasing in CPD starting with solicitors who had just qualified was a response to consultation. The commitment to the development of CPD was seen as a necessity following developments in other professions. The Law Society ultimately imposed CPD as the governing professional body after consultation. This process was driven by solicitors who wanted learning about change in the law to be high quality, practical and relevant. Solicitors have a professional obligation to ensure continuous updating of knowledge and skills. The scheme is intended to assist firms in providing an efficient and effective service to their clients. The first phase took effect in 1994, the second phase starts in 1998.

Solicitors used to be able to start their professional life with a concept of a career. The traditional specialisms of the high street solicitor such as conveyancing are being eroded. These processes are changing the level of security within the profession. The very effective sole practitioner working from home with low overheads, a high degree of personal attention, personal service and low charges is almost a new cottage industry. The alternative for high street practices is to train junior staff to support solicitors dealing with aspects of the transaction, be highly computerised, and be very aware of the rapid changes in the predominant work relating to domestic conveyancing and divorce.

Solicitors with three years at university, two years on a vocational course, and two years in articles will be expected to take on responsibility as quickly as possible after qualification and are expected to be much more aware of commercial and management aspects of practice generally at a much earlier stage than has previously been the case. The expansion of higher education led to an overexpansion of the provision of law courses. The output of 12,000 a year recently was roughly three times what the profession could absorb.

The Law Society is attempting to create a different culture, through its practice management standard. Appraisal and an evaluation of performance define the training needs for the individual. The provision of training and development opportunities will maximise their contribution to the business objectives of the firm. Investors in People is being encouraged for this reason. Firms are willing to pay for CPD when it supports their business priorities. Though the vast majority of courses are on new law, courses such as Self-Presentation, and Handling Difficult People are examples of recent personal development courses.

The ultimate aim of CPD for the Law Society is a practitioner, who can reflect intelligently on experience. The development of problem solving skills exemplifies this. This has to be combined with a strengthening of the management based on a clear vision of where the practice is going. The Law Society officers see little practical significance in the distinction between self-regulation and state regulation. Self-regulation depends on the powers allowed by the state and there is some indirect control of these powers. This alleged major benefit of the traditional profession was not as highly valued as had been anticipated, and may have implications for the General Teaching Council.

Solicitors' policy statements

From *Continuing Professional Development Information Pack.*

CAREER PLANNING AND DEVELOPMENT – 'PROACTION NOT REACTION'
Career progression should be planned and should take account not only of future goals but current role development needs. The following are the stages which should be included in planning career development:
1. Devise a career plan.
2. Analyse and prioritise training needs.
3. Consider the most appropriate methods to meet these needs.
4. Plan and prioritise training activities.
5. Evaluate the training undertaken.
6. Review achievements and career plan.
Analyse and prioritise individual training needs
Current role training needs analysis:
1. List key areas of work and identify job tasks
2. Consider your present level of expertise in each area
3. From this list . . . identify which areas needs to be developed and analyse the training needs
4. Prioritise the list of training needs in order of urgency and importance
Future goals training needs analysis
1. List short, medium and long term career goals
2. Identify which areas need to be developed and to what level
3. Assess whether any of the training undertaken for the current role will meet or contribute to these needs
4. Decide what further training would be needed to meet future goals.

CONCLUSION

The cultures of these five professions are distinctive. What is clear is that there has been a tremendous increase in the commitment to CPD in the last few years, driven by the professions themselves. The applications are in different contexts. There is however a great deal that the education service can learn from this experience. The focus on lifelong learning and learning organisations is powerful. The leadership given by the professions in demanding higher standards of their members is exemplary and necessary to survive. These changes are driven by a recognition that the employment market for professionals requires a commitment to ever higher demonstrable standards of performance. The professions selected represent a range of approaches to CPD which will help those making policy for the teaching profession understand the wider context. It should also make clear to the teaching profession, and individual teachers, that they are responsible for their own destiny.

BIBLIOGRAPHY

ARCHITECTS
Royal Institute of British Architects, *A Guide to Continuing Professional Development*

DOCTORS
Royal College of General Practitioners, (December 1993) *Portfolio-based Learning in General Medical Practice*
Royal College of General Practitioners, (December 1994) *Education and Training for General Practice*
Royal College of General Practitioners, (January 1996) *The Nature of General Medical Practice*

ENGINEERS
Engineering Council, (1994) *Continuing Professional Development: The Practical Guide to Good Practice*
Engineering Council, (January 1995) *Competence and Commitment: The Engineering Council's proposals for a new system of engineering formation and registration*
Institution of Mechanical Engineers, (1996) *Continuing Professional Development: A Guide for Mechanical Engineers*

NURSES
Royal College of Nursing (November 1995) *Nursing Update Information Pack*
UKCC (1994) *The Future of Professional Practice – The Council's Standards for Practice following Registration*
UKCC (1995) *PREP and You*

SOLICITORS
Law Society (March 1995) Continuing Professional Development Information Pack

Questions for discussion

What are the differences in these five professions in the interpretation of professionalism?

How would you characterise the distinctiveness of teaching as a profession?

What can teachers learn about CPD from other professions?

3

Teaching as a Profession: The Role of Professional Development

VIV GARRETT WITH COLIN BOWLES

This chapter will explore how professional development is used in schools to enhance professionalism. It will explore the different roles of in-service training and staff development to explain the types of development and training currently used in schools. It will address the links between individual and whole school development and will use a case study of staff development initiatives in a large community college to illustrate the support for the development of the teacher as a professional working towards school improvement.

First of all it may be useful to clarify the meanings of the various terms associated with continuing professional development: staff development, in-service training (INSET), and professional development. They have been used interchangeably over the last few years often reflecting the terminology associated with various funding mechanisms. O'Neill (1994, p. 287) uses *training* for individuals or groups with like needs about an externally identified subject and is essentially short-term in nature in that it fills a gap; *staff development* is for whole staff on a subject identified by teachers or whole school as priority and is medium-term; *professional development* is for individuals or groups with like needs identified by them or the school, is career-orientated or personal and is longer-term. He decides to use *professional development* as a generic term to cover all. I will do the same and will use the other terms as appropriate.

It may also be useful to consider the meaning of the term 'professional' when applied to teachers. I would like to offer three key dimensions to this role:

- A professional will have undergone a lengthy period of professional training in a body of abstract knowledge (Goode, 1960; Coulson, 1986; Hughes, 1985), and will have experience in the relevant field, in this case teaching.
- A professional is controlled by a code of ethics and professional values (Barber, 1963, 1978; Coulson, 1986; Hughes, 1985).
- A professional is committed to the core business of the organisation, i.e. the quality of student learning (Coulson, 1986).

(adapted from Garrett, 1996)

We can now attempt to connect the two by considering what are the aims of what we will now call professional development. They are well-documented (see for example: Main, 1985; Bolam, 1987; Brown and Earley, 1990; Madden and Mitchell, 1993; Institute of Management, 1995). However they do not make explicit the link between professional development and the teacher as a professional. I will therefore suggest an amalgam which takes into account the above dimensions of the professional.

The ultimate aim of professional development in schools is to improve the quality of learning and teaching. This can be achieved by recognising the status of the teacher as a professional and ensuring opportunities for that teacher to update and extend his/her knowledge and skills. It should provide opportunities for reflection and learning from experience as well as training and development for new roles and responsibilities to ensure the effectiveness of the individual teacher in contributing to the development of the whole school.

PROFESSIONAL DEVELOPMENT IN SCHOOLS

I would now like to explore the roles played by the different types of professional development currently in use by schools. Hargreaves and Fullan (1992, p. 2) cite three different approaches to 'training or improving the teaching force':

1. *Teacher development as knowledge and skills development,* where teachers are equipped 'with the necessary knowledge and skills to provide pupils improved opportunities to learn'.
2. *Teacher Development as Self-Understanding,* where the focus is upon the teacher as a person.
3. *Teacher Development as Ecological Change,* which highlights the importance of the context of the working environment.

I would like to use Hargreaves and Fullan's typology to consider each of the areas in turn and relate them to current practice and thinking where appropriate.

Teacher development as knowledge and skills development

This is often the prime focus of teacher development and could be said to fulfil the *training* aspect of O'Neill's descriptions, in which knowledge and skills training is normally used to plug identified gaps in the teaching or management practices of individuals or groups. This could be in response to inadequacies highlighted by OFSTED inspections, Investors in People (IIP) reports or a change in curriculum. On the other hand this approach is also widely used to update teachers in the knowledge and skills required for new developments and responsibilities, such as GNVQs or special educational needs. Although acknowledged as an important component of teacher development (for example, Hargreaves and Fullan, 1992), this approach is no longer considered the single most effective way of developing teachers' skills. There are a number of reasons for this.

First, this type of development has traditionally been delivered away from the school by outside experts and is what Joyce and Weil (1996) refer to as *workshop learning* rather than *workplace learning*. Although it can be an extremely cost-effective and efficient way to train large numbers of people in, for example, new teaching methodologies, there is no guarantee that the learning from the workshop will be developed into new or improved practices in the classroom. The devolvement of staff development monies to schools has meant that schools are becoming increasingly demanding of value for money in terms of identifiable outcomes. However, it is quite difficult to attempt to evaluate specific training in terms of changed practice and improved outcomes for students; this is an area for development which has been highlighted both by schools themselves and by the TTA.

Second, the development funds are usually targeted towards the trainer rather then the teacher, with the result that little is left for buying release time for teachers to work together and further develop ideas and materials specific to their school.

Third, there can be unease with the underpinning rationale of the 'right' way to do things, based on 'positive knowledge' (Webb, 1996) gained from research or driven by government. Using this rationale, there is a danger that the dominant external expert disregards the professional experience and expertise of the teacher. Hargreaves (1996, p. 1), in his Teacher Training Agency (TTA) lecture, highlights this gap between educational researchers and practitioners: 'If the defects in the way educational research is organised were remedied, research would play a more effective role in advancing the professional quality and standing of teachers.' Hargreaves and Fullan (1992, p. 5) also note the perceived superiority of the 'hard research knowledge of experts' to the 'soft practical wisdom of teachers'.

Fourth, this approach can be seen as top-down and imposed upon teachers by school management or external bodies. There is then the danger of a lack of ownership by staff of both the training and the development itself.

Some schools are attempting to overcome the weaknesses of this approach by organising their own training on-site. Much of this function was previously undertaken by Local Education Authorities (LEAs) but given the decreasing numbers of in-service trainers and advisers still in post, many schools are looking for the expertise elsewhere, either within their own workforce or by buying in from outside. This in turn can lead to its own problems. The internal experts may not have the necessary skills in the training of adults, and their use can contribute to the creation of an inward-looking organisation. Tempting though it may be for schools to use all their staff development resources for release time and supply cover, there is a danger of development becoming incestuous and stagnant without external stimulus and challenge. There are also disadvantages associated with the use of external experts who can be expensive and vary in quality, and it can be difficult for them to fully understand the context and culture of the school in which they are working.

Many of us involved in the training and development function, who are at the same time committed to school improvement, are anxious to remedy the unease associated with this approach by collaborating with teachers in planning development activities and relating them closely to the workplace. This can take various forms: after-school workshops with groups of teachers from one school, or from a local cluster of schools; joint training side by side with teachers, providing the very best internal and external expertise; training school professional development co-ordinators; school projects undertaken by individuals or groups of teachers and supported by externals; or the trainer as consultant and supporter working with teachers in the classroom or relevant area. In this way, resources can be used both for external stimulus and expert support as well as for release time for those teachers who in turn will be supporting others.

It can be seen above how this approach is changing to meet the needs of teachers who are keen to learn new knowledge and skills and at the same time contribute to whole school improvement. However it does not necessarily address the personal development needs of individuals who may have aspirations outside the areas in which they are at present working.

Teacher development as self-understanding

The basis for this term comes from Hargreaves' and Fullan's suggestions that beliefs and behaviours are bound together and that reflection on personal and professional practice may come before changes in behaviour. They cite Nias and Leithwood who both have strong philosophies of personal development underpinning teacher development and identify three important dimensions (Nias, 1989; Leithwood, 1991). First, the stages of development as a person, where personal maturity may affect professional development. Second, the phases of development associated with the life-cycle, where energy and commitment may be dependant on age and affect attitudes to change and improvement. And third, the experience of the teaching career which may bring positive or negative attitudes towards further development. All point to the importance of recognising the teacher as a person and not a mere item in the resource bank of a school.

It is within this approach that understanding of motivation and individual motivators plays a strong part. Motivating has been recognised by Bollington et al. (1990) as 'perhaps the most neglected of managerial functions'. They go on to say that 'In education, this is often explained away as a consequence of working with 'professionals' who, in theory at least, are self-motivating' (p. 89). While teachers early in their careers may still have the energy, enthusiasm and commitment that 'they can make a difference', it is those teachers in mid-career who have not gained, or sought, promotion who may be most at risk from demotivation. Morant (1981) identified four areas of professional needs which were further developed by Garrett et al. (1992): Induction, Extension, Refreshment and Conversion. It is the area of conversion needs which best demonstrates the demotivating aspect of changed ways of working and ability to cope with new challenges and demands.

Hargreaves and Fullan (1992) rightly point out the difficulties of over-indulgence of this viewpoint where the individual is separated from the context and has to take on a great deal of personal responsibility for professional development. On the other hand, the non-recognition of the teacher as an individual leads to many stresses and tensions in the implementation of staff development policies. How can we accommodate this approach as part of professional development? The best examples of appraisal in schools encourage individuals to reflect on their experience and question their practice in the tradition of the reflective practitioner (Schon, 1983). These teachers working towards self-understanding are a substantial percentage of those undertaking long award-bearing courses which, in turn, may also support the development of the reflective practitioner. A considerable number of teachers will come to decisions affecting their long-term career planning while studying.

It is worth noting that even though changes in beliefs may occur as a result of the self-understanding approach, it does not necessarily follow that changes in practice will occur. Those may depend on the context in which the teacher is working as much as on their improved knowledge. It is no surprise therefore that the third approach focuses on the context of teaching.

Teacher development as ecological change

I believe that effective teacher development cannot take place alienated from the context of practice. This context can vary across schools and within schools and can be influenced by both the formal organisation of the school, i.e. its structures and strategies, as well as the informal organisation, i.e. the way things really get done. (Plant, 1987; Garrett, 1997) A working environment that is unsupportive can make the difference between effective and unsatisfactory teaching, and can come about as the result of several factors.

First, resourcing issues can severely affect the environment in terms of poor accommodation, inadequate materials and insufficient time to work with colleagues on development work. The 'hygiene' factors associated with the physical surroundings can have a negative effect on both teachers' and students' motivation to work. If that is linked to an apparently disinterested management in the school and a meagre level of resourcing for materials and release time for development work, then disaffection can easily occur all round.

Second, disinterested colleagues can make an enthusiastic teacher feel isolated and affect the climate of development in a school or curriculum area. How many teachers have returned from courses full of enthusiasm and ideas, only to have cold water poured on any new initiatives suggested by them?

Third, and following on from the above two points, the standard of leadership is crucial to the success of new initiatives. Leaders, whether whole school or departmental, need to show commitment and active involvement to teacher development (Garrett, 1997). By actively sponsoring teachers' new ideas and helping them plan and prepare implementation, leaders are developing a supportive work environment. Headteachers can, by openly valuing teacher contributions to decision making, establish a collaborative work culture in the school which directly underpins the most successful school improvement strategies.

FITTING IT ALL TOGETHER

So how can we ensure that all aspects of professional development contribute to a meaningful whole both for the individual and the school? Meaningful for individual teachers in that their knowledge and skills have been updated or extended; they have been trained for new responsibilities or changing roles; and they feel an effectiveness in their professional life which culminates in job satisfaction (Madden and Mitchell, 1993). At the same time, this development for individuals must feed into whole school development and improvement. How can we make sure all this is achieved?

One mechanism we have at hand is appraisal. In spite of its weaknesses and faults, there are some examples of good practice which could be developed more widely. The best type of appraisal is one which encompasses a formative development function and is linked to professional development resourcing. At the same time, it has to be recognised that there is an accountability function to appraisal which is satisfied in the best cases by supported goal-setting and effective follow-up. The most recent review of appraisal (TTA and OFSTED, 1996) highlights the relationship with whole-school improvement: 'appraisal should be a central strand in how a school manages, evaluates and seeks to improve its own performance and that of all those working in it' (p. 5). As well as pointing out various identified weaknesses of the current system including excessive paperwork and bureaucracy, it makes an enlightened comment about widespread misinterpretation of the confidentiality of targets. It is felt that this has contributed to the failure to link appraisal to school development plans and training and has hampered plans for whole school improvement. The relationship between appraisal, professional development and school improvement is therefore made quite explicit and included in two of the key principles. First, that appraisal should be 'integrated with the other annual management processes and information systems directed at school improvement'. Second, that appraisal should 'address more consistently and systematically how well teachers are performing their essential tasks and what would be required to assist their professional development' (p. 5).

Other mechanisms used by schools are external quality assurance initiatives: popular at the moment is IIP. In fact, it is the external stimulus which is very often used as a change agent in schools. The biggest change agent is undoubtedly the OFSTED inspection. These may vary in quality and may not always be a pleasant experience for those concerned, but they are bringing about a considerable culture change in schools and forcing them to focus on a school improvement agenda which incorporates monitoring and evaluation at its centre.

The following case study demonstrates how one school is attempting to address the issue of providing an integrated package of staff development and school improvement.

RAWLINS COMMUNITY COLLEGE CASE STUDY

Introduction

Rawlins Community College is a large upper school and community college in Quorn, Leicestershire. It has 1200 students on roll from ages 14 to 19 and employs approximately 80 teachers. My post, as a member of the Senior Management Team (SMT), gives me responsibility for many aspects of staffing and staff development, including teacher appraisal. There were a number of related issues which made us decide to look critically at staff development at Rawlins. These were:

- Our OFSTED inspection highlighted the roles and responsibilities of middle management as a key issue.
- Staff development is one of the five priority headings in the College Development Plan.
- The staff recently voted against joining the Investors in People (IIP) initiative.
- Our appraisal system had lapsed, having completed the first two-year cycle. We had had no evaluation and no discussion as to how we would proceed.

This case study then is the story of our progress. It is by no means the perfect answer, and the process has not been easy, but it is the way we at Rawlins have chosen to proceed.

The Context

Rawlins certainly has a long history of supporting and developing its staff, but they turned their collective back on Investors in People. Why? The distinguishing features of Rawlins, including the structures, the culture, the workforce itself and its morale – all of which will probably affect the principles of a staff development policy and are certain to affect the methods used to implement the policy – have been affected by recent financial difficulties. These include:

- A major restructuring of the Senior Management tier (from three vice-principals to one) has resulted in a leaner, less expensive structure. This has inevitably caused some cutbacks: one of particular relevance is the role of professional tutor which has now been shared amongst other SMT members all of whom have other major responsibilities and have insufficient time to perform the professional tutor role properly.
- The recent loss of 8+ teaching posts, many with major responsibilities, and some non-teaching posts has increased the workload for many of those who remain.
- An understandable desire to maximise the use of reducing resources available for development purposes created an explicitly stated policy of linking

training opportunities to institutional needs.

Some observations on the workforce itself are relevant at this point:

- the age profile of the remaining teaching staff is heavily skewed to the 35+ age group;
- the number of years service at Rawlins is equally skewed to 15+ years;
- of the few new teachers recruited in recent years, only some were newly qualified teachers (NQTs);
- for many years, almost all promoted posts have been filled by internal candidates;
- few teachers have moved on to other schools;
- the recent restructuring of the Senior Management tier is likely to limit further opportunities for middle managers to move upwards.

This has created a tier of middle managers many of whom have 'grown up' within Rawlins; some have been on the same pay scale or in the same post for many years. I have already mentioned our OFSTED inspection which high-lighted the need 'to engage more middle managers in decision making and in identifying and implementing whole school policies'. Part of our response was that we would 'improve the professional development and status of staff responsible for major curriculum areas'. This we had been working on but had proved difficult to achieve to date. Our vision was to combine increased responsibility for whole-school decision and policy making (with systems for monitoring and evaluation by senior managers) and revised appraisal and mentoring systems; then to present the whole as an integrated and coherent package for staff development and school improvement.

Staff had worked hard to implement a fair, considered and acceptable appraisal model, with long consultation with many teachers. Although there were many – valid – criticisms, I believe that most appraisees and appraisers found the experience useful. Rawlins has never coped well with externally imposed schemes and systems (unless it can manipulate them to its advantage!), so appraisal may become more acceptable when we can create a revised model that is ours. Development planning is well-established at Rawlins; it has a high profile and real attempts are made to involve all teachers in the teams' plans. However we needed to ensure that the planning process not only involves but affects all staff by drawing up individual staff development plans in parallel to our normal curriculum and overall institutional plans.

There is not the space to discuss all the issues these factors about the workforce raise, for example whether they add up to stability or stagnation in the staffroom, or whether the accusation that Rawlins looks after its own is confirmed. Certainly none of them seem to directly connect with the rejection of IIP, but they are connected to morale in the staffroom which in turn is related to the institutional culture.

The culture of Rawlins – in which autonomy and initiative have historically been highly valued, and outside interference and imposed change have been resented – has meant that the flood of external legislation, and more recently the financial cuts, have been hard to cope with. Being forced to lose valued members of staff was especially threatening, and morale among those who survived was badly affected; it was not perhaps a good time for the management to be talking about valuing people. What's more, we managed to unwittingly reinforce the message that people didn't matter: for example, at the very moment we needed to give people individual time to discuss their personal development, we withdrew it, or rather there was no-one with the time to do it.

Research at Rawlins

Staff development had already been agreed as a main priority area for the year 1996/7. After the rejected IIP bid, the SMT set up a small working party with the brief of deciding how the College should move forward on the issue of staff development. As convenor of this group, I asked more people to join in, making around 15 staff in total and representing most departments.

I was aware of our vision of an integrated package of staff development central to which was a broadening of the decision making base, the revision of appraisal and mentoring, and a much higher profile for monitoring and evaluation. There were loads of things to do but we needed to take everyone along with us. We needed to openly recognise teachers' concerns about their professional development by asking them their views and trying to fulfil some of their needs. Therefore, with the twin aims of raising the profile of staff development among the staff and actually carrying out the kind of full consultation that was to have been the first part of an IIP bid, the group designed a questionnaire. We looked at various questionnaires, in particular those that would have been used as part of the initial IIP investigation. Partly because we didn't like any of these very much, and partly because we felt it was important to tailor at least some of the questions specifically to Rawlins, we decided to create our own. It was divided into five sections, based on the issues the group had identified as significant.

Briefly, the sections covered these issues:

1. The extent to which staff felt there were opportunities for development within the existing structure. Also, how the present structures could be improved, in particular whether there is sufficient support after the development activity to enable any learning to be acted upon.
2. The areas in which staff would like to improve or develop – using a list created by the group.
3. After some discussion about whether to include questions about facilities available and activities that were more related to welfare than personal development, we decided to do so because of their links with the climate in the school and levels of individual motivation.
4. We put the more philosophical questions about staff development at the end (they started off at the beginning) in the hope that staff would now be tuned in to the issues being raised.
5. Questions on the first experience of appraisal.

The Results and Recommendations

We were very pleased with the level of response to the questionnaire: more than three quarters of the staff answered it.

In Section 1, there were generally positive levels of satisfaction expressed with external courses, training days and department meetings. However, given the time invested in training days (30 hours a year for full-time staff), scores were disappointing. We therefore recommended that there should be more consultation with staff on the content of training days, and more staff involved in their delivery.

In Section 2, significant numbers of staff were interested in most of the areas suggested, and particularly those relating to assorted management skills. We recommended setting up sessions on some of the most popular subjects, using in-house expertise where appropriate.

Section 3 gave staff the opportunity to express dissatisfaction about the College facilities open to them. In particular they wanted access to the swimming pool and to Community Education classes. We were able to look into that.

Section 4 highlighted some interesting issues, in particular whether staff development was a right or an entitlement, and the need for individual guidance from a line manager or professional tutor. These points were to be included in an updated Staff Development policy.

The recommendations emanating from the section of the questionnaire on appraisal were rather more detailed, because we felt that, with effective and supportive systems in place, many of the problems associated with identifying development needs and finding ways of meeting those needs would be reduced. We therefore recommended that we should create separate systems for appraisal and mentoring and develop a set of principles for each. We also noted that we would need to train line managers particularly in a more active role necessary to make appraisal and mentoring successful, and that had resource implications.

The Outcomes

So, what has happened since our awareness raising exercise with staff? We needed to ensure that we were able to fulfil some of the needs highlighted by the questionnaire as well as trying to satisfy some of the demands for improvement we had identified earlier. On reflection, our outcomes are considerable and begin to address our earlier vision.

- We have reconsidered the roles and responsibilities of the members of SMT and made some changes to them to allow for some development work. I have been allowed a welcome break from arranging the daily lesson cover in order to concentrate more on staffing and staff development. These changes also mean that we will be better able to provide the individual consultations and professional guidance for staff which many felt had been lacking in recent years.
- We have enlarged the SMT by one person to include a secondment on a one year rolling programme as a development opportunity for that member of

staff. This has meant that there are cascading opportunities for others to take on the roles made vacant by the temporary promotions.

- Each member of SMT has taken responsibility for some curriculum areas: we now have a direct monitoring and evaluation link between the curriculum areas and SMT. We have one special SMT meeting per month devoted to sharing and discussing information and issues from contacts with the curriculum areas. This initiative is affecting a considerable number of people: SMT members, curriculum managers and staff, and is slowly bringing about a cultural change in the school.

- As a result of the above, we have now developed new job descriptions for curriculum managers which are far more specific about their leadership and developmental role than before. We acknowledge that there will be staff development implications here, and we recognise that training should start at the level of senior managers in order to develop some role models.

- More staff are becoming involved with policy making through membership of working groups and involvement with an extended SMT (ESMT).

- We have developed a Staff Handbook not just as a reference book, but as an active process which we can use to appraise our working procedures and raise discussion about what we do.

- We now have a new mentoring system in place for all newly qualified teachers (NQTs) as well as those teachers new to the school and new to post. We hope to include other interested staff later on. Our LEA has set up a local support group for mentors, but we recognise there may also be a need for some training.

- We have developed a new set of principles for appraisal taking into account the external requirements and our internal needs. We are now working on the actual process of appraisal and have set up a group to take this vital aspect of staff development further.

- We have reviewed and reduced the number of meetings in school and allowed additional opportunities for groups to meet during normal school time as well as allowing individual teachers more time for preparation and marking.

- We have negotiated free entry for staff to adult classes of their choice in the Community College programme and have arranged special staff sessions for the swimming pool.

- And last, but by no means least, we have created a new budget heading for staff development with additional subsidies from the school and therefore given it the high priority it deserves.

Conclusion

At the time of writing this case study, we are only a few months into the implementation of these developments. However it may be useful to identify factors that have enabled us to be implementing so many changes at one time. First, a large scale approach does have advantages. We were able to have discussions on some of the philosophical issues underpinning development for the professional, for example, whether it is a right or a responsibility, and the balance between personal and institutional needs. This was seen as important as was the inclusion of staff welfare and facilities which were not strictly development issues but perceived by many as affecting teachers' motivation and therefore their enthusiasm for development.

Second, the entire process of identifying concerns, developing the questionnaire, processing the responses and making recommendations was done by a working party with open membership – this was necessary for any recommendations to have credibility with staff. It was also important to keep SMT informed of progress without constraining the deliberations of the working party; this balancing act became more difficult as the summer term progressed and decisions about next year were needed!

Third, if the negative response to 'Investors in People' was a clear message to management that staff were deeply unhappy about staffing cutbacks, the pendulum was soon to swing back. The work of the group seemed to catch the mood of the staff which was that change was in fact needed but not via an external agent like IIP.

The result is that the majority of changes now being made are seen as directly relating to recommendations from the group; and also, importantly, that this started with changes at senior management level.

Most of the above list of outcomes are providing development opportunities for the staff involved, at all levels, as well as directly contributing towards our drive for school improvement. Our vision was to introduce an integrated package of changes. I believe that all teachers at Rawlins would acknowledge that there have been changes – hopefully for the better – but they may not yet see these changes as integrated. The element not yet in place, which is probably the most critical test of our success, is the creation of a revised appraisal system. This would be one which encourages teachers to review their experience and question their practice, and to regularly produce agreed targets which are followed up. It must also be one which ties into the overall institutional development planning process, the ultimate aim of which is school improvement.

COMMENT

The above case study illustrates how one school is tackling the combined issues of school improvement and professional development in ways in which the whole staff are involved. The staff feel some degree of ownership of the many changes taking place in the school and the responsibility of being accepted as a professional. They recognise the benefits of learning for adults as well as children; after all they do work in a community college. The SMT has made changes to ensure that its members can resume offering guidance to staff on an individual basis and have further shown their support for staff by addressing issues of staff welfare and facilities. The introduction of the mentoring scheme to teachers other than NQTs also shows how staff are valued. It may be no small coincidence that the cultural norms identified by Stoll and Fink (1996) as underpinning successful school improvement are gradually becoming very evident in the changing culture of Rawlins Community College.

1. Shared goals – 'we know where we're going'
2. Responsibility for success – 'we must succeed'
3. Collegiality – 'we're working on this together'
4. Continuous improvement – 'we can get better'
5. Lifelong Learning – 'learning is for everyone'
6. Risk taking – 'we learn by trying something new'
7. Support – 'there's always someone there to help'
8. Mutual respect – 'everyone has something to offer'
9. Openness – 'we can discuss our differences'
10. Celebration and humour – 'we feel good about ourselves'.

(Stoll and Fink, 1996)

It is also evident that this school is trying hard to fit together the three approaches to professional development outlined earlier in the chapter: knowledge and skills development, self-understanding, and ecological change. Once the new system of appraisal is in place with its explicit links to professional development and school development planning, then the staff will have an integrated package of which they can be proud. I know of many schools which are implementing excellent models of professional development. The most effective of them are those which start from *where the school is* and do not seek to impose external solutions on individual school issues without full consultation and support from staff. This is the strength of the Rawlins model: it has been designed for the staff by the staff themselves as a whole school process leading ultimately to improvement for all.

Questions for discussion

How satisfactory is the teacher development as knowledge and skills development, as self-understanding and ecological change model?

How does or should appraisal relate to professional development?

What can be learned from the case study about the relationship of professional development and school improvement?

4

Values and Ethical Issues in the Effective Management of Continuing Professional Development

PAULINE SMITH

As CPD moves into an increasingly 'hard-nosed' era where only the TTA defined 'right teachers' get the 'right training', it is important to identify and value those elements in the management of CPD which have contributed to its effectiveness in the past. This chapter argues that the collaborative approaches to managing CPD, particularly in managing the initiatives of appraisal, NQT induction, mentoring and more recently HEADLAMP, the new headteacher management development and training programme, should be examined in terms of their contributions to efficiency and effectiveness. An investment in the ethical values of mutual respect, entitlement and genuine support has underpinned many collaborative LEA/HE/school-based in-service developments in recent years. The beneficial effects of this investment in terms of building an open organisational culture, in developing expertise and teacher professionalism during a period of considerable change are identified, and the argument is developed that these benefits should be valued and embodied within recent TTA CPD initiatives.

CLIMATE, ETHICS AND VALUES IN CPD

Although competitiveness may be high on the political agenda, experience affirms that a different set of values underpins much effective CPD activity in the profession to date. Collaboration, it can be argued, has proved to be an essential element in the successful implementation of the challenging human resource management processes of induction, mentoring and appraisal. Partnerships between School/LEA and HEI provide a substantial track record of effective and efficient 'on the job' support for the development of vital professional skills and processes, over a lengthy period of INSET funded years.

Amongst the most vital and transferable of these professional development skills are those engaged in our complex interpersonal communication processes. The author's own experiences in working with schools and LEAs within the initiatives of appraisal and the mentoring of NQTs and new headteachers have provided a rich source of evidence which constantly affirms the importance of these management skills in the effective implementation of these challenging professional development activities. The processes of critical self-reflection, needs identification, observation of classroom or management task, constructive feedback and review interviewing, leading to target setting – which are common to both appraisal and mentoring – require skilful management involving high order interpersonal and intrapersonal skills in order to be implemented effectively. Much of the HE/LEA collaboratively designed and delivered appraisal, mentor and HEADLAMP training to date has focused on the development of these generic management skills and processes and has stressed the importance of the climate surrounding the initiatives. Both appraisal and mentoring, it is argued, require a climate of respect and a relationship of trust in order to be accepted and to become effective in school.

It can be argued therefore that the TTA, in developing the National Standards and Assessment Criteria for both teaching and leadership and in designing the ensuing national training and development programmes, would benefit from sharing the experiences of tutors, trainers and teachers who have been involved in appraisal/mentor training over recent turbulent years. These trainers have developed a clear understanding of the importance of climate and ethics in ensuring the effectiveness of challenging professional development activities in school. Thus, the values of mutual respect, empathy and fairness have underpinned much of this GEST funded training in appraisal and mentoring undertaken over the past five years. Such a targeted investment in ethical CPD processes needs therefore to be closely analysed for its contribution to school effectiveness as we move into a more centrally controlled period of professional development; since, as Burford argued at the 1995 BEMAS Conference: 'when schools are tightly coupled to ethics there is no problem with quality'.

The author suggests therefore, that the ethical collaborative approach to CPD, evident within the recent initiatives of appraisal and NQT mentoring which has concentrated on the importance of relationship building, integrity and support in the development of professional competence, has been to good effect. This chapter goes on to examine and to reinforce the importance of the role, qualities and skills of the appraiser/mentor in ensuring the effectiveness of the staff development process and quality of the outcomes, all of which it is argued need to be fully recognised and built upon in future CPD initiatives.

At the point of writing the TTA has not yet published its criteria for the 'expert' teacher or 'subject leader'; it seems unarguable, however, that expertise in mentorship or in appraisal must form an essential dimension in the impending TTA definitives. The essential interpersonal communication skills already identified as vital to the effective human resource management processes of CPD must surely be valued in our National Standards for 'expert teachers' and 'subject school leaders'. Indeed, it can be argued strongly that the two management roles of mentor and subject leader are inseparable; since it is difficult, if not impossible, to lead subject teams effectively and to develop teachers' classroom competence, unless the manager is also competent in her professional development role. Experts in subject leadership and management need, therefore, high order mentoring/appraisal skills and as Drucker and Mintzberg have identified clearly a 'commitment to moral values' in order to be effective leaders.

THE VALUE OF RESPECT – OPENNESS, INTEGRITY, FAIRNESS AND ENTHUSIASM

Perhaps the most powerful of these moral values in CPD is respect which can be seen to be at its most creative when involving a 'five-fold attitude of respect' – for oneself, for other people, for the environment, for beauty and for truth (Watson and Ashton, 1995). As these authors reveal a person who genuinely pursues respect in their professional lives will tend to develop certain 'shared values' and 'qualities' such as 'openness', 'integrity' 'a concern for fairness for all' and 'enthusiasm'. It is important to consider the relevance of these values in relation to the changing context and culture of CPE in Britain.

Openness – Watson and Ashton (1995) suggest that openness, when properly understood has four components:

1. Openness to fresh evidence – the opposite of a closed mind. This type of openness leads to a 'more perceptive interpretation' of the world.
2. Openness to the experience of others, seeking to affirm their insights. A lack of interest in what others believe and value, and a failure to weight these carefully in a positive way, we are told is 'the mark of an immature, selfish attitude to life'.
3. Openness to appreciating the real needs and situations of other people – for example their sensibilities, their level of understanding and their need for affirmation.
4. Openness to critical assessment of the ease with which people, including oneself can be self-deluded.

It is interesting to compare this concept of openness and its clear benefits to the profession in terms of relationship building, empathy and respect for teacher/managers' experiences and needs with the management of recent CPD initiatives. For example, the TTA consultation process for the National Professional Qualification for Headship NPQH and the ensuing bidding system for Regional Training and Development and Assessment Centres does not yet appear to affirm the successful experiences of many existing providers or receivers in this field, notably LEAs, their partner HEIs and school teachers. Whereas the management of appraisal across five years has been characterised by the value of openness to the experiences of the profession and in particular a successful affirmation of the appraisees' real needs.

Integrity is concerned with honesty and wholeness and it is surely unarguable that personal and professional integrity is a vital ingredient in effective

CPD. Having concern for one's integrity ensures the search for honest and trustworthy convictions and inevitably leads to the critical affirmation of others' experiences and insights, including one's own. Further it involves the vigorous use of our critical faculties in order to develop a sounder understanding of our beliefs and a commitment to principled behaviour.

One question might be whether our existing CPD provision helps to develop this holistic and sound personal and professional integrity through a critical approach to knowledge, understanding and beliefs. Or, whether a utilitarian approach to CPD is dominant, where the relevance of facts, tasks and skills are uppermost and a system of conditioning or indoctrination is then possible. The dangers of the narrow, mechanistic technique style of professional and management training, including a restrictive use of the teaching and management competences, is discussed later in this chapter. If integrity means having a commitment to moral values that have been critically tested then our CPD activities need to encourage the development of a critical awareness or 'questioning culture' which ensures that each course participant analyses the values and assumptions which underpin their training, the tasks they are undertaking and the way in which those teaching or management tasks should be carried out. Can we say, with all honesty, that this is the case; especially when considering the short term or one off type of training that is a feature of school-based professional development activity. Do existing funding mechanisms for CPD encourage this longer-term development of a critical consciousness?

Fairness – relates to a sense of justice, equity and consideration for the rights of others. Notions of 'entitlement' have underpinned the provision of CPD over the past ten years to the extent that CPD is at present a firmly established expectation of all NQTs and experienced teachers. Even the increasing targeting of professional development funds and activities is accepted as fair by many teachers, who are educated (or is it conditioned?) into the School Development Planning Process and its agreed priorities. The sense of justice in the fact that all staff development support increasingly needs to be tightly integrated into the school's priorities is a notable feature of the author's evaluative work on appraisal with Manchester and Oldham teachers.

Up until now, notions of equity of access and provision still largely pervade much LEA, HE and school professional development programmes. Further, where the rights of the individual teacher to expect equal respect and a freedom to take up professional development opportunities have been infringed, the author finds that teachers are increasingly willing to criticise the effectiveness of their management systems. However, with the imminence of increased targeting of CPD funding only on those teachers fulfilling the TTA 'eligibility criteria', one wonders whether teachers' sense of fairness, justice and equity will be stretched to the point of publicly voiced criticism. Or, whether the 'powerful social norms against talking about public issues in social settings' identified by Professors Crewe and Searing (TES 7/6/96, p. 14) will therefore inhibit any such public criticism of national CPD developments. Certainly, at the point of writing the teacher professional associations do not appear to be challenging this social norm and their voice on recent CPD changes remains relatively unheard in the national media.

Enthusiasm – this last quality generated through a commitment to the value of respect is, as Watson and Ashton (1995) identify, of great importance as a major motivating factor in undertaking self-education and thus CPE. It is important therefore to evaluate how motivated or enthused teachers have been through particular types of CPD training and development.

In one example, the author's evaluation of the implementation of appraisal in Oldham and Manchester has revealed the importance of effective training in review interviewing skills, helping teachers to recognise their real achievements in a period of change and instability. The importance of the high-order inter-personal skills of active listening and giving constructive feedback, or affirmation as described earlier in this chapter, are paramount here in maintaining teachers' motivation or enthusiasm to continue their own professional development. This is perhaps especially true when the morale of teachers is depressed by unrealistic notions of external accountability, and when overload and teacher stress are commonly perceived features of the life and culture of our schools.

THE ORGANISATIONAL CULTURE OF CPD

The culture of any organisation is not static as Bennett (1995) has ably identified, and is susceptible to 'shaping by management' as well as being potentially resistant to change. It can be argued that a key management task is to shape a CPD culture in school or college in order to promote life long learning in the profession. However, those aspects of culture which are susceptible to this sort of influence by managers need firstly to be identified and the ethics of any such influence and action carefully considered. The work of Young (1983) reveals the importance of understanding the individual values, assumptions, beliefs and constructs underpinning the ways in which groups come to interact, negotiate and share common values; which in turn determine standards of acceptable and appropriate behaviour in any organisation. If a key management task (of TTA or senior manager in school) is to promote a CPD culture then it is important to research into this two-way interactive process of individual teachers or sub-groups with the dominant culture. At this point, it is tempting to ponder whether the recent TTA initiative to promote 'excellence in teaching', through its focus on *Teaching as a Research-based Profession* (TTA 1996k) and the encouragement of teachers to play a more active role in research through the pilot scheme of research grants, might result in this type of organisational or cultural research that could help therefore to open up the issue of values and ethics in education to critical debate.

The dominant view of organisational culture in much management writing and evident in recent TTA literature relating to HEADLAMP and NPQH is that a clear relationship exists between a homogenous culture and a successful organisation. The strong 'culture of collaboration' in three schools identified by Nias *et al.* (1989) and referred to by Bennett (1995) in his book *Managing Professional Teachers* is attributed clearly to the organisation's leaders and their acts of openness, sensitivity, tolerance and flexibility. This leadership behaviour which exemplifies a certain set of values, described previously in this chapter as respect and its associated qualities, leads to reciprocal action by other staff members and thus it is argued a self-perpetuating culture of collaboration and mutual support.

The author's research into Oldham and Manchester teachers' perceptions of school culture through the case study of appraisal, echoes the work of Nias revealing the importance of the supportive climate established by the head-teacher. The pivotal nature of this leadership role in creating a conducive culture and in establishing publicly a clear set of values and expectations of behaviour can also, it is argued, be seen within the TTA HEADLAMP tasks and abilities and in the Draft Principles for Aspiring Headteachers (TTA 1995b, 1996d).

The importance of the effective management of a positive CPD culture where respect for the professional development of self and others is uppermost is clear therefore when viewed from an integrationist perspective on organisational culture (Martin and Mayerson, 1988). If, however, a perspective of differentiation is adopted then the reality of individual interests and the challenge of reaching agreement on the values underpinning most whole school policies and practices is made visible. Again, the value of critical reflection on self and organisation and further research into the effect of cultures of differentiation and fragmentation on schools is indicated. This type of research would be helpful in our open search for greater understanding of the complex social interactions at play within CPD and could lead to greater effectiveness in its management. Such research might also question whether the present TTA moves to establish Regional Training and Development and Assessment Centres and centrally defined eligibility criteria are more likely to lead to Mintzberg's (1979) 'divisionalised' form of organisational structure or perhaps the 'ambiguity' defined by Bush (1995) – and thus, it is argued, less effectiveness. At the point of writing, the relationship between intention, practice and outcome in relation to the professionally developed expert teacher/leader unfortunately appears most uncertain.

APPRAISAL – A CASE STUDY IN RESPECT

We are informed by TTA in their Review of Headteacher and Teacher Appraisal (June 1996, p. 6) that, to 'date, £54 million has been spent on the preparation and implementation of the current appraisal process.' Whatever the 'real' figure, it can be argued that this targeted money has been well spent in establishing a national system of appraisal strongly founded on respect which has developed major strengths in terms of:

- the opportunity teachers have to discuss their teaching and career development, and

- the value of positive feedback, recognition of achievement and constructive critical comment.

The above strengths are identified by TTA (June 1996) and supported by this author's own research using questionnaire and interview data from Oldham and Manchester teachers (Smith 1995, 1996). However, a major difference in findings occurs between the TTA review evidence and the Oldham/Manchester research and is illuminated particularly in the choice of TTA words that the above strengths 'were not often seen in practice.' Such a finding is strongly challenged by the views of 312 teachers who completed questionnaires and were interviewed by the author and team of LEA evaluators, during the period 1995–6. In general terms three out of four teachers in both Oldham and Manchester found appraisal to be a beneficial professional process and valued highly the opportunities for self-review and constructive feedback. In particular, the survey revealed that teachers valued most highly the appraisal interview or dialogue in both Oldham and Manchester and referred to the benefits of 'feeling valued', of 'improved communications' and 'openness' throughout their responses. It is also important to record that over fifty per cent of teachers in both LEAs identified specific improvements to their teaching and management practices as a result of the appraisal process. Another finding in opposition to the recent TTA report on appraisal.

One particular question in the survey asked teachers about whether appraisal has influenced the school organisation or climate in any way. This was followed up by interview questions on the management style/culture of the school and its relationship to appraisal. These responses are particularly pertinent to this chapter as we consider the importance of climate and culture in the effectiveness of CPD.

In relation to the question: *The management style/culture of the school – how would you describe it? How does this dominant style relate to appraisal?* the dominant culture was described as a 'team approach' where 'staff feel valued'. A collaborative, consultative style of management seems therefore to dominate both Oldham and Manchester schools where 'communication between staff is good' and as at least one teacher put it 'mutual respect is present and essential'. Clearly, 'team work', 'confidentiality' and 'trust' are uppermost in these teachers' responses who feel that these 'values' or 'qualities' are important in the successful implementation of appraisal in school. As one interviewee put it 'the climate took the pressure off appraisal'.

These responses provide sound evidence of the importance of leadership in CPD and of the successful ways in which leaders can promote the values they wish to become the basis of the appraisal culture in their schools. I would suggest that the LEA working closely with its Professional Associations acted strongly as the culture founders for appraisal as Schein (1991) and Nias *et al.* (1989) have identified. Certainly the expert training and documentation provided by the LEA established the values of 'respect, empathy and genuineness' in the processes of appraisal and made a heavy investment in the development of interpersonal/communication skills through interactive, role play sessions designed to 'open-up' the challenging processes of observation and feedback to critical analysis and debate.

In relation to the question: *Has appraisal influenced the school organisation or climate in any way?* approximately fifty per cent of teachers recorded an affirmative response and went on to identify 'the greater understanding of one another's needs' and feelings of 'not being alone'. These are important values for us to note. Several headteachers answered this question positively and referred to the 'more open constructive atmosphere' resulting from appraisal; and the building of stronger relationships/team building. Others referred to 'increased teacher self-esteem' an important 'attitude' of respect, identified earlier in this chapter. One head wrote that appraisal had provided a 'means of giving praise to staff who work hard and are successful'. It was not only heads who wrote of these changes in climate since teachers also referred to the 'opening of classroom doors'; 'improved relationships with colleagues'; how appraisal has 'helped us to support each other' and that staff are now 'more willing to discuss their practice in a constructive atmosphere'.

Generally, then, these positive responses focused around the improvements in climate associated with the 'raising of esteem', 'feelings of value' and 'improved communications and reflections in school'. These are clearly important benefits from appraisal for these teacher/managers. TTA does confirm several of these benefits in its recent review of appraisal, but then casts doubt on their occurrence in practice. Perhaps further research is called for on those schools where these practices or values are clearly perceived to be in place in order to isolate their contribution to school effectiveness – in this case through the implementation of the challenging CPD processes of appraisal.

It is interesting to note that the perceived benefits and improvements emanating from appraisal are almost always closely related by Oldham and Manchester teachers to the *skills of their appraiser and observer*. Further, the majority of teachers in these two metropolitan boroughs did not regard the process of observation as problematic or stressful in any way. The reasons given by respondents related to the 'observer's personal skills' and their experience of 'working alongside the appraiser'. Again these are vital skills and qualities developed through experience which the profession can build upon in the next stage of 'managing teacher performance'. Especially perhaps in relation to 'monitoring the implementation of policies' – an area of need identified by OFSTED and TTA. Observations of practice, followed by constructive feedback are vital in the professional development of the student, NQT and CPD teacher/manager and the use of peer observation has provided some increased opportunity for teachers to benefit from the process within appraisal. Many observers in appraisal (as well as in mentoring, monitoring and inspection) have found the process to be highly demanding and challenging on a personal and professional level, thus supporting the argument of 'high order' professional skills. It is also interesting to record that many observers have found the process of observation highly valuable to their own professional development and deem it a privilege.

Certainly, the *codes of practice* established within both appraisal and OFSTED inspection processes have proved to be vital documents identifying the ethics of the process of observation and the values and qualities to be demonstrated by observer. The importance of training and development that focuses on values and ethics as a part of such a sensitive CPD activity cannot therefore be over-emphasised. The success of appraisal in Manchester and Oldham can clearly be linked therefore to the heavy investment made by both authorities in the high quality training for appraisal using expert trainers. (The same might be claimed for the early OFSTED secondary training underpinned by a strong code of practice, but this requires much greater analysis than is possible at this point in time.)

This investment in skills training and the implementation of a code of practice and standards of behaviour which embody respect and its related qualities of fairness, integrity, openness and enthusiasm can perhaps best be seen *in the role of the appraiser and the appraisal interview* (or dialogue as it is known in Oldham). This was cited by teachers as being the most valuable part of the appraisal process and well 'worth fighting for' (Smith 1995, 1996). The vast majority of teachers found their appraiser to be 'competent, sensitive and supportive'. The importance of receiving constructive feedback from 'well-informed and experienced colleagues' was identified as 'confidence-building' and leading to 'raised self-esteem'. Several Manchester and Oldham teachers revealed the importance of the affirmation discussed earlier in this chapter when they referred to their pleasure at 'feeling valued', of their satisfaction on learning they are 'on the right track', resulting in 'renewed confidence and faith in oneself as a teacher'. Important effects in the light of the increased perceptions of overload and stress discussed earlier.

The dissemination of good practice across team, department or school is, it can be argued, greatly enhanced by the use of observation and it is clear that several schools are now incorporating the observation of teaching and learning facilitated by appraisal into their *school and curriculum monitoring processes*. Staff are needing to agree their fundamental values and ethical purposes in this monitoring process, in order to determine how far the practice is one of senior management 'accountability' or observation for 'professional development, mentoring and ongoing support'.

It can be argued that if observation is to remain a valuable tool in developing teacher/manager competence then schools and teachers must be able to use observation dominantly as a method of gathering data for self-improvement – facilitating the openness to evidence, needs, experiences and assessment described earlier in this chapter. Observation from this perspective and the experiences of appraisal shared here remain therefore powerful tools in the further development of a self-critical community of professionals, within an action research framework, rather than it being used dominantly in a narrow assessment or accountability model.

Surely, we need now to build *on* the benefits that appraisal – its skills and processes – has already brought and to build *in* the increased rigour and quality of outcomes that can be achieved most effectively, it is argued, within a collaborative culture where respect for the individual within the organisation is a dominant value.

RESPECT AND RIGOUR – COMPETENCES, INDICATORS AND BENCHMARKS

The importance of increased rigour is evident in TTA's 'Key Principle' for the appraisal of the future in that the process should *both* encourage, recognise and value good work by teachers *and* point up firmly any weaknesses, taking appropriate follow-up action (TTA 1996i). In this section it is argued that improvements in the areas of focusing and target setting in appraisal and CPD generally should help to develop increased rigour and improve effectiveness. The use of performance indicators, competences or benchmarks in the processes of review and target setting is also discussed in the light of the author's experiences with NQTs and new headteachers.

The desirability of sharper, more challenging targets for professional development was identified by Manchester/Oldham teachers to the author and can also be seen in the TTA survey. Many of the author's respondents felt they had 'opted for a safe focus' the first time round in appraisal and wished to 'choose a much narrower focus next time'.

'Finding an appropriate focus' and 'setting targets' are identified therefore as areas for further training and support by many teachers/managers. Yet, the use of performance indicators competences or even benchmarks for the purposes of self-review in CPD is still very limited to date. This fact is perhaps all the more surprising when one considers the maturity of school-based Initial Teacher Education, the use of *The Competences of Teaching* and the NQT Professional Development Profiles developed over the past five years through collaborative HE/LEA partnerships.

The Competences of Teaching (DFE 9/92 and 14/93) are perhaps the clearest example of indicators or National Standards in use which enable the measurement of performance against specific objectives. It can be argued that this *specificity of objectives* can lead to the increased rigour or effectiveness desired by the profession since they can be used to 'point up' success (and weakness) and enable the efficient targeting of CPD resources at the point of need. From this perspective, then, the use of performance indicators, such as the Competences of Teaching are signals of success (Rogers and Badham, 1994) which can be used to indicate whether agreed objectives have been achieved. As such, they can contribute to the ethical management of CPD. Much depends, however, on how these indicators, competences or benchmarks have been determined and most importantly the purposes of the assessments made against these specific criteria.

The author's own experiences with NQT competences and the piloting of the new TTA Career Entry Profile reinforces the vital contribution, to any ethical or efficient CPD process of *the role of the mentor*. Mentoring an NQT opens up areas of professional competence to critical scrutiny for both mentor and mentee and demands as much the qualities of integrity, openness and fairness argued earlier in the chapter as does the role of appraiser. The role of mentor, like that of appraiser or other manager of professional development requires therefore high order interpersonal communication skills in order to be successful (Smith and West-Burnham, 1993). After five years of mentor and NQT development work in local authorities, the author finds that mentors are requesting still further training and development in the challenging skills and processes of observation, review, interviewing and target setting/action planning. These experienced mentors express the need for their own ongoing professional development support – that is their own mentoring.

Some teachers/schools, but not many, have made a link between the skills and processes of mentoring and appraisal and have used this understanding to bring both CPD systems together and to build on the investments already made. In this way, it can be argued, the values of respect, empathy and genuine support that have underpinned the introduction of appraisal to date can now be disseminated into mentoring and hopefully into the co-ordinating and monitoring activities of the school. In this way TTA's 'key principle' that appraisal 'should be a central strand in how a school manages, evaluates and seeks to improve its own performance and that of all working within it' (TTA 1996i) can become an ethical reality.

The increased use of competences, for example in the TTA HEADLAMP and National Professional Qualification for Headteachers, which are defined as the tasks and abilities of headship, could therefore, encourage a rigorous and focused self-review and collection of appropriate evidence against a set of 'benchmarks or success criteria'. This rigorous and supportive process could then lead to the setting of clear targets, linked to the school training and development plan, thus resulting in further improvements in the quality of teaching and management, and the performance of the school as a whole. The potential for this improvement lies as this chapter has argued in the respect and sense of fairness afforded to the process by all players and the attendant high order interpersonal skills demonstrated by the mentor. Similarly, in collaborative CPD activities, it is the quality of the relationship between partners in this process of CPD and the values and standards of behaviour established by the leader and adopted by all partners which are vital characteristics of effectiveness.

A relationship of collaboration, trust and mutual respect has existed between Manchester Metropolitan University, Crewe School of Education and its local LEAs for a significant period of time. Recent work with Cheshire LEA and its new headteachers has revealed the value of a set of clear criteria against which the new headteacher diagnoses needs and action plans professional development, with the skilled support of the mentor/advisor. After successful three day conferences focusing on the 'core' tasks of strategic management and leadership Cheshire HEADLAMP heads are formed into 'action-learning sets' across the county where the relationships of mutual support are maintained and collaborative research and development in the areas of leadership and management are more easily facilitated through expert support.

CONCLUSION

In summary the competences, tasks, abilities, performance criteria, benchmarks, assessment criteria and the Professional Development Portfolios for staff rapidly being developed are, it is argued, useful tools to aid effective CPD. Yet they are only effective in the hands of a skilled and reflective practitioner who with mentoring support engages in the double loop learning identified by Schon (1983) and who therefore values the questioning of underlying assumptions and engages in critical problem-solving through a process of enquiry. This critical self-reflection on and in action is dialectically and, it is argued, *essentially* related to the value of respect in CPD already propounded in this chapter. Such a value promotes the ethics of openness, professional integrity, enthusiasm for learning and hopefully fairness in all our behaviour. These qualities, it is argued here, have been promoted most effectively through the expert collaborative training and development provided by LEA and HEI, based on a relationship of trust which has made efficient use of the pool of expertise in teacher development built up over a lengthy period of DFE and HEFC funded years. It is surely important to value this national investment now and to promote a *continuity* of support for further teacher development – and thereby school improvement – rather than a potential fragmentation of provision.

Questions for discussion

How do you interpret the differences between appraisal and mentoring?

How fully do openness, integrity, fairness and enthusiasm underpin CPD in practice?

What is the relationship between organisational culture and a climate for successful CPD?

5

Privatising Policies and Marketising Relationships: Continuing Professional Development in Schools, LEAs and Higher Education

SUE LAW

The last decade has seen a significant reformulation and marketisation of the education system, characterised by a strengthening emphasis on 'account-ability' and 'choice' and seen by successive Conservative governments as a catalyst for raising standards, pursuing curriculum reform, and locating management within the schools themselves. These changes reflect, to some degree, both national and international trends towards redefining education policy and the role of education (Macpherson, 1996). Within the British context, for example, the 1988 Education Reform Act and subsequent legislation has de-centralised responsibilities to schools, making them increasingly accountable not only for the funding and management of pupils' learning, but also for the training and development of staff at all levels.

Alongside this decentralisation of management responsibility, there has been a simultaneous and progressive centralisation of control and curricula in government hands – established through a diminution in local education authority (LEA) power, an enhancement in ministerial power, and the growth of educational 'quangocracies' like the Office for Standards in Education (OFSTED), the agency charged with national school inspections. Another quango (or 'EGO' – extra government organisation – as it is sometimes known) the Teacher Training Agency (TTA), was created in 1994 with, initially, a role focused on initial teacher training (ITT) funding. However, responding to a request from the Secretary of State, TTA rapidly absorbed continuing professional development (CPD) into its remit, reviewed INSET spending and gained control of higher education's INSET funds (Graham, 1996; HEFCE 1995).

This centralisation of control and decentralisation of responsibility is part of a long-developing policy shift. The apparently cosy 'liberal education consensus' characterising the post-war period, revealed as a triangle of tension (Briault, 1976) during the 1970s was, by the late 1980s, being characterised as a discourse of derision (Ball, 1990), as in the post-1979 election period, New Right Think Tanks increasingly reviled the apparent 'rampant progressivism' of LEAs, teacher unions and the 'educational establishment', and encouraged successive Thatcher and Major governments to 'think the unthinkable' in education policy terms.

Since 1988, educational reform in relation to schools has been pursued in three major areas. Initially, the government focused on the curriculum and structures of *compulsory schooling* with, for example, the introduction of the National Curriculum and local management of schools (LMS). Scrutiny then fell on the curriculum and structures of *initial teacher education*, with the introduction of school-based or school-centred training, a growing emphasis on competences and, more recently, plans for a national teacher training curriculum. Most recently, the curriculum and structures of *inservice education and training* (INSET) have seen fundamental changes to INSET funding and organisation, leaving schools as the locus of decision-making, and the government committed to introducing 'model' professional development curricula like the National Professional Qualification for Headship (NPQH).

This chapter focuses on issues of professional development reform since, despite a number of piecemeal changes to structures and relationships over the last decade, strategic INSET planning at a national level remains a relatively recent phenomenon, largely pursued under the auspices of and co-ordinated by the TTA. Following a brief review of the policy backdrop framing the newly marketised INSET, I examine the metamorphosis in relationships between providers and schools, the roles of LEAs, higher education and private consultancy, and the influence of OFSTED and TTA. On the basis of research data gathered through the Keele Effective Educators Project (KEEP), it is argued that certain organisational elements are needed if an effective CPD culture is to be established (Glover and Law, 1996). Lastly, the developing 'delegated' leadership role of the Professional Development Co-ordinator (PDC) is examined.

CHANGING INSET POLICY

During the post-war period, continuing professional development (CPD) and inservice education and training (INSET) in England and Wales was often the subject of 'recommendation and pragmatic action' (Burgess *et al.*, 1993), largely ignored by government in policy debates, and frequently side-stepped in legislation. In effect, INSET became the 'Cinderella' of teacher education (Williams, 1991). During the 1980s, even as successive Thatcher governments focused attention on reforming education in schools, colleges and initial teacher education, issues concerning continuing professional development initially retained a relatively low policy profile and priority on government agendas. Where changes in INSET occurred, they did so almost silently – seemingly the by-product of national funding constraints and the impact of the new diversified market in education.

Despite the James Report's commitment to teachers' professional development (DES, 1972a), later echoed by the government's Advisory Committee on the Supply and Training of Teachers (ACSTT, 1978), and reaffirmed by the Advisory Committee on the Supply and Education of Teachers (ACSET, 1984), professional development structures established during the post-war period did not change radically until the mid-1980s – with even then change being pursued on an *ad hoc*, piecemeal basis, driven by revised national funding priorities. The recent rise of the TTA brought a rapid review of provision and a stated concern to place longer term, national and planned structural change on the agenda – although the degree to which imposed structural change for INSET is effective in both gaining teacher commitment and stimulating improvements in classroom and management practice remains a complex and difficult question.

Nevertheless, the importance of INSET has been increasingly formally recognised over the past decade. For example, the *Better Schools* white paper argued that 'individual teachers need support and encouragement for their professional development at all stages of their career' (DES, 1985), while the School Teachers' Pay and Conditions of Employment proposals (1987) introduced teacher appraisal, and highlighted the importance of teacher development, specifically identifying five 'professional development days' a year for those working in schools and colleges.

Various training initiatives established during the 1980s also encouraged a re-framing of professional development. The government's experience with the introduction of TVEI (1983), alongside lessons learned from 'cascading' GCSE training (1986) and the implications of the proposed National Curriculum (1987), stimulated a review of both the costs and strategies in developing new initiatives and emphasised, in the government's mind, the importance of encouraging INSET which was directly relevant to classroom practice, rather than focused on general principles (Glickman and Dale, 1990).

Although government commitment to teacher development in the 1970s and 1980s was reflected in a gradual movement towards school-focused inservice education (Bolam, 1982), significant change really only began with the publication of Circular 6/86 (DES, 1986) which established the Local Education Authority Training Grants Scheme (LEATGS). This development marked an end to the relatively longstanding 'pool' of INSET funding which had enabled the more opportunist LEAs to provide long-term development opportunities for their teachers. The 'pool' was, in effect a relatively open-ended government funding commitment which some LEAs exploited to benefit their own teaching force. Changes to a more systematic approach through LEATGS represented the first moves towards more nationally-prioritised, government-directed INSET funding – while still retaining a locally-prioritised (i.e. LEA-directed) element. Consequently, traditional INSET relationships between government, schools, LEAs and higher education altered as, initially, LEAs became more centrally involved in planning and structuring professional development. However, the government's 'scrutiny' report on INSET (Glickman and Dale,

1990) was followed by the introduction of GEST (Grant for Education Support and Training), (DfE, 1992) replacing LEATGS and ESGs (Education Support Grants) which were rolled up into one unitary grant – effectively ending the opportunity for 'local' (i.e. LEA) funding priorities.

During the early 1990s, the government's teacher education focus rested on a continuing delegation of responsibility and funding to schools – aimed at locating ITT within 'partnership' schools and, wherever possible, breaking a perceived HE monopoly of ITT management, curriculum and funding (echoing Secretary of State, Kenneth Baker's description of its 'producer capture' in the 1980s) through establishing Schools' Consortia for Initial Teacher Training (SCITT) and, later, the 'brokerage' of the Teacher Training Agency. However, while policy-makers were active with respect to the funding, organisation and curricula of schools and the links with initial teacher education during the early 1990s, professional development hovered in uneasy policy limbo – left, as the White Paper *Choice and Diversity* states, to the 'education market': 'The Government expects that increasingly the private sector will step in to provide such services'. (DfE, 1992, p. 32.)

While schools have for some time been expected to think strategically about school development planning, government planning strategies *vis-à-vis* INSET effectively only rose the top of the education policy agenda in March 1995 with an acknowledgement by Gillian Shepherd, Secretary of State for Education, that 'it is an area about which we know relatively little. We cannot afford that ignorance . . . INSET funding amounts to a huge investment nationally; if we count the cost of the five "non-contact" days in the teachers' contract, it is around £400m a year'.

While government INSET funding priorities have been announced annually since the mid-1980s, school leaders constrained by tightening budgets have found it increasingly problematic to establish long-term institutional strategies for professional development. In addition, as government-funded and longer-term award-bearing INSET diminished, the number of registered MEd research students for example, fell from 2,000 to 200 a year over a five year period (Wragg, cited in Low, 1995), largely to be replaced by part-timers with short-term 'training immediacy' needs resulting from newly-imposed government initiatives. In effect, professional development practice reflected the development of 'government directed' and 'school-centred' education policy.

In this period of rapid (albeit relatively low-key) change to the funding and climate of professional development, the wider INSET community endeavoured to sustain a focus on identifying issues, documenting practices and offering potential examplars of good practice (Bolam 1993; Glover and Law 1993; Bradley, Connor and Southworth, 1994). However, funding changes substantially destabilised providers' attempts to plan proactively for long-term development. With a government focused on annual and changing CPD priorities and funding strategies, providers were pushed towards short-termist, 'flavour of the month' approaches, which inhibited strategic staff planning, and encouraged reliance on part-time, contracted staff to support 'quick response' programmes.

CHANGING LEAS: FROM CONTROL TO CONTRACT

During the 1980s, LEATGS arrangements had enabled many LEAs to develop more 'formalised and coherent' systems for managing INSET (DES 1989, Harland *et al.*, 1993), establishing a greater professionalism in needs identification and consultancy largely provided through a cadre of newly recruited advisory teachers in support of advisers and inspectors (Baker, 1986). Arguably, these developments created a professional environment which allowed many LEAs to survive (and in some cases, even thrive on) the marketisation of INSET heralded by the introduction of GEST, as schools became purchasers and customers.

The impact of the marketplace has, nevertheless, dramatically changed LEA structures, destroying numerous long established alliances and systems (Morris, 1990), and shifting the centre of power: schools are now pivotal in determining the level and range of professional development provided for their staff. Headteachers are, for example, far less willing than formerly to release staff for offsite course attendance – stressing the problems of 'teaching time lost which you can't get back'. In addition, the amount of 'personal time' rather than 'professional time' being used for teacher development is increasingly significant as efforts to establish a national staff development strategy gain momentum (Hewton and Jolley, 1991).

The introduction of GEST and later, new OFSTED inspection structures also forced LEAs to rethink their operations in order to become examples of 'new public management' (NPM) – 'leaner and fitter', better able to survive a decimation of role and diversity of competition. Effectively, the marketisation of CPD led to narrower ranges of LEA provision and a diminution in their responsiveness to school needs across the broad range of areas. For example, schools responding to the KEEP surveys over several years readily acknowledge that, as the Audit commission (1989) noted, LEAs have 'lost an empire' but have yet to 'find a role'. Redefined as only partial INSET providers, LEAs are no longer strategic 'command and control' authorities: they are moving, instead from 'management by control' to 'management by contract' (Harland *et al.*, 1993) and 'evolving a new philosophy of local administration based on partnership' (Low, 1995).

These changes are highlighted by the fact that, since 1993, LEA-based inspection posts have declined by a quarter, advisory teacher posts by a third, and some LEAs no longer have advisory teacher posts at all (Mann, 1995). Moreover, the need to fund posts through OFSTED inspection contracts has meant that, as inspectors and advisers noted in a national survey, they are only able to devote 'half-a-day to one-and-a-half days a week to specialist support in schools'. In addition, some LEAs are only able to provide advisory teacher/adviser support in a limited number of curriculum areas (Mann 1995, Education 1996).

CHANGING HIGHER EDUCATION: LEARNING TO SUPPORT

The fluidity and uncertainty of LEA provision nationally is echoed by developments within higher education institutions (HEI), traditionally the other major providers of formal teacher development opportunities. The increasing 'marginalisation of HE' during the 1980s (Day, 1989) was largely driven by changing government funding priorities and exacerbated by the consequent ascendancy of LEA-managed provision. In the post-1993 era, as school-based professional development gathered pace and LEA advisory personnel were 'forced' to sell their expertise to OFSTED, HEIs experienced a similarly confused and uneven pattern of contraction and growth. On the one hand, they were confronted with often significant 'training' demands to facilitate National Curriculum, assessment and management development needs, balanced on the other, by an often rapid decline in other less high profile curriculum areas and in more sustained 'education' courses.

Historically, higher education provided teachers with long-term development opportunities through termly or yearly secondments onto award-bearing programmes (e.g. Masters degrees and advanced Diplomas), offering a ready-made research base with direct links into a 'community of scholars' (Dempster 1991). The abandonment of the 'pool' funding system brought a relatively rapid decline in registrations for long courses in HEIs, with GEST reinforcing this trend as funding focused increasingly on national priorities and local priority funding was eroded. 'Teacher-as-consumer' pressures have also pushed higher education away from traditional 'provider-recipient' relationships with schools towards, on one side, professional training 'partnerships' linked to ITT and 'customer-marketeer' relationships where schools negotiate and purchase specific services on the other. Universities and colleges no longer have security of role as recognised 'expert-providers' and, arguably, need to metamorphose into 'learning support agencies', reflecting moves towards a user-led rather than provider-led market (Gilroy and Day, 1993).

Thus, in essence, many higher education institutions are struggling with the twin pressures of educational consumerism and quality assessment. This is leading many to review their activities – by developing, for example, distance learning, self-supported study programmes, school-based courses and school–HEI partnership research. Like LEAs, HEIs need to satisfy consumer demand within an increasingly constrained 1990s economic climate, where government-determined funding priorities are the central and driving force and 'the client is king'. In addition, they need to ensure that courses are delivered, monitored and evaluated effectively, meeting the 'quality' imperative, with standards set by a range of monitoring and auditing bodies – the Higher Education Funding Council for England (HEFCE) and the Higher Education Quality Council (HEQC) and OFSTED – despite the difficulties in defining precisely what the elusive concept of 'quality' really means (Pfeffer and Coote, 1991).

CHANGING CONSULTANCIES: PRIVATISING SUPPORT?

The expansion of private consultancies has also characterised the growing marketisation of professional development. As schools initially pushed for 'value for money' within a climate of diminishing funds, the early 1990s saw a rapid growth in consultancy provision (often comprising former LEA, HEI and HMI 'grey power' expertise), although the pattern of development was very uneven across institutions and over time. In addition, consultant quality has become a major concern for schools, with many of the newer providers initially criticised as 'cowboy consultants' showing 'quick fix' and 'hit and run' tendencies (Law and Glover 1995).

In the case of both HEI and private consultancies, KEEP research data shows that schools are consistently critical of the way many consultancies have retained traditional provider infrastructures which they consider are insufficiently adapted to meet increasingly sophisticated school needs. Some of the HEI and private consultancies, as well as the older LEA advisory services are seen as 'inflexible' and 'amateurish' by comparison with the best of the newer LEA 'agencies' which are thought as having developed greater 'closeness to the customer' (Peters and Waterman, 1982). Nevertheless, schools also concede that the rise of consultancy has forced them to hone their negotiation skills and sharpen their financial acumen in developing purchaser–provider relationships.

CHANGING SCHOOLS: NEW ROLES AND RESPONSIBILITIES

As the traditional relationships linking schools, LEAs and higher education have become realigned and competition-driven, schools have metamorphosed into 'ring holders' – funding agents, organisers and consumers of inservice education and training – undertaking many traditional LEA planning and decision-making roles regarding training-needs identification and personnel management. New responsibilities as 'training schools', initially in relation to ITT and increasingly for INSET, have encouraged some schools to establish a stronger professional development ethos and resource base to cater for wider professional needs – e.g. for trainee teachers, supply staff, classroom assistants and other 'para-professionals', as well as permanent full-time and increasingly, part-time, teaching staff. Arguably, therefore, schools may be poised to become 'learning shops' – echoing American models for improving access to learning materials and information as advocated by the *National Commission On Education* (NCE, 1993, p. 94).

This emphasis echoes some business management notions that 'learning organisations' are those able 'to tap people's commitment and capacity to learn at all levels' (Senge, 1990); that learning is vital for institutional survival; and that the rate of learning within organisations needs to be equal to or greater than the rate of change occurring within the wider environment (Garrett, 1987). If this emphasis is correct, schools need to be effective learning organisations with each headteacher becoming the 'head learner' and 'a catalyst assisting teacher growth' (Barth, 1990).

Drives away from off-site, *course-focused* INSET towards site-based *consultancy-led* approaches reflect the changing locus of INSET activity, reflecting greater staff participation. Stimulated by a dramatic decline in government-funded secondments and twilight/evening award-bearing classes in HE institutions (Butt, 1989) schools increasingly endeavour to utilise site-based INSET to maximise cost-effectiveness, minimise disruption and maintain the pace of development. However, meeting a range of legitimate agendas is complex and difficult as whole school, departmental and individual needs all joggle for attention. The tight funding climate, has also brought significant levels of 'hidden investment' in schools, as a support for both *human* and *physical* resources – through increasingly self-funded teacher development and community support for physical resources. However, as a Chartered Institute of Public Finance and Accountancy (CIPFA) national survey found, while contributions from parent-teacher associations (PTA) amounted to £52m a year, fund-raising is increasingly difficult since 'increasing numbers of parents were fed up by the pressure to make financial donations for essentials' (Education 1996).

Furthermore, delegated budgets have altered more than the funding balance for teacher development. Even if teachers increasingly support their own development, schools now face overt personnel *management* responsibilities, having strategically important roles as guardians of 'whole-career' or 'life-long' learning opportunities for their staff – from initial training stage, through induction to long-term development (Bolam 1990; Ball and Goodson 1985). Decentralisation and administrative pressures mean that headteachers and Professional Development Co-ordinators are increasingly arbiters of institutionally-led professional support – ultimately controlling time, opportunities and sometimes the funding support of colleagues.

TOWARDS A PROFESSIONAL DEVELOPMENT CULTURE

In order to manage school improvement and attempt to resolve a multiplicity of tensions arising within the newly privatised INSET, many schools have acknowledged the need to provide a more coherent framework for professional development which can provide a platform and be a catalyst for school improvement.

The Keele Effective Educators Project (KEEP) has, between 1993 and 1996, developed both a quantitative database of over 300 primary and secondary schools and compiled extensive interview data through work with key staff in twelve case study schools (i.e. headteacher; PDC/deputy head, head of department and main scale member of staff). Thus far, KEEP survey and interview data shows that where schools are able to manage five fundamental organisational aspects of professional development, they have the basis for a secure and supportive professional development culture in which staff and pupils are able to thrive (Glover and Law, 1996). These five key elements comprise:

- the effective management of *information/communication* flows;
- shared and open *planning processes*;

- clearly defined *resource allocation procedures* with focused aims and targets;
- a clear *evaluation strategy* which provides a structure for ongoing review and development;
- open *networking opportunities* to facilitate mutual support and reflection.

By auditing their organisational status quo in relation to these elements and then targeting specific aspects, schools are better placed to integrate teacher development within whole school development agendas. Three kinds of 'typical' professional development situations may be loosely characterised within schools:

- *Adverse situations*: these situations tend to inhibit development, largely because opportunities are frequently either random, unplanned or unrelated to the institution's overall aims and objectives as identified through both departmental and school development planning processes;
- *Neutral situations*: these situations neither inhibit nor enhance development, most frequently because they are regarded as 'one-off' and limited in focus, designed to meet specific and relatively narrow needs, where the full significance and potential is not fully appreciated;
- *Positive situations*: these situations facilitate opportunities and strategies which enable staff associated with an activity to develop and grow professionally because their potential for achievement is released and supported, and the interaction between opportunities and possibilities for development is recognised at *all* levels within the institution.

When used in combination, the five organisational elements and three situational descriptors outlined above provide a possible framework for developing a baseline audit of the prevailing development culture within a school or other organisation (see Figure 5.1). Most schools are likely to demonstrate a mixture of adverse, neutral and supportive elements, with few institutions being at one extreme or another. However, by aggregating a range of staff perceptions in relation to each of the key elements, it is possible to create a clearer picture of the school's 'INSET ethos' and, consequently, to identify areas in which CPD strategies may be improved – for example, where there are confused or unclear management practices, or where departments, groups or individuals are 'at odds' with, or unaware of, formally agreed practices.

THE ROLE OF THE PDC

With LEAs no longer virtual monopoly providers of teacher development opportunities (Baker, 1986; Harland, Kinder and Keys, 1993), the role of the designated Professional Development Co-ordinator in schools has become increasingly central. In 1993, for example, 70 per cent of KEEP survey schools had a designated Professional Development Co-ordinator (PDC); by 1995, the figure was 97 per cent. As a multiplicity of providers 'bid' for business, PDCs

	Development support for Individuals	Development support for Departments	Development support for Whole School
Adverse situation	Random information; No encouragement to participate outside the school; Appraisal targets ignored.	Little coherence, information haphazard; Resources on a wait and see basis; No networking; No regular evaluation.	Multiple management of information; Plans imposed rather than discussed; Minimal participation by ordinary staff.
Neutral situation	Policy of bidding to DH on basis of notices of courses; Allocation on first come first served system; Evaluation by filed report; Networking limited.	Department holds information and makes it available if requested; Tendency to be pragmatic in approach; Little reporting back.	Programme developed from SDP discussion but imposed on staff; Resources 'bespoke'; Limited evaluation of activities, no link to appraisal etc.
Supportive situation	Appraisal targets notified and related to SDP; Funding to meet some development if possible; Established networks and others encouraged.	Departmental policies according to needs; Funding made available for department use; Networking and evaluation maintained; Participative decision making linked to whole school and individual targets.	Staff discussion establishes priorities; Information sought, bids managed, resources allocated according to programme; Thorough and published evaluation; Networks established.

Figure 5.1. Towards a Professional Development Culture (Glover and Law, 1996)

operate as institutional purchasing agents, 'playing' the new INSET market and overseeing CPD budgets which may range from as little as £2,000 to as much as £85,000 a year (Glover and Law, 1996).

Although it has been argued that neither headteachers nor deputy heads are best placed to operate as PDCs because of the counselling skills and degree of informality required (Warwick 1975), Deputy Heads were CPD postholders in over three-quarters of secondary schools surveyed in 1995, while it was the remit of Senior Teachers in only 8 per cent of schools, and the responsibility of Heads of Department in a further 12 per cent. The TTA survey (Page and Fisher Jones, 1995, p. 4) points to the link between planning and co-ordination responsibilities within schools, noting unsurprisingly that schools with PDCs were 'more likely to have a planned programme than where a head or deputy takes responsibility'. KEEP research data over several years shows that PDCs feel increasingly pressured by the need to show they are 'obtaining value for money' while developing efficient and effective administration skills to cope with 'the masses of paperwork'.

In addition, there is a strong emphasis in interviews and survey returns from senior managers on the need for improved PDC training and development opportunities – especially in connection with their administrative, personnel and financial responsibilities. As 'school effectiveness' and school improvement issues have gained in importance, the PDC role has become more closely linked with developing coherent 'school improvement' processes. KEEP research evidence also shows that for both *ad hoc* and more deliberate reorganisational reasons, the reduction in the number of deputy heads (a phenomenon particularly apparent in larger schools) has brought a gathering together of management responsibilities into a more rationalised 'Personnel Deputy' role, involving a range of people-related aspects like appraisal, initial teacher training links, supply cover and inservice education. In relation to INSET, personnel deputies are often responsible for managing and processing information; managing development planning and programming; matching whole school, departmental and individual needs; overseeing financial administration and facilitating networking and administrative arrangements to ease development (e.g. through supply and staff replacement).

Clearly, the PDC role is likely to evolve further – particularly as TTA developments gather pace and a formal TTA-driven training pathway is linked to professional accreditation. Building on earlier experience with the Head-teacher Leadership and Administration Programme (HEADLAMP), the TTA's National Professional Qualification for Headteachers (NPQH) initiative emphasises work-related needs identification for aspiring headteachers. It is, however, only the first element in a four-stage development plan, which also incorporates a focus on the needs of newly qualified teachers, 'expert teachers' and 'subject leaders'. With additional rather than fewer CPD responsibilities in train, it is vital that PDC's existing concerns and training needs are fully acknowledged if implementation is to be productive at the grass roots level. KEEP investigations show that PDCs have major anxieties in relation to:

- 'being swamped by all the administration so that there's no time to talk to people';
- being hindered by non-existent or limited administrative back-up;
- 'a chronic lack of time' to do all the tasks;
- the lack of support and the active participation of middle management colleagues/heads of department who too often see CPD as 'not really part of my job';
- feeling marginalised or lacking in status when the PDC role remains outside the Senior Management Team;
- the 'ever increasing bureaucracy involved in INSET . . . with one new initiative after another', which a number of PDCs fear is endangering flexibility – their own, other colleagues' and their organisation's response to needs;

- insufficient and poorly targeted PDC training and development – especially in personnel, counselling, negotiation and administration skills, to enable them, as one PDC comments, to 'select, employ and evaluate what is being offered, so that we can satisfy the needs of the staff, and ensure the development of the school'.

Although basic INSET administrative training is usually provided by LEAs when PDCs come into post, comprehensive development opportunities remain limited: only half of PDCs contributing to the research had had any specific PDC training, with no discussion of the conceptual framework for CPD work or support in establishing an appropriate institutional INSET ethos within their schools. Although accreditation for school-based CPD may be supportive of PDC development, informal teacher development networks are seen by PDCs as crucial support mechanisms for filling the development gaps that both they and their colleagues experience.

DELEGATING LEADERSHIP AND TEACHER DEVELOPMENT

Leadership skills are not simply the prerogative of headteachers or principals (Fullan 1993; Blase and Blase 1994). The concept that 'all teachers are managers' has been stressed (Buckley and Styan, 1988) alongside the view that teachers, as adult learners, lead their own development (Knowles 1980). Furthermore, the centrality of middle management leadership roles is becoming increasingly emphasised (Earley and Fletcher-Campbell 1989; Harris *et al.* 1995). Nevertheless, the tensions and dilemmas surrounding the nature of leadership and the value of delegation is also well documented: 'The dialectic between strong leadership and delegation is never resolved in the learning organization, at least according to the literature: it requires individuals who are able to operate in the forefront and the background at different points in time' (Louis, 1994, p. 21).

For Louis and Kruse (1995), shared norms and values 'are the bedrock upon which all other aspects of professional community are built', while Van Hoewijk (1993, p. 37) argues that headteachers cannot directly stimulate teacher learning on their own, because they are often trapped into being 'knowing' leaders rather than operating as 'searching' leaders. Schools are consequently poor examples of learning organisations, since their 'leaders are not trained in learning', but are rather 'socialised in a leadership model that prescribes knowing the answers instead of searching for the answers . . . they themselves must unlearn the knowing leadership model and learn how to think, feel and behave in a searching leadership model'.

KEEP research suggests that success can come through a policy of structured collaboration and delegated leadership – where the 'bridging abilities' of the PDC, as a relatively senior member of staff who has significant credibility with most staff in an institution are a critical aspect of success. Professional Development Co-ordinators (PDC) who work very closely with or as part of a senior management team appear to be highly effective INSET leaders and facilitators – especially where CPD is *integrated* as part of overall school improvement strategies, within a school-set development agenda, like that articulated by the School Management Task Force (DES 1990). Both interviews and recent survey data indicates that PDC leadership roles are most successful in the hands of a 'personnel deputy' who is

- able to combine and embody both top-down and bottom up CPD strategies;
- listened to because s/he has sufficient management seniority or 'clout';
- capable of 'situational empathy' – most often achieved through individual counselling;
- in control of the appropriate CPD budgets;
- able to facilitate, encourage and offer opportunities for both internal and external networking;
- aware of in-house staffing priorities and development issues, based on an apparently 'global knowledge' of key development concerns not normally found in other school staff; and
- actively able to influence and shape the professional culture(s) of the school through membership of key 'development' committees or working groups.

Nevertheless, some aspects of organisational life make PDC roles potentially problematic. For example, where schools predominantly experience top-down leadership rather than more consultative approaches, the organisational structure acts as an inhibitor (McMahon 1994). Further, as Bullock *et al.* (1994) suggest, 'the delegation of tasks may be simpler than the delegation of authority'. Overall, however, interviews and open comments in questionnaires indicate that many staff regard clearly structured '*delegated leadership*' approaches are best placed to engender a more effective CPD culture – conducive to whole school and personal teacher development, which supports pupil achievement.

CONCLUSION

While much importance still attaches to the leadership role of school leader or headteacher, Professional Development Co-ordinators are increasingly valued for their delegated leadership responsibilities – particularly as school-managed and school-focused professional development gains ground. KEEP research shows that a diversity of professional development cultures and leadership styles are being utilised in managing INSET in schools. It also shows that in those institutions which offer an *integrated* approach and take account of key organisational elements, the PDC can be 'a catalyst for co-operation' (Hughes 1975) and the prospects for effective INSET to become a central element in school improvement are much increased. Where, however, there is relatively inflexible or bureaucratic leadership, what Hughes called 'the autocratic initiator', INSET is often counter-productive, *ad hoc*, misdirected or poorly organised – stimulating little more than a lip-service response from staff and only limited attempts at CPD-focused team work.

While policy makers, policy advisers and some teachers still see headteachers as *the* strategic decision-makers and determinants of institutional direction (Woodhead, 1995), there is growing recognition that 'delegated leadership', (where the parameters of power and task are clear) is crucial to institutional success. Delegated leaders need to both 'be accessible' and 'have access': 'someone who, basically understands the problems we're facing and who's around to deal with them' but, importantly, someone who also has an entrée into senior management decision-making and planning processes. Where a PDC is a senior manager rather than a teacher only able to 'look in on the SMT', both staff and PDCs themselves are generally more positive about the potential for INSET development: 'it's important that there's someone there who knows the nitty gritty'. Nevertheless, the issue of professional support, training and development for these key change activists remains a major issue – particularly in view of what seems to be an increasingly instrumentalist and managerialist educational environment.

Questions for discussion

How do you interpret the changing role of LEAs and Higher Education?

Consider the strengths and weaknesses of the model Towards a Professional Development Culture.

Is the argument for the Professional Development Coordinator (PDC) role successfully made?

6

Initial Teacher Training: Providing a Foundation for a Career

DAVID TURNER

The Teacher Training Agency (TTA) in its brief two year existence has had more impact on ITT than any other organisation since the Board of Education and Inspectorate abandoned payment by results. Since its inception it has been reviled and resisted by individuals such as Ian Kane, Chair of the Universities Council for the Education of Teachers (UCET) in a particularly acrimonious public debate, by the former Chair of the Committee for the Accreditation of Teacher Education (CATE), William Taylor in more measured tones, by lecturers' and teachers' unions and by institutions providing training. Paradoxically at the same time that this public criticism was being voiced, like the French under the Vichy regime, institutions and individuals were queuing up for funds to take part in TTA pilot schemes to offer new courses and increase student numbers. The author will endeavour to examine this enigma, to see exactly what changes have been made as a result of the TTA, what its real impact on schools and institutions has been and, how far it has fulfilled its mission. What are the issues that lie ahead? Will and can institutions resist further encroachments upon their autonomy? Is such resistance desirable or merely the opposition of an entrenched élite unwilling to change?

The TTA is especially subject to hostility because of its overtly political nature as a quango directly accountable to the Secretary of State and whose Board members are government nominees. This subservience was made dramatically explicit by Mrs Shephard on 12 June 1996 when addressing the first anniversary meeting of the Improving Schools Programme. She declared

> We have set up the TTA to push forward our reforms. For the first time we have a body with responsibilities across the full range of teacher training. Ofsted can report on the quality of courses and the TTA can close the bad ones . . . We need to move further and faster to ensure all new teachers are trained to use the most effective techniques. To meet the most urgent need the TTA will draw up tighter rules for primary teacher training in English and Mathematics. For the first time we will define the essential content of training courses. This is just a start. I intend over time to recast all initial and in-service teacher training within a full scale professional framework. It will cover course content and qualifications for everyone from brand new teacher to the experienced head'.

Most of us will know that this is not in fact the first time central government has intervened in the content of ITT for Mrs Shephard's immediate predecessors also specified hours, subjects and content. Such a tradition of control goes back to Kay Shuttleworth and the first voluntary colleges in the mid 19th century. This system of direct intervention was part of the voluntary and public sector which university departments of education, emerging and developing fully only in this century, never inherited. Indeed when the university run ATOs and Institutes were set up they themselves took on this role of controller of the satellite colleges (Dent 1977 p.120). Wilkin (1996) has shown that political or central government intervention in teacher training is not a recent development. She quotes Thompson as stating in 1974 'Teacher Education is fundamentally a political question' and she argues that earlier in the 1960s setting up the Robbins Committee was

> both a political and an ideological act . . . and the selection of committee members was tactical. In its aims and its substantive proposals – including those for ITT it reflected the principles of social democracy. The government could be confident that their choice would also be social democratic in tenor because this was the prevailing social climate at the time.
>
> (Wilkin, 1996, pp. 59–60)

In some ways the 1970s was an aberrant decade with the professionals, principally through CNAA, setting the pace, and with a tendency for the public sector institutions, especially the Polytechnics to break away from the rigid academic disciplines of the old universities in many ways anticipating the TTA's belief in professionally orientated courses with closer school links.

The climate of the 1980s under Mrs Thatcher's government was ripe for further intervention since Prime Minister Callaghan in his Ruskin speech had alerted the nation and the political parties to deficiencies in the education system. The context was also ripe because of the increase in the power of the DES and the Inspectorate and decrease in that of the teachers' unions and the LEAs. 'I am not satisfied with the present content of teacher training', said Sir Keith Joseph in 1983. Governmental control over teacher training was steadily increased by issuing circulars, establishing CATE, bringing about the demise of CNAA and transforming the Inspectorate. These measures particularly affected the élite training departments with single PGCE courses in the old universities who, without the experience of CNAA and rigorous inspections, felt threatened and expressed this through a variety of channels, including UCET, which they had dominated and had run almost as a private club for Professors of Education. Mr Clarke's outburst at the North of England Conference in January 1992 had particularly upset them when he declared emphatically that 'university based training had not been successful and secondary ITT at least must be shifted to schools' (Trafford 1996 p.10). Critics from the entire education establishment opposed these changes, seeing in them the influence of the right wing think tank authors such as Sheila Lawlor (1990) whose polemical and ideologically motivated pamphlets appeared to have had the ear of the Prime Minister. It is not surprising that after the election of 1992 the new Secretary of State, John Patten announced his intention to set up the TTA. Its continuing existence will depend upon its fulfilling its political *raison d'être*. The TTA is as aware of this dilemma as its critics and recognises the parameters within which it must work. Is it too much to ask that educationalists too accept the political reality, ask rather what has been achieved and explore whether the TTA has a professional agenda of its own, instead of resisting its every move? One might debate whether or not any of its reforms can or need to be undone or one might even venture to suggest that many of them were long overdue. With a general election in sight it is not surprising that we see the Government desperately accelerating its programme and pressurising the TTA to pronounce on more and more areas and the TTA trying genuinely, perhaps in order to survive a change of government, to broaden its base and work with all interested parties where possible. After listening to David Blunkett in Sheffield and browsing through Labour Party documents, the author has no doubt that a Labour Government would retain the TTA with perhaps some modifications, a few cosmetic changes and new appointments to the Board. Its work has already been so extensive and penetrated so deeply into the system that it is doubtful if it could be undone even if it were desirable.

To make some assessment of this penetration we need to examine its own declared aims set out in the first Corporate Plan 1995 and reviewed in 1996. Its purpose which it repeatedly and properly reiterates at all meetings is 'to improve the quality of teaching, to raise the standards of teacher education and training, and to promote teaching as a profession, in order to improve the standards of pupils' achievement and the quality of their learning'. No one would quarrel with these high ideals especially when we are reminded that the focus of all this activity is the pupil's progress and achievement. The TTA seeks to meet this purpose through seven aims.

1 To secure a diversity of high quality and cost effective initial training which ensures that new teachers have the knowledge, understanding and skills to teach pupils effectively.
2 To secure the effective involvement of schools in all forms of ITT.
3 To ensure that the teaching profession attracts high quality candidates in sufficient numbers to meet the needs of schools.
4 To promote well targeted, effective and co-ordinated continuing professional development.
5 To promote high quality teaching and teacher education through the investigation and dissemination of key features of effective classroom and training practice.
6 To advise the Secretary of State and others on matters concerning teacher education.
7 To manage effectively and keep under review all aspects of the Teacher Training Agency's own work and make best use of the abilities of its staff.

It will in its work promote choice, diversity, efficiency and accountability. It is important that in assessing the TTA's success and impact we use these aims as a yardstick. In this chapter the main emphasis will be on the changes introduced in ITT. None of the aims listed has a party political dimension though advice proffered to the Secretary of State may and indeed has to be couched in terms that she is likely to accept, and once accepted the TTA has no control over what she makes of it. Executive members of the agency having experience and knowledge of both ITT and teaching, have also previously worked for government agencies. As a result they have a clear overview of some of the deficiencies in the system and a determination to make an impact, which of course may not be unconnected with their personal future careers and the continuance of the agency. The work of this agency can be assessed solely on its effectiveness and not on its political colouring. Its first aim is very wide and in some aspects it is too early to judge success or failure, but on at least two counts the nature and location of ITT has been profoundly affected. There is now in theory a greater diversity of training than ever before with School Centred ITT schemes (SCITT), Licensed teachers, one, two, three and four year routes into QTS, part-time and full-time. Proposals for more subject based primary courses, for Key Stage 2/3 courses and for 14–19 training are being suggested or even piloted. Diversity has certainly been achieved and more is to come, but a close scrutiny of 1995/6 figures show that wholly school based schemes are still very few (19 in 1995) and in spite of encouragement and financial inducements from the DfEE there is a reluctance on the part of schools to form consortia. A survey by the University of Warwick (1994) for the Association of Teachers and Lecturers (ATL) confirmed that secondary schools preferred partnership arrangements with Higher Education Institutions rather than SCITT programmes. The Modes of Teacher Education (MOTE) research team reported in July 1996 that 'by far the largest segment of provision still conformed to what might be called conventional course structures: one year post graduate courses or four year undergraduate courses' (Barton *et al.*, 1996, p. 11). Diversity has indeed been achieved and in its 1996 Corporate Plan the TTA states its intention to promote more diversity 'not only from new providers of training, but from new routes, whether offered by current or new providers' (TTA 1996a, p. 15). As with many TTA statements there is an implied threat to existing providers which can only increase the feeling of vulnerability of those institutions offering single courses. The TTA itself was not responsible for introducing the SCITT or other schemes as they arose from earlier ministerial initiatives. For instance institutions were encouraged to move from four to three year courses by the veiled hint of incentive monies. None of this money has materialised and the TTA disclaims any responsibility for the promises made by the DfEE. In this instance there has been a financial saving to the Treasury through the removal of a whole year's costs of undergraduate training, a cost almost entirely borne by the new universities and colleges of higher education who mainly provided four year BEd courses. This has resulted in loss of income for those institutions with no recompense except a relocation of lost student numbers. In hard financial times and with diminishing grant support students are finding the new three year courses attractive and the four year courses may well be doomed. In fairness to the TTA it has not tried to influence institutions in this area other than the general exhortation to diversity. Additionally as institutions fall into line with the proposals in circulars 9/92 and 14/93 they have taken the opportunity to replace BEd degrees by BA or a BSc but again none of this was due to TTA pressure. The most startling recent change and perhaps the most ominous and threatening for one year full-time PGCE courses is the emergence of the Open University as the largest single provider of ITT in the country with its eighteen month part-time PGCE primary and secondary courses. This is probably the only area in which ITT might make a claim to be cost effective, one of the TTA's aims, but again the Open University initiative predates the TTA, although it now has its full support, and in its early days received financial support from the government. All other sources indicate that moving to full part-nerships with schools has not resulted in any financial saving but has actually in-creased the costs of ITT and that the most expensive form of ITT is the SCITT scheme which was also poorly rated in the HMCI annual report for 1994/95 (p. 63).

It is in the area of funding and cost effectiveness that the TTA is currently having its biggest impact on ITT. The legislation establishing the TTA charged it with the sole responsibility for the allocation of student numbers and fund-ing. In its first corporate plan in 1995 the TTA declared its intention of de-veloping an appropriate methodology for the allocation of funding. One problem for both the TTA and institutions was that these changes would have to be met within existing funding since the government and Treasury made it clear that there would be no additional resources. The TTA commissioned Coopers & Lybrand to undertake a study of these issues and following the publication of their report and a short period of consultation the TTA pro-duced its *Report on the Outcomes of Consultation* in March 1996. New arrangements operable from 1997/8 include the following innovations:

- Funding will be student-led at standard rates for the subject and phase of the course.
- A range of incentives will be introduced to promote improvements in quality. Providers of high quality training will be given priority in the alloca-tion of places.
- Support for diversity of training taking into account national and regional needs.
- Longer contracts over a three year rolling programme to allow for strategic planning.
- Adjustment of funding where institutions over or under recruited and where students failed to complete courses.
- An Expansion Fund to help providers increase student numbers in second-ary subjects.

When the consultation paper was issued it was met with at best lukewarm acceptance of the inevitable, so much so that Anthea Millett was moved to respond in the THES on 1 December 1995. Much of the criticism revolved around the question of quality – how was it to be measured and how valid were any pronouncements on quality? The notion of quality was not new and was consistent with the views of the Secretary of State and the TTA. The Coopers & Lybrand Report (para. 503) reiterated the notion of a five point scale of quality as recommended by Ofsted in its 1993 criteria for the Inspection of Training courses. In the new universities with well established Quality Assurance procedures and the systems of self evaluation developed by the funding council HEFCE such ideas were not alien.

The related key issue of applying these quality assurance procedures to a wide variety of schools when looking at partnership issues will be considered but in this instance it is the reliance upon Ofsted grading of quality that causes most concern. When BEMAS published its compendium on Improving ITT (McCulloch and Fidler 1994) many contributors raised the issue of the measurement of quality. There was a fear of a narrow reliance on the assessment of competences according to the criteria laid down in the 1993 Working Papers for the Inspection of secondary ITT by Ofsted. Trafford (1996) is highly critical of the concentration of attention upon the concept of satisfactory and very good. Recent pronouncements following the sweep of all primary courses by Ofsted and a seeming determination by HMCI and the Secretary of State to downgrade some of the primary training courses by a reinterpretation of 'satisfactory' currently defined as 'sound but unremarkable (shortcomings balanced by good features)' to something less than satisfactory is a grave cause for concern. This coupled with the Secretary of State's request to the TTA and Ofsted to review appraisal procedures caused apprehension. At the point of writing this situation has not been clarified.

The achievement of high quality gradings is a key issue in the new funding mechanism since only those institutions with a high quality rating will be able to bid for new numbers or be assured of long term contracts. Trafford (1996) suggests that a rigorous inspection procedure should concentrate upon identifying and helping to improve the unsatisfactory rather than 'draw fine distinctions on the basis of sometimes unsafe evidence, between providers of attested quality' (p. 95). In an ideal world this might be possible but in the climate created by central government, the TTA and Ofsted such advice is unrealistic, maybe even complacent in its assumption that we the providers can readily recognise 'attested quality'. Underlying this is a real concern by students, teachers and the general public, as well as the TTA that a consistent and quite high number of primary providers are failing in one or more areas. When surveyed (TES 13.9.96) four out of five Primary Headteachers expressed concern about ITT provision. Anthea Millett reported in the THES (5.7.96) that of the inspection reports published to date 14 per cent contain one or more unsatisfactory grades, triggering the TTA procedures for withdrawing accreditation. That rate of failure compares to only 2 per cent of schools that have been deemed by Ofsted to be 'failing'. Institutions and professional organisations may seek in the next few years to persuade the TTA and Ofsted to broaden their criteria for assessing quality, and eventually may be able to develop an acceptable form of self assessment or even peer evaluation. In the meantime it does not seem unreasonable that all training institutions are subject to the same inspection criteria and have the same opportunities equally to demonstrate their excellence or otherwise. Certainly the TTA and Ofsted together have had a tremendous impact on Teacher Training. All institutions know that inspection is a reality, it is likely to be frequent and may have serious consequences not only for their future funding but even their very existence – a far cry from the days when in some institutions inspectors paid courtesy visits and if they made a report it was not published.

Another significant issue as seen by the TTA was the wide disparity of costs incurred in the different institutions for what appeared to be similar courses, since the TTA had inherited from the HEFCE a funding system based on average units of funding (known as Average Units of Council Funding – AUCF) which permitted these wide variations in per capita payments. Anthea Millett in the THES (1.12.95) noted 'the current system pays between £810 and £3,721 to different providers for the same provision'. Institutions of course claimed that there were historic and geographical explanations for such differences and that in any case, particularly in the monotechnic and denominational sector arcane methods of establishing exact costs accounted for the difference. Further complicating the picture is the practice of top slicing by most institutions, so that many training departments were unaware of the real costs and income attributable to teacher training. The new funding from 1997 and the separation of TTA funds from those of HEFCE has forced institutions to clarify and modify their accounting systems, not always willingly. Those within teacher training departments especially in large institutions have not been entirely unsympathetic to the changes and some see them as potentially beneficial. Other groups may lose the protection and subsidies granted by their institutions. It is not surprising that in this area it is difficult to establish an accurate picture. The recent MOTE survey (1996) found that course leaders were reluctant to comment on funding either through ignorance or because of the sensitivity of the information. Top slicing for central services usually amounted to between 30 and 40 per cent of the total. A discussion paper at the MOTE dissemination seminar (13.7.96) *Partnership and Costs; Emerging Developments and Dilemmas* (p. 4) contrasted the views of two providers responding to the survey. One senior management team pointed out 'with a bit of luck we will get improved funding, although the degree of improvement will depend on how things equalise but we've been grossly underfunded so that . . . we might receive better levels of funding. I think the particular issue for us is the link between quality and length of planning and if we get a good grade from Ofsted for the first time we will be into a three year planning cycle and that should make a substantial difference to us'. The contrary view expressed by senior management in a near monotechnic was 'there is just a single issue . . . if they abandon the idea of historic costs . . . and fix a standard unit price . . . and the standard unit price is bound to be more or less the average unit of funding at the moment and we're something (considerably) above the standard. So we stand to lose (£s) per student – a thousand students. That is such an issue that anything else just fades into insignificance'. In this arena of funding therefore the TTA is having its deepest impact. The new funding formula does allow a period of phasing in for those institutions whose costs are well above average, but if they fail to bring down these costs in the time allowed their future ability to remain in teacher training could be seriously jeopardised. Providers with suitable quality gradings and ambitions to expand or diversify may make bids immediately for funding in 1997/98, 1998/99 and 1999/2000. The long term implications are that some institutions may flourish and expand others may decline or some may decide voluntarily to withdraw from teacher training. Partnership arrangements with schools are another crucial factor in both the funding and future developments and secondary courses currently are more deeply affected by the changes than primary courses.

The second of the TTA's aims is 'to secure effective involvement of schools in all forms of ITT' which to date has had the most identifiable impact upon institutions. Again the directives in circulars 9/92 and 14/93 to HEI's were from the DFE but the TTA has taken on the role of developing partnerships with a zealous single minded determination to shift the balance towards schools. The Secretary of State's original view was that schools would be the leading partner, but this has been somewhat modified. Ofsted is now giving more attention to school partnerships and has published guidelines for good practice. In trying to gauge the effectiveness of the TTA in this field there are a number of specific issues which merit attention and a number of questions to be raised. How far have the nature of courses changed to meet these new needs? How far have the roles of both school and provider changed? In what ways has the shift towards school domination urged by Kenneth Clarke actually taken place? Has the TTA further plans in this area and what further issues have arisen as a result of the changes?

Secondary courses have so far seen the most changes principally because circular 9/92 has now been implemented in all institutions and new partnership arrangements are entering their third or fourth year in some. This rapid progress is well illustrated by the TTA pack of working papers, *Effective Training Through Partnership* (TTA 1996e), which provided examples of good practice in secondary schools. A series of conferences followed in which the TTA specified that representatives of partnership schools should be in the overwhelming majority (four school representatives to one HEI representative was suggested). The purpose of these meetings was to discuss the examples and further develop policy. At the conferences the school representatives were actually outnumbered by those from HEIs, which pinpoints one of the TTA's main problems, namely that schools are not rushing to sign up partnership contracts with HEIs and are even less keen to set up on their own in SCITT consortia. Evidence from a variety of sources supports this view. To counter this reluctance the TTA is actively engaged as a propagandist and is pursuing its purpose with a missionary zeal, perhaps encouraged by the Secretary of State. As a result attractive pamphlets have been sent to primary and secondary schools with a separate one directed at governors extolling the virtues and benefits of partnership. One cannot help noticing that all materials emanating from Portland House have a distinctive appearance, good quality glossy paper, often in full colour designed both to attract and to be read. These publications reflect clearly the TTA's aims and its success, though resource starved schools and HEIs have been known to raise a few eyebrows when they estimate the cost of so much publicity material. The TTA has yet to publish its promised pack on primary partnership practice, again indicative of the slower and less radical progress in the primary field.

From the standpoint of the providers the first and most drastic consequence of the new partnership arrangements was the requirement that schools be paid out of HEI funds for their services and that no particular fee level was to be recommended, enabling market forces to prevail. Institutions were forced to confront several issues. Some Vice-Chancellors and Principals whose education departments were small with a single course, seriously considered phasing out teacher training not solely because of the financial damage to income but because of the accompanying loss of autonomy. That they have not withdrawn to date is a tribute to the tenacity and good standing of their education departments. The Secretary of State's declared intention of laying down a curriculum for ITT may now finally provoke those institutions who value their autonomy to abandon ITT particularly if the results of the Research Assessment Exercise (RAE) due in December 1996 give a further steer in that direction. Payments to schools varied from £200 to £1,000 per student on secondary courses with some fierce competition between institutions to secure places and some bargaining by headteachers to secure higher payments, a move encouraged by the Secondary Heads Association (SHA) which demanded a higher rate. By 1996 the situation had stabilised and the monetary payment was less prominent in discussions on partnership agreements though still a major factor. There remains a wide variation in payments between institutions although enhanced packages often include INSET deals and access to university or college facilities. A very clear indicator of the impact of this policy on HEI has been the increased number of early retirements, voluntary redundancies and nonreplacement of secondary tutors especially in the field of education and professional studies whose work was downgraded by circular 9/92. Consequently this shift in resources to schools has resulted in the loss of a vast amount of expertise and the fragmentation of specialist teams in HEI.

Another significant change has been in the design and shape of programmes of ITT partly resulting from closer school partnerships in the secondary field though the scene has been complicated by the simultaneous introduction of semesterisation and modular programmes in HEI. I can best illustrate this by a brief summary of the radical changes which have taken place at Sheffield Hallam University though similar new courses have been produced at Sunderland, Wolverhampton and elsewhere. In order to strengthen the reality of partnership involvement at Sheffield Hallam University, representatives of secondary schools were from the outset invited to join as full members of planning committees for the new programme and they formed a majority on the school experience planning group. Schools in this region were insistent that the placement pattern had to be simple, consistent and extensive if they were to be fully involved. The working group scrutinised the competences laid down by circular 9/92 and added a few more perhaps to emphasise their independence but also to embrace their concept of the reflective critical beginning teacher. The scheme that finally emerged with their full support consisted of a single comprehensive programme which embraced a variety of undergraduate and postgraduate routes. A three year BSc/BSc Hons route for Design and Technology, Mathematics, Physical Education and Science students was introduced in which the first year contained foundation work in skills development and education together with subject study. Five days only were spent in a primary school. The second year was entirely subject based with a direct entry for the two year BSc/BSc Hons routes in Design and Technology, Mathematics and Science, the shortage subjects. Students on a two year PGCE route in the shortage subject areas of Design and Technology, Mathematics and Modern Languages also enter the programme at this stage in order to enhance the subject content of their first degrees. The third and final year of the programme is a common professional year in which all existing students are joined by one year PGCE students of Business Education, Design and Technology, English, Mathematics, Modern Languages, Religious Education and Science. As directed in circular 9/92 students spend 24 out of 36 weeks in secondary schools or colleges. Schools in the region insisted that they could only cope with the additional time in school if there was a common pattern for all placements. They also believed as did the School of Education that since all these students would ultimately be working together in the same schools as professionals, it would have been invidious to separate them out during their training. Finally, if the schools were to work closely with the university in developing competences a common pattern was essential. The programme has now moved into its third year and schools are still insistent that they do not wish to make any major changes to the pattern beyond simplifying the competences profile. Additionally, schools are pressing the university to extend subject choice so that a single partnership can encompass all national curriculum subjects. The TTA has not yet responded to this view. It is fair to say that the changes made were not universally welcomed by all university tutors or students a minority of whom would have preferred to remain with the long established traditional pattern of continuing contact with schools in all three years. Students who have completed the course so far have not felt disadvantaged, nor have they suffered in the jobs market. The primary course at Sheffield Hallam University has also been reduced more recently from a four to a three year route with a change in name from BEd to BA in response to circular 14/93, but a common programme for undergraduates and postgraduates was not introduced. Partnerships with primary schools have been developed, indeed pilot schemes began several years ago, but have not yet been extended to all schools.

The TTA sees the partnerships with schools as pivotal to its reforms but evidence is accumulating that changes in this respect may not be as effective in practice as they appear on the surface or in written agreements. There appears to be a point beyond which schools are unwilling to go. The MOTE project (Barton *et al.*, 1996) pp. 63–4 noted that:

- students were spending more time in school during their training;
- teachers were more involved in the training process;
- teachers had received some minimal form of training to support them in their new role in teacher education. All such moves are supportive of the TTA's aims but at the same time institutions were working with large numbers of schools, basing relatively small numbers of students in each school;
- universities were finding difficulty in recruiting schools for their partnerships;
- universities were unable to impose their desired criteria when selecting schools;
- universities had found it necessary to establish different contractual relations with different groups of schools.

Another important point was that

> although teachers were significantly more involved in the training of students than in the past, that participation was primarily limited to supporting and assessing students in the practice of teaching; teachers had much less involvement in other dimensions of the TE programmes and comparatively little role in leading, designing and the day to day management of programmes. With reducing staff–student ratios in HEI there were fewer opportunities than in the past for HEI staff and school staff routinely to collaborate in support of students' school based work.

The TTA has further impacted on HEI by requiring the development of mentor training programmes as part of the partnership contracts. There were of course some well publicised schemes, such as the Oxford University Department internee programme, established well before the TTA was created, but there is no doubt that the huge development and variety of mentor training schemes, as well as training videos and books on the subject, are directly attributable to the transitional funding provided to institutions for that purpose. The MOTE report (Barton *et al.*, 1996) revealed a huge disparity in training, both in hours and purposes, and highlighted the fact that many class or subject teachers working on a day to day basis with students had not received training in so far as it had cascaded down from designated trained mentors. Institutions are tackling this issue, often clearly set out in partnership agreements but they are finding that training is much affected by resources or lack of time. Most institutions were surprised when it became apparent that there was an annual turnover of about 30 per cent of mentors, so that more training for new mentors as well as upgrading existing mentors would have to be provided. The TTA has recognised this need, if somewhat late, and provided funds for the continuance of this crucial mentor training in 1995/96. Whether this expensive exercise can continue annually is debatable and both the TTA and Ofsted would prefer that schools took a greater part not only in training their own mentors but acting as quality assurance agents across schools. Because of the current competition between schools and because of the resource implications secondary schools in this region have not responded to university requests to pilot such schemes. Perhaps the TTA and Ofsted will provide a steer by funding them. The whole question of organising the ITT programme, developing new partnerships, running a placement office, securing appropriate school experience for over a thousand students, dealing with travel and postage costs is a vast drain upon HEI resources and a source of constant stress to those involved at the cutting edge. One must ask will diversity and the encouraging a thousand flowers to bloom really benefit ITT or be the most cost effective way of running a system? Is this really a partnership of equals when so much is expected of one partner and in reality there are no imposable sanctions against school partners who fail, often for good reason, to meet their obligations? One can imagine the reaction if any HEI tried to recover monies if a school failed to deliver.

It is not surprising therefore that the remaining area of real concern to the HEI is the question of quality assurance. The new universities in particular have well developed quality assurance systems and are naturally anxious to maintain their high standards and the reputation of their awards. How can they be certain that such controls as are now in use will be properly extended to as many as five hundred primary and secondary schools in the region, and in some cases in far distant regions? Some HEIs might consider terminating their ITT if they cannot be certain that they can have control over the quality of students emerging from their courses. To prevent this there are some positive developments taking place which are being actively encouraged by the TTA and Ofsted. The TTA's *Effective Training through Partnership Pack: Paper 4 Assuring the Quality of Partnerships* 1996 is one example. Some key principles and practices are emerging, for instance the careful listing of teaching competences and the further refining of these in the TTA's recently piloted Career Entry Profiles in which attempts at consistency of judgement are being made through the use of a common format with universally understood definitions. Careful documentation with the specific outlining of responsibilities and requirements of both sides in partnership agreements is improving. Joint assessments with moderators and a changing role for external examiners to include assessment of the process in schools rather than judgement of individual students on a single lesson, are some of the changes which are contributing to quality assurance. Where partnerships have matured there is now a willingness by both sides to share concerns and no longer 'ring fence' areas as beyond the jurisdiction of one or other of the partners. Perhaps this is an area where HEIs with experience in the field will be allowed to take a lead and help the schools move towards more valid forms of self-assessment. The Open University has provided a well used package for the SCITT schools.

There are other listed aims of the TTA which are having an impact on ITT including its recruiting campaigns, its distribution of bursary money for shortage subjects (too little and too late) and its long term plans for staged professional development from new qualified beginner to headteacher as well as the rather meagre research grants given to teachers for very small scale projects, (TES 13.9.96) surely hardly in line with the suggestion made by Hargreaves (1996) in his TTA lecture on research.

The TTA has without doubt had a major impact on ITT, driving it down the new routes recommended by the government, routes heavily geared to competences and school based. It has thus forced HEIs to contemplate more equal forms of partnership, new relationships with schools, greater diversity and choice for students, less emphasis on the eighteen-year-old school leaver and more on the mature adult preferably with an industrial, business or service background. The TTA has displayed a single minded missionary zeal for training as opposed to education. It has attempted perhaps an over-ambitious programme of reform which at times has clogged its administrative channels in spite of its proclaimed charter of good service. The bungling of bursary bids, and its failure to realise that there would be a serious shortage of secondary students early in the next century, hence its sudden volte-face over numbers allocated or rather not allocated, highlighted its fallibility. At the same time it has produced an enormous quantity of readable and useful material, it has stimulated debate and innovation as well as kept a clear focus on the importance of the pupil as central to the process. Its consultation papers are legion and infamous for their short response time – nevertheless they have been published and may even have been modified as a result. Yet the apparent diversity and choice is in reality limited, with few schools wanting to take SCITT routes, and partnership schools unwilling to venture in many cases beyond the assessment of the QT competences, believing in spite of all the propaganda that university and college lecturers are best placed to deliver degree and postgraduate level work and the schools' first duty is to the pupils, the national curriculum, GCSE and A levels. The TTA has not had the luxury of being able to pump-prime its initiatives in latter days so all its clients complain of the lack of realistic funding. Universities are losing resources to schools yet have had to face increased costs in developing and maintaining partnerships, running mentor training schemes, providing the management and organisational framework for the partnerships and quality assurance systems needed to maintain the courses. Subject to dual control by the TTA and Ofsted increasingly working together, with further threats to their autonomy through a national curriculum for teacher training some institutions may be tempted to shed ITT altogether. Others may be forced out because of failure to reduce their historic high costs and a further group may be closed by the TTA following adverse Ofsted reports. Most institutions however have shown an unseemly private eagerness to work with the TTA as the full and exhaustive list of contributors to the pack on *Effective Training through Partnership* reveals.

Questions for discussion

How do you respond to this interpretation of the role of the Teacher Training Agency (TTA) for Initial Teacher Training (ITT)?

How do you interpret the changes in ITT which have occurred?

How is teacher education a political question?

7

The Early Years of the Teacher's Career: Induction into the Profession

KEN JONES AND PETER STAMMERS

A short while ago, staff teaching on a primary B.A. (Education) programme invited former students who had recently qualified as teachers to return for an informal reunion. It was in the last week of the Autumn Term, just before Christmas, so spirits were high. The ex-students were now qualified primary school teachers and most of them were just about to complete their first full term's work.

There was much to talk about. What no one had anticipated was the torrent of discussion which met the question: *'Well, what has your first term as a teacher been like?'*. The floodgates opened. Students who had said little during their four years of studying to be teachers interrupted others to describe their experiences. Those who had always held court as students had even more to say. They talked about the children in their classes; being a member of staff; facing parents for the first time; the Christmas concert; coping with tiredness; planning; taking on the role of a curriculum leader; dealing with behavioural problems; having to be a counsellor, social worker, nurse, secretary, manager, planner, leader, law enforcer, parent substitute, diplomat, taxi driver, sports team manager, computer wizard, artist, musician. . . .

When, over 45 minutes later, the initial hubbub had subsided we began to compare experiences more systematically and to examine the expectations which heads, colleagues and the community as a whole had of these 'rookies'. They were expected by parents of the children in their class to be expert on everything to do with schools and education and to be specialists in all of the National Curriculum subjects (including Welsh for this particular group). They were expected to keep discipline, manage their classrooms, differentiate their work to extend all children, support those with special educational needs, assess, record and report the children's progress, maintain an effective learning environment through the use of display and make their lessons interesting and enjoyable.

They were expected by head teachers to take responsibility for at least one curriculum area ('I know you've only just started but we do need someone to take charge of science, geography and PE. You can begin by drawing up a policy . . .').

They were expected by their teaching colleagues to be the fonts of all up-to-date knowledge on the National Curriculum and teaching styles . . . but only when asked. For the majority of the new teachers, to offer unsolicited advice was to court rejection.

They were expected by their partners and friends at home to be sociable and human.

What became clear at a very early stage was the diversity of experiences and expectations these new teachers were encountering. Some were teaching in large urban primary schools with 12 or more staff; some in small rural primary schools with 4 staff and vertically integrated classes spanning Key Stages 1 and 2. Some were in socially disadvantaged areas, others in leafy suburbs. Some reported occasions of physical aggression by parents; some were more concerned about the intellectual challenge of verbally aggressive behaviour from articulate parents.

Some were responsible for co-ordinating the National Curriculum subject in which they had specialised; others had been employed by the school because they looked good all-round teachers. One ex-student who had specialised in Key Stage 2 English had been employed in a very socially disadvantaged school to teach the Reception class and take responsibility for Science. She had been employed because she looked as if she could cope with this difficult class; her subject specialism didn't matter. Of more significance, this new teacher had been employed because she was cheap. For a governing body working to a possible budget deficit this was a key consideration.

Most of the ex-students at the reunion were in full time, permanent positions. Others were in one-year or, in two cases, one-term posts. One had been unable to find a full-time position and was acting as a supply teacher. Some were extremely contented and, in spite of the hard work, were obviously enjoying the experiences. A minority were struggling – personally and professionally – to cope with the demands of primary school teaching.

It was clear that there was little which their four year initial training course could have done to prepare them for such a variety of experience, and even less could have been achieved on a one-year PGCE programme. It was also clear that much of the need to share their new experiences came from a sense of isolation. When they were students they formed a large group with common needs and experiences. As newly qualified teachers (NQTs) they were often alone.

They all felt that it was essential for new teachers to be supported in their schools during their induction period and for those responsible for providing this support to be familiar with the personal and training backgrounds of these new professionals. In particular, it was essential that their 'mentors' were aware of the routes by which these NQTs had entered teaching – and the entry routes have multiplied significantly in recent years.

ROUTES INTO TEACHING

Gone is the easy distinction of a one year PGCE after a university course or a four year B.Ed; with that distinction, those providing induction programmes were aware of the differences in skills and knowledge afforded by the two routes and planned their programmes accordingly. Now, the multifarious routes include B.A. (with qualified teacher status), B.Ed (three or four year versions are running across the country), PGCE, the articled teacher scheme, the licensed teacher scheme, the Open University programme, and school based programmes (SCITT). Added to that, as always was the case, NQTs arrive in schools with different experiences *within* these routes as they come from different training institutions and from different training environments. Whereas this once could be seen as a richness to be exploited for benefit within a well planned induction programme, the current plethora of entry routes, together with the struggle to make viable groups within an ever constraining financial stringency, now causes more difficulties than advantages.

DIMENSIONS OF INDUCTION

Most would agree that a new teacher's understanding of classroom situations is partial and simplistic – it takes years to comprehend fully the richness of the many interactions constantly taking place in a classroom, at different levels, between more than thirty youngsters energetically growing. Schemp, *et al.* (1993) found that the number of decisions, the variety of the tasks and the immediacy of the demands forced 'novice teachers to use instinctive reactions, adopt time-honoured traditions and management routines and import lessons from related experiences' and that the fluid, immediate and dynamic pressures of school life did not permit teachers time to reflect on a problem before attempting a solution. Doyle (1986) has called this the 'multi-dimensionality, simultaneity, immediacy, unpredictability, publicness and history' of the job and, not surprisingly, it is this that leads to the greater stress that is observed in novice teachers in their first year in the profession.

In fact the DES (1989) conceded that the full complexities of teaching cannot be covered before entering the profession, '. . . it would be unreasonable to suppose that initial training could prepare all teachers for all aspects of their professional work . . .'. Indeed, it is frequently misconstrued that the newly qualified teacher is fully trained and capable of coping with the same work as a teacher with twenty years' experience. Initial training is too short and inevitably much is omitted or necessarily dealt with superficially.

The DES (1989) emphasised that 'Some aspects of training cannot be developed in depth until the [NQT] is in post' and that it is unreasonable ' . . . for schools to expect that they will receive fully fledged practitioners' from colleges. Unlike most other professions, there is a loneliness in teaching – teaching is typically an *isolated* job with teachers in rooms surrounded by juveniles, the essence of their professionality demanding a high *personal* element and involvement, and because of this the danger of 'failure' becomes greater and if it occurs, it has the potential to be traumatic.

This interconnection between the personal and professional, so essential in good teaching, makes the task of learning to teach so demanding and never more so than in a teacher's first year before the robe of experience has afforded a measure of confidence. It takes time – years – for the complexity of the personal/professional interconnection in teaching to mature and be a positive resource, and in the first years of teaching that interconnection may serve more as a complication than as a tool of the trade. It takes time to be alert to the strengths, as well as to the dangers of these interconnections and crucially it takes time to reflect upon, and to discuss with others, their embryonic growth.

McIntyre (1994) has identified four specific problems associated with a novice's understanding of classroom situations. Firstly there is the 'invisibility of skilled performance': the problem of learning by observation is that one has to understand the skill that one is supposed to be observing. Secondly there are the 'practical difficulties of cueing' where significant things to be learned are clearly pointed out as they happen. The point is made that a teacher cannot give a 'running commentary' to the novice as can, say, a driving instructor in a car. Thirdly, there is the 'teachers' difficulty in articulating their expertise': experienced teachers, according to McIntyre, take their expertise for granted and are 'generally unaware of the sophisticated judgements and decision making in which they routinely engage'. Finally there is the 'non-acceptance of teacher models' where the novice tends to see only 'global pictures'. There 'may well not be a good match between the pictures they see of individual teachers and their own often naive and idealised conceptions of good teaching'. They therefore tend to 'dismiss [such experienced teachers] as people from whom they have little to learn'.

Colleagues, students, and administrators can exert an enormous pressure on beginning teachers (Zeichner et al., 1987). Schemp et al. (1993) showed that veteran teachers have established traditions and perceptions that the novice teacher must accept, reject, modify or accommodate. Sometimes, they assert, the newcomer 'walked a thin line between alienating these teachers and injecting his or her own brand of pedagogy'. Schemp et al. were surprised to discover the number of 'uncaring teachers' who were 'too burned out or simply too busy for matters pertaining to the education of children.' Furthermore, frequently, teachers in their first year of the profession refer to the feeling of 'isolation' – the isolation felt by a novice amongst experienced fellow professionals – often made all the more acute by only a scant understanding of a school's 'taken for granted' customs and practices. Even the pupils, for whose learning the novice teacher has a professional responsibility, are more in tune with, and knowledgeable about, such school customs and practices – even to the extent of the mere geography and layout of the school premises!

Schemp et al. (1993), showed that in shaping their roles in schools, NQTs struggle both to understand and exercise power within the school culture. Further, in their survey, Schemp et al. found that 'explicit' demands (such as classroom management and grading work) were seldom made explicit. It was assumed by all (administrators, peers, students and other teachers) that the

NQT would know what it was they were supposed to do and have a good idea of how to do it. The demands were only made explicit when a difference in perception or assumption occurred (such as 'We don't do that here' or 'This is the way we have always done it'). Little wonder, then, that the typical response of NQTs to their pupils is to become more *custodial* and more *authoritarian* and that, as Tischer (1984), and How and Rees (1977) showed, the first year of teaching sees the novice shift very rapidly from being concerned with helping pupils to learn, to becoming more concerned with *controlling* their behaviour. Teachers are expected to establish themselves as authority figures over students (Waller, 1932) and it is incumbent upon teachers to demonstrate the power and authority they hold over students to those outside the classroom (Feinman-Nemser and Floden, 1986).

Establishing authority over students is essential for the NQT to be accepted by all members of the school community (Schemp *et al.* 1993). Put another way, teachers' control over students is a taken-for-granted assumption in schools and Schemp *et al.*, showed that subject expertise was more often used for establishing authority in the classroom than it was for furthering the education of students. It must be remembered that if the NQT does not have the *structured* opportunity to discuss these phenomena with colleagues and to discover from other NQTs that *it is a frequent and typical experience* for teachers in their first years then the overwhelming sense of professional failure can be very depressing indeed. Forced to handle it in isolation, without the opportunity to be reassured that the true professional can get through the primarily 'custodial' teacher–pupil relationship, then it is not surprising that the teacher wastage rate is worse than that for World War II Bomber Command crews! (In 1991 the DES acknowledged that *35 per cent* of teachers leave within the first five years of entering the profession.) In such circumstances any allocation of resources in an induction programme for newly qualified teachers should be seen *not* as an item of *expenditure* but as an *investment*!

Moreover, teachers in their first year are often seen to be of inferior status and yet, as has been shown earlier, they have to take the same full professional responsibilities as their colleagues. Almost all other professions allow the novice to be eased into the profession, only taking on certain duties on their own and requiring them to take full responsibilities only after a period of induction – airline pilots and doctors being good examples. However, given the intertwined nature of the personal and professional in teaching, together with the polarising capacity of the loneliness aspect referred to above, teachers' work is much less easily segmented in this way.

Even so, we need to distinguish between a process that *formally* recognises the NQT as a fully fledged 'qualified' teacher (what used to be the 'probationary period') and a programme which is designed to smooth the transition from student-learner to teacher-professional *and* begin what is to be hoped is a career-long interaction with professional/staff development.

THE INDUCTION OF NEWLY QUALIFIED TEACHERS: A WELSH OFFICE PROJECT

In recognition of the need to support the induction of newly qualified teachers, the Welsh Office funded a research and development project from 1992 to 1994 (Bolam et al., 1994; Bolam et al., 1995). The collaborative project involved colleagues from several higher education institutions, all Welsh local education authorities, representatives from primary and secondary schools in Wales and OHMCI Wales.

For the first stage of the project, material was gathered from a range of sources to compile and trial two practical handbooks (Clark et al., 1994 and Jones et al., 1994). The second stage of the project consisted of a survey of induction in schools throughout Wales. It used as a focus four aspects of induction which were perceived as central to the concept of a continuum of professional development: the provision of support networks for newly qualified teachers, the nature of mentoring in schools, the use of competence statements to define and enable support for NQTs and the development of professional development profiles. These were seen to be key links in the transition from initial training and education into induction and from the status of newly qualified teacher to that of experienced and reflective practitioner.

The findings of the project are significant and highlight the contextual changes which newly qualified teachers face when beginning their careers. They also provide indicators for action which needs to be taken at school, local and national levels if the induction of new teachers is to be effective and if the notion of a continuum of professional development is to become a reality.

The existence of support networks

Lawson (1992, p. 164) highlights the fact that 'becoming a teacher is not a simple transition from one role to another; it is a social process involving complex interactions between and among prospective and experienced teachers and their social situations'. Drawing on research into induction carried out in the USA he notes that 'neither teacher education nor induction could be viewed as a linear, one-way process of socialisation wherein recruits are "induced" into the profession's way of defining and performing work'. This socialisation process involves formal, professional support alongside the reassurance provided informally from peers and others sympathetic to the challenges and opportunities arising within the early years of teaching.

The increased autonomy of schools in England and Wales since the Education Reform Act has given governing bodies and headteachers much greater authority in the appointment of new teachers. However, the subsequent demise of local education authorities in this period has removed a great deal of organised support for the NQT. The 1992 HMI survey of new teachers in England and Wales (OHMCI, 1993) commented that 'With the changes in arrangements for funding for professional development many LEAs were less well placed to offer induction programmes than in previous surveys. Where inspectors and advisers observed their teaching, the new teachers generally found the feedback very helpful' (para 1.29).

The need for a local professional network to be as active as possible is apparent from the project's findings. A web of interaction is needed enabling a sharing of expertise between the new teacher and other colleagues from within the team in school, outside the team in school, tutors from ITE programmes, LEA representatives and, most important, other NQTs. Without this extended professional contact, induction will be to the school and not to the profession. The success of induction will be hit and miss and the coherence in terms of experience and career progression will be lessened.

Support from mentors

Although the project was carried out in the early days of mentoring and school-based ITT there were already clear signs of the growing importance of mentoring. What was less clear was the exact nature of the mentor's role and the amount of support given to mentors to enable them to carry out their role effectively. There was no consistency in the way in which the role of mentor was interpreted. In some schools the mentor was a senior member of staff, in others a colleague with a similar teaching commitment. Some were line managers; others were 'confidantes' so that the appraisal process did not interfere with the need for open support. Some received a time allowance for the role; others received none. Some were responsible for student teachers; others solely for NQTs. Most had received training; some had been given the role after the mentor training programmes had finished.

There is no shortage of literature and research evidence on the role of the mentor in the induction process and as the role becomes more central in the management structures of all schools it is inevitable that support in school for NQTs will become more structured and effective.

The use of competences and professional development profiles

At the time of the project little development had taken place on the use of competence statements and even less on teacher profiles. The responses from schools and NQTs showed a lack of awareness of both. Since this time, however, there have been further developments in both and the use of 'competency profiles' (Tolley, Biddulph and Fisher, 1996) and personal development portfolios which avoid the use of competence statements (East Midlands 9, 1993) and it is clear that as the uses of professional development profiles are refined they will play a central role in the linkage of all parts of a teacher's continuing professional development (Turner, 1995).

Two areas of concern arose from the project. Firstly, the increasing tendency for new teachers to be appointed on temporary and short-term contracts. Secondly, the increasing difference between primary and secondary school provision of induction support and experience.

Contractual changes

As well as removing a tier of pastoral support, this individualism on the part of schools has reduced the availability of an overview of a pattern of appointments. LEAs had a local perspective on entry into the profession and, rightly or wrongly, could influence and moderate the effects of advantage and disadvantage of individual schools. In many cases, new teachers were appointed not to the individual school but to a 'pool' of new teachers managed by the local authority and, in the best cases, they were supported as a group with common needs in a coherent way. This arrangement was particularly advantageous to smaller primary schools and the existence of the 'pool' of new teachers frequently helped both the new teacher and the partner schools in the local authority.

It is now accepted that a school's governing body will appoint a new teacher with regard to its own individual situation. The 'pool' arrangement is being replaced by independent commercial regional and national agencies who exist to find placements for new teachers. The broader and longer term effects of this on the profession as a whole and on the continuing professional development of individual teachers are little understood.

The emerging pattern in Wales in 1994 was clearly shown in the survey's questionnaire responses from schools (Table 7.1).

Table 7.1 The employment contracts of new teachers – questionnaire responses adapted from the Welsh Office Report

Question	Primary		Secondary	
	N	%	N	%
How many NQTs have permanent contracts?	67	27.5	137	70.98
How many NQTs have temporary contracts?	177	72.5	46	29.02
Of those on temporary contracts, how many are on:				
1 year contracts?	114	64.4	41	89.1
2 term contracts?	36	20.3	4	8.7
1 term contracts?	27	15.3	1	2.17
How many of the NQTs were previously student teachers in the school?	38	15.6	28	15.3

Source: Adapted from Bolam et al., 1994.

The responses show that only just over one quarter of newly qualified teachers in primary schools were on permanent contracts. Of more concern is the fact that, of the new teachers in primary schools on temporary contracts, over one third were on one or two term contracts. The implications of this for continuity and coherence of both professional development of the teacher and of teaching and learning may well be considerable. It is also of concern that no authority exists to either monitor or act on this trend. The psychological contract, let alone the legal contract of employment for the new teacher, becomes less secure. Planning becomes more difficult and, in the worst scenario, continuity becomes impossible.

It is probable, of course, that the new teachers appointed on short term contracts were retained and eventually became full time and established members of staff as soon as the school budget allowed. However, a glance at the appointments pages in the Times Educational Supplement for the academic year 1996–1997 indicates that the trend is firmly established and illustrated by block advertisements placed by the new independent agencies which announce the availability of one term, two term and one year contracts for newly qualified teachers.

Differences between NQTs in primary and secondary schools

The survey also highlighted significant differences between the primary and secondary phases of education. Table 7.1 shows a situation in secondary schools which still merits concern but which, in comparison with the situation in the primary phase, is much less extreme. The differences are accentuated by the fact that less than 10 per cent of the primary schools responding to the survey indicated that their NQTs were given a reduced teaching load compared with over one third of secondary NQTs who had a teaching load below the norm for the average classroom teacher in the school.

It must therefore be a cause of concern that so many new primary school teachers are entering the profession on short term contracts with a one hundred per cent class contact commitment. It is no wonder that the challenge of the first term of teaching is, for some, a totally different experience to their initial teacher training rather than a progression from it.

INDUCTION AND PROFESSIONAL DEVELOPMENT

One programme organised by the authors had as its main aim: 'To smooth the transition from student-learner to *teacher-professional*'. It was important to recognise publicly the *professional status* of the NQT. Even during the years when NQTs underwent a probationary period it was crucial for the induction programme to recognise that the participants *were* teacher professionals and were no longer college students. As such, a prime objective of such an induction programme was to ease the college–school transition and, along with that, to promote the initial development of the teacher as a *professional* typically holding a wider professional concept of the task of teaching (and being more than a mere 'clockwatcher' for 1265 hours).

NQTs often find their beliefs vigorously challenged as they attempt to meet the demands and expectations pressed upon them by schools (Veeneman, 1984) and the dialectic process of induction reshapes the actions and beliefs of both the individual and the school (Schemp and Graber, 1992). NQTs change as they affiliate with an institution and the organisation changes as new members usher in fresh ideas and unique ways of acting. It is during those first crucial, formative years (and none more so than that first year) that a teacher must be helped to form appropriate 'skills' and 'habits'and struggle against the tendency to fall back on mere instruction and control. That is a purpose of an induction programme, along with the task of helping a teacher to develop appropriate professional attitudes towards teaching and to refrain from taking on the negatively sceptical and misanthropic outlook of the cynic. As Thompson (1991) has pointed out, 'induction is about more than performing competently'. Indeed, experience from successful induction programmes has shown that job satisfaction has increased and 'drop out' has been reduced amongst the attending NQTs.

From this evolves the question: what *is* it we are inducting the NQT *into*? Those who have ever been involved in induction programmes will know that of immediate, crucial, concern to the NQT is knowledge about, and feeling comfortable with, the school and the work group. They are two of the most decisive and determining *dimensions* of induction – but there are more. It is important to consider an induction programme as comprising *dimensions*. Those of the school and the individual's work group, mentioned above, are normally the two considered of most immediate concern by NQTs during their first year or so in the profession. But the NQT *is* working in a *profession* and with professionals, with all that that means in terms of commitment, obligation, responsibility, accountability, duty, trust, and so on. It is an aspect of induction into teaching that, however well a school can support a teacher, there is a necessity for a wider platform to be provided, especially in the face of the national call for ever higher standards, principles and ideals from the *profession*.

Thus a key dimension of an induction programme that is of national interest is the ways in which the newly-qualified teacher is supported on entry into a *profession*. For this aspect of induction to be fully successful it is necessary for colleagues outside the immediate school environment to be involved. Historically and to a limited extent today it is provided by Local Education Authorities and in some recent isolated cases it has been provided by Higher Education institutions, but it has all become too piecemeal and too haphazard, a newly qualified teacher's experience of induction into the wider profession of teaching depending too much on the serendipity of location and programme content. LEAs also used to induct NQTs 'into the LEA', into the local area and into the local policies, concerns and procedures. In particular, in the best LEA induction programmes, NQTs would learn about local ethnic groupings and relationships, as well as key developments and links that had evolved, and significant local resources that could be tapped.

The full professional advantages of all of these assets could be detailed and described more comprehensively and more richly in a *regional* induction programme, drawing on the experiences from a group of schools, than could any single school's induction programme – however well designed and funded. Indeed, in those areas where the induction programmes considered such a *regional dimension* the benefits *to the school as a whole* deriving from the NQT's participation were freely acknowledged.

Finally, at the other end of the spectrum is the *individual dimension* of an induction programme. This is the part of the programme that deals with the teacher *qua* individual. It is the most immediate and personal element and the part of which typically the school's mentor will be cognisant and which, experience shows, is typically given more weight by mentors.

For a full development of the teaching force, therefore, there is a need for induction programmes to be run on the individual, working group and school dimensions, as now, but in addition the regional and professional dimensions must not be omitted from the programmes of planned support.

The DES findings of 1992 well supported the experience of those who had run regional induction programmes that, more than anything else, new teachers found the chance to meet and talk with other new teachers most useful and, in the long run, very professionally supportive and strengthening. In contrast, in 1988, HMI found that some 40 per cent of schools still had expectations of new teachers that were too high (DES, 1988) and by 1992 HMI were particularly concerned that there was a failure in many cases for the individual needs of the newly-qualified teacher to be differentiated (DES, 1992).

INDUCTION – THE WEAK LINK IN THE PROFESSIONAL DEVELOPMENT CONTINUUM?

Bolam *et al.* (1995) point out that 'For more than a generation there has been broad agreement, in England and Wales, between the profession, local authority employers and successive Governments, that the induction of newly-qualified teachers (NQTs) is inadequate and ought to be improved' (p. 247). They go on to argue that 'It is, therefore, both puzzling and worrying that so little has apparently been achieved over such a considerable period of time' (p. 248). In retrospect, the notion of a continuum of the three I's (initial, induction, and in-service education) proposed by the James Report in 1972 could only have been a pipe dream.

At that time there was no common philosophy underpinning teacher professional development; no continuity between the stages of a teacher's career; very little professional interaction between schools and those responsible for supervising student teachers; and a culture in education and in society which made it unlikely that a uniform national structure would be imposed.

The importance of induction as a managed and coherent part of a teacher's continuing professional development is closer to fruition in 1997 than it has been at any other time. We have seen in earlier chapters that the move to provide coherent support for CPD has been piecemeal. The identification of comparable routes in the initial education and training of teachers is ideologically bound and at the time of writing the shape of a 'National Curriculum' for ITT and how it will prepare the teachers described at the beginning of this chapter for their varied experiences remain to be seen. The development of National Standards for middle and senior managers and for other elements within the profession will add more to the coherence and continuity of professional development but will possibly not impact on every teacher. They may also constrain and limit the effectiveness of individuals rather than build on the creativity and enthusiasm of new entrants to the profession. The management of in-service support is still fragmented and, on an individual basis, poorly funded.

In effect, the progression from student teacher to experienced professional is still one of discontinuity rather than being a continuum. The period of induction sits uneasily between the diversity of initial training routes and the fragmented support offered from individual schools in an increasingly devolved system of professional development. In spite of the existence of a National Curriculum and the development of National Standards, the diversity within the systems of schooling and education in England and Wales will remain. It will be imperative that the key strands of support for new teachers in schools are clearly articulated if children and teachers are not to be disadvantaged.

And yet they do not have to be, for we are working with a very willing group – new teachers' commitments and enthusiasms are immense – possibly higher than at any other stage in their career and so many schools have, even in the face of intense budgetary constraints, appointed 'mentors' who have attended specialist courses (some of them accredited at Master's level). Even as recently as 1992 HMI found that new teachers who attended induction programmes showed 'interest, enthusiasm and commitment, a desire to improve professionally, and a willingness to share experiences and support each other' (DES 1992) and that this was so even when after-school meetings were held when the inexperienced new teachers were more tired than their more seasoned colleagues.

As O'Sullivan *et al.* (1988) point out, 'to use the objectivity of new teachers to comment on ways in which curriculum or other developments might be approached may be of use to the school and of value to the new teacher'. New entrants into any profession have the potential to offer ideas, to see things anew, to suggest new approaches and to take up the challenge in a *two way* process where the NQT is not seen as merely an *encumbrance*, lacking in skill and to be 'inducted' at vast expense and trouble but as a positive addition, a welcome breath of fresh air and ideas coming to support a beleaguered staff team!

Questions for discussion

What are the particular problems for newly qualified teachers entering the profession?

How can the new career-entry profiles be used to assist the process of induction?

Is induction the weak link in the professional development continuum?

8

Energising Middle Management

JEFF JONES AND FERGUS O'SULLIVAN

In most sectors of education we have seen a dramatic increase in the involvement of promoted post-holders (and, indeed, every member of staff) in the task of management. In primary schools there has been the rise of curriculum leaders since the introduction of the National Curriculum and in secondary schools the expansion of the role of faculty/department and pastoral heads has become a common feature.

An important issue identified in the reports published as a result of the OFSTED inspection system has been an affirmation of the key role of the head-teacher – a factor that has been well established through both the effective schools and the school improvement movements. However, the importance of middle management in schools in maintaining and developing school effective-ness, although mentioned, is less clearly articulated

The significance of the middle management role in schools has been targeted by the Teacher Training Agency (TTA) in their stated intention to develop 'stand-ards' of competence for the roles of the 'expert teacher' and the 'expert subject leader' to add to those being tested through Headteacher Leadership and Man-agement Programme (HEADLAMP) and the National Professional Qualification for Headship(NPQH) and to those which have already been implemented for the newly qualified/beginning teacher.

With increasing evidence of government funding for staff development being 'hypothecated' or targeted at improvement of performance through reference to such a framework of 'standards', schools will need to clarify their understanding of not only the competencies involved in the standards relevant to each stage in the Continuing Professional Development (CPD) continuum but also of how each stage relates to the next and how the whole process of school improvement can be supported and enhanced.

This chapter will build on the framework of policy and practice in CPD at the macro level covered in the first part of the chapter and map out the issues as they relate to those who form the vast bulk of management and leadership potential in schools – the experienced classroom teacher and the subject/section leader. The dual aspect of the middle management role as both a career in itself and a preparation for the next stage will be discussed, as will recent trends in management and organisational development in order to set the scene for the development of a competency-based approach to school middle management development.

In the second part of the chapter, this introduction to issues in the development of middle management in schools will be followed by a case study applying the principles in the context of one particular school. The role of the 'external' management developer will be explored from the point of view of the need for an organisation to utilise external expertise in the form of a 'critical friend' and from the point of view of the emerging role of the LEA towards newly autonomous schools in the area.

The final section will identify key issues for the future in the development of middle management as an under-used but vital ingredient in school improvement for the 21st Century.

TRENDS IN MANAGEMENT DEVELOPMENT

The increasing significance of middle management in organisations is partly a result of what are often termed 'megatrends' in society and the global economy generally (see for example Beare and Slaughter, 1993) and partly a response to the management's perception of the competitive position of the organisation itself. Of course, these two are inextricably linked, as a focus on competitive advantage at the level of the individual organisation has been identified as one of the 'megatrends'. Thus moving decision making down to the point of production or delivery of the service and setting up pseudo-competitive arrangements between 'service units' or 'agencies' which were formally divisions of a larger organisation impacts directly upon middle management at a time when

Table 8.1 Social and information megatrends

Social Megatrends	Information Megatrends
• Decline of the nuclear family • Changing age profile • Increasing cultural distinctiveness – multiculturalism	• Increasing quality and quantity • Globalisation of communication • Capacity/cost ratio changes exponentially (things get cheaper, quicker)
• Decline of Welfare State and other individual and family support	• Replacing symbolic knowledge and the organisations which provide them (established wisdom challenged)
• Emergence of an underclass – the 'have nots' – in all countries • Changing gender roles	• Access to anything, anywhere by anybody • The rise of 'information crime' – hacking, viruses, plagiarism, 'chip piracy'
• Rise of the global competitive market	• Growth of the 'information black market'
• Transnational companies – contrasted with increasing autonomy and flatter organisational structures at the work unit level	• Integrated media – tele and video conferencing, interactive video and TV

delayering and downsizing has begun to drastically reduce the numbers of middle managers available to handle this new autonomy and responsibility.

So how does this affect the continuing professional development of middle managers generally and heads of subject/section in schools in particular? One way of approaching this is to look at the curriculum of senior management development courses and qualifications in order to determine how top management envision the task of management. Here it can be clearly seen that the focus is moving from management to leadership (HEADLAMP, NPQH, Management Charter Initiative, Senior Management Standards etc.). This implies a more 'people' orientation with emphasis on creating a vision, empowerment, team building, motivation, decision making, negotiation. However, the nitty-gritty tasks of management still have to be carried out (what the Americans call 'doing the numbers') and it is these which have moved down to the middle management level.

In schools, a common response to this has been to set up development plan priorities and budget or cost centres at the section or subject level. Curriculum co-ordinators, heads of department/subject or section have, for many years, expected to produce an account of progress in their area of responsibility even if this was merely an indication of how the capitation was spent. Now, with teacher assessment, SATs, cognitive ability tests and public examination results as well as expenditure and budget variance returns, the data-base available is much larger and the expected level of accountability correspondingly greater. All this increases the number of management skills required of middle managers and their level of accountability and responsibility – at a time when they are struggling with another revision of the National Curriculum and continued ongoing debate about 'standards', testing, league tables and all the panoply of local management/governance of schools.

An interesting approach in successful organisations has been an attention to improving performance through focusing on leadership at senior management level and consequently increasing the level of management skills required at middle management level. Coupled to this is the move away from a hierarchical view of the task with specified objectives, narrow but detailed job descriptions and line and branch appraisal and management approaches to flatter organisational structures. This is paralleled in some of the more successful organisations with a new emphasis on values, the worthwhileness of the enterprise, environmentally green approaches and a 'learning organisation' orientation as a response to rapid change in society and political economy.

To recap, two most powerful findings from both studies on school effectiveness/improvement and the OFSTED inspection process have been the crucial importance of the headteacher on the one hand and the under-use or ineffectiveness of middle management. This is not to say that individual middle managers cannot be very effective in their own areas of responsibility but that *as a group* they are less effective than they could be . To put this another way, the effectiveness of the whole middle management group is *not* greater than the sum of the effectiveness of each individual middle manager.

It is towards this latter objective – to achieve a more effective performance from both senior and middle management – that two of the four TTA 'standards' are those for leaders of schools and for subject leaders. Whilst it is probably an important stage in the process to map out the individual skills, competencies and abilities required at each level (and, indeed a process which the MCI initiative in business also found necessary in their search for a more qualified management workforce), it is counterproductive in the long run if this is seen as the end product. The beneficial effects come from the way in which the upskilled managers and leaders work together as a group and from the processes which they use to facilitate their own learning about how to respond to changing circumstances within the organisation and its environment. It is this search for the benefits of 'synergy' where the whole *is* greater than the sum of the parts, that characterises the best of middle management development and is a crucial characteristic of 'learning organisations'.

DEVELOPING COMPETENCY IN MIDDLE MANAGERS

One of the key shifts in management development, paralleled by the movement to a skills based curriculum in vocational qualifications as exemplified by programmes designed to the specifications of the National Council for Vocational Qualifications, has been the rise of competency-based approaches. Previously, most INSET for middle managers focused either on the acquisition of new knowledge about their subject or area of expertise or were 'hints and tips' about being a successful promoted post holder. Not that this type of INSET is bad or unhelpful, on the contrary, as a mechanism for passing on good practice, there is still little to beat a workshop run by a talented and experienced practitioner. However, the emphasis is on contexts external to the individual's own self-development.

As attention has moved to identifying excellence in organisations – that which distinguishes the 'best from the rest' – more emphasis has been placed on the attributes possessed by and required of the individual in the organisation. It is these attributes which have come to be termed 'competence' or 'competency'. In characterising the development of competence/competency, two main approaches can be identified. Taking the model developed by Trotter (Davies and Ellison 1997) the 'competence' model is based on a functional

Table 8.2   Characteristics of competence and competency

Competence	Competency
• outputs for minimum standards	• inputs for superior performance
• concern for what the job requires	• concern for what people bring to the job
• sociological focus	• psychological focus
• reductionist	• holistic

Source: Davies and Ellison, 1997.

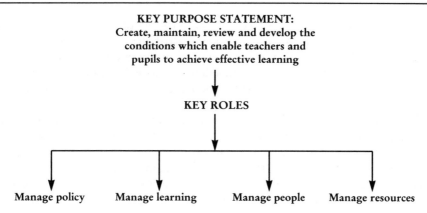

KEY PURPOSE STATEMENT:
Create, maintain, review and develop the
conditions which enable teachers and
pupils to achieve effective learning

KEY ROLES

Manage policy   Manage learning   Manage people   Manage resources

Figure 8.1 School Management South Competence framework
Source: Adapted from Earley (1992a)

analysis of the specific skills required by the job or task in hand and centres on the outputs required of the individual charged with this task, whereas the 'competency' model is based on the inputs that the manager brings to the role and therefore the underlying generic skills which are, once acquired, transferable to many different tasks.

One example of how the Competence version can be applied in practice for school managers is the School Management South consortium's formulation of middle management skills. This focuses on the range of tasks that have to be carried out, as shown in Figure 8.1.

In contrast the National Educational Assessment Centre's approach, which is based on 15 years of development work carried out in the USA by the North American Secondary School Principals Association, focuses on the individual skills which a school manager needs to bring to the job, as shown in Figure 8.2.

NEAC: 12 COMPETENCIES

ADMINISTRATIVE

1. Problem analysis
2. Judgement
3. Organisational ability
4. Decisiveness

INTERPERSONAL

5. Leadership
6. Sensitivity
7. Stress tolerance

COMMUNICATIVE

8. Oral communication
9. Written communication

PERSONAL BREADTH

10. Range of interest
11. Personal motivation
12. Educational values

Figure 8.2 The NEAC competencies for successful school leaders

Both of these approaches are equally valid for middle and senior managers as there are aspects of the school leader's attributes (as represented by the NEAC list) which need also to be developed in the middle manager, for example judgement, sensitivity and leadership. Likewise the headteacher needs to retain an ability to carry out some functional tasks, particularly as regards the budget and personnel.

In order to begin to understand how all this applies to the development of middle managers in schools we need to return to the basic question 'what exactly *is* the task of management?' The definition most apposite to the middle manager in schools is one of those given by Kemp and Nathan (1989, p. 8): 'getting things done through people with the most effective use of resources'. To this we can add the element of strategic thinking. It used to be said that management was far too important to be left to managers; now the focus for headteachers is moving to leadership we can extend this thinking to leadership being too important to leave to leaders. Indeed, as noted earlier, one of the 'megatrends' in business is the adoption of flatter organisational hierarchies ('flatarchies') with devolved responsibilities and a concern for process rather than structure. In such a scenario, the capacity for strategic thinking has to reside throughout the organisation, although it is true that those in the more senior positions will have this as a, if not the, major part of their role whereas middle managers' strategic thinking will properly focus on development in their area of expertise with some appreciation of the general environmental and professional context. The middle manager has to strike a balance between managing people and managing resources, between strategy and operational decisions, between managing policy and managing learning and all the while adopting the appropriate range of skills, attributes and competencies.

How can this be achieved? Is there a model which integrates several of these approaches? Do you learn with experience? Or is leadership just something with which you are born? One model which links the style of leadership to the experience of the team being led is discussed in the next section but there is a very powerful model of personal competencies that explores the tensions and paradoxes in the task of management and relates them to the way in which the organisation is seen (see Figure 8.3). The four conceptual models of the organisation covered are the human relations model, the open systems model, the internal process model and the rational goal model and within each model there are three main competencies – the skill of the manager is to determine their normal behaviour and then work out the most appropriate balance for the task.

MIDDLE MANAGEMENT IN SCHOOLS – A NEGLECTED RESOURCE?

This section will focus on the effects of 'flatarchies', self-directed work teams and devolved leadership on middle management in schools. It will look at learning organisations and situational leadership in order to set an agenda for the particular balance of skills and attributes a middle manager will need to have to make a successful contribution to school improvement.

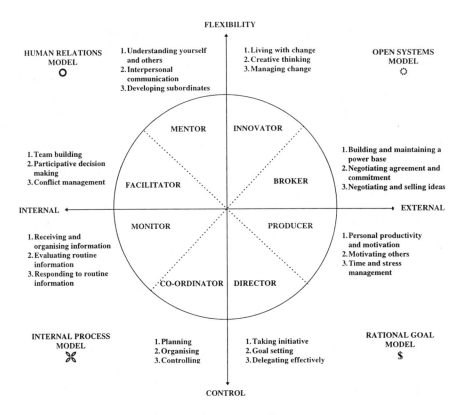

FLEXIBILITY

HUMAN RELATIONS
MODEL
O

1. Understanding yourself
   and others
2. Interpersonal
   communication
3. Developing subordinates

1. Living with change
2. Creative thinking
3. Managing change

OPEN SYSTEMS
MODEL

MENTOR   INNOVATOR

1. Team building
2. Participative decision
   making
3. Conflict management

FACILITATOR   BROKER

1. Building and maintaining a
   power base
2. Negotiating agreement and
   commitment
3. Negotiating and selling ideas

INTERNAL ←   → EXTERNAL

MONITOR   PRODUCER

1. Receiving and
   organising information
2. Evaluating routine
   information
3. Responding to routine
   information

CO-ORDINATOR   DIRECTOR

1. Personal productivity
   and motivation
2. Motivating others
3. Time and stress
   management

INTERNAL PROCESS
MODEL

1. Planning
2. Organising
3. Controlling

1. Taking initiative
2. Goal setting
3. Delegating effectively

RATIONAL GOAL
MODEL
$

CONTROL

Figure 8.3 A Competency framework (Quinn *et al.*, 1996)
Source: R. E. Quinn (1996) *Becoming a Master Manager*, New York, Wiley, p.16.

It is a truism that we live in a time of rapid change: 'the only constant factor in contemporary society is the exponential increase in the rate of change' (anon.). This can be illustrated by the oft quoted statistic that over 90 per cent of all the scientists that ever lived are still alive today. In our age the engine driving such change is technology. You wear on your wrist more computing power than existed *in the world* before 1950. Just as the curriculum for school children has shifted from a knowledge focus to that of understanding the processes, principles, concepts and relationships which link rapidly changing facts, so there is a need for organisations to move away from structures, line and branch management and detailed job descriptions to a more holistic and process-based approach in order to respond to the changing environment of competition.

There are many ways of achieving this, for instance Total Quality Management, Self-directed Work Teams, Quality Circles, Just-in-Time processes and so on, however, the one which promises to be the most appropriate for schools is the re-creation of the school as a 'learning organisation'. It seems paradoxical that the idea of the whole organisation 'learning to learn' should be so novel at this time – surely schools *are*, by definition, learning organisations? Certainly it is true that (most!) schools are *concerned* with learning, both at the levels of the pupils and, with staff development and governor training, at the adult level as well. But do they actually mobilise the learning power of *all* their people effectively? Barber, Hargreaves, Caldwell, Fullan and many other educational thinkers have drawn attention to the fact that schools (especially secondary schools) were designed for the factory system of the early twentieth century with its division and specialisation of labour, bureaucratic administration and hierarchical management systems. As we have seen earlier in this chapter, business has moved on and is increasingly more flexible, task-orientated and customer driven.

So how *should* schools be responding to the changes in society and what role should middle management play? It has always been the case that middle managers probably represent the real 'intelligence' of the organisation. Senior executives, in developing their 'helicopter' view and strategic perspective, inevitably lose grip on the detail. In the case of schools, it is those who both continue to teach for much of the time as well as manage others in their section (age-group or curriculum area) that have the up-to-date knowledge, experience and expertise of what it means to teach today's children today. So why are such middle managers so often brought to task for failing to carry out the task of management and leadership? We believe this arises from two main sources:

1. senior managers are not well trained in management and leadership styles which are responsive to the varying needs of their middle managers; and
2. middle managers are given too little training generally in the skills of *managing adults*.

In short, the focus on the vital importance of the headteacher as the single most significant factor in school success has distorted the range of leadership styles seen as most appropriate for the task of developing the school as a learning organisation. It puts an unfair and overloaded burden on the individual head and leads to the development of a dependency culture among the middle management of the school. You only have to look at the draft list of National Standards for new headteachers (TTA 1996f) to realise that heads are expected to be proficient in twenty-three task areas, fourteen skills and abilities and eight areas of knowledge and understanding. Any cursory glance at the detail of this list will show that the majority of these will actually be done by academic or administrative middle managers.

Although middle management positions are often characterised as being the 'training ground' for future school leaders, in practice the great majority of holders of such posts are not going to become headteachers. They will, however, continue to progress in experience and expertise so there is a need to see the development of middle management as a career in its own right. The TTA's approach to competence standards is a step in this direction, another is for senior management training to encourage approaches to leadership which

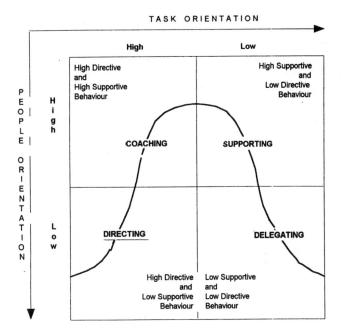

LEADERSHIP STYLE

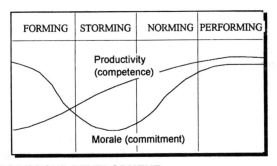

STAGES OF GROUP DEVELOPMENT

Figure 8.4 Situational leadership: matching leadership style to stage of group development
Source: Adapted from Blanchard, Carew and Parisi-Carew (1992) *The One Minute Manager Builds High Performing Teams*. London, Harper Collins p. 79

are much more responsive to the needs and growing expertise of middle managers. The model developed by Blanchard *et al*. (1992) is offered here as an example of one such approach.

The key to understanding this model is its basis in the level of maturity (or experience in the task) of the middle management team. In the early stages, when they are inexpert in the task, the leader needs to adopt a strongly task centred role, contributing his/her direction, vision and technical expertise. As the group matures the leader can focus more on the people dimension and take progressively coaching, and supporting stances. When the team is expert both in the task and in managing its own interpersonal relationships, full delegation is most appropriate.

What is particularly powerful in this model is the movement between the four leadership styles *along the bell shaped curve, one step at a time*. In new contexts and changing team membership, there will be the need to move back to an earlier leadership style, so, in practice, the skilful leader will be tailoring his or her style to the developing maturity of the team, moving subtly from style to style.

Such a model, allied with a competency approach for the detail of the skills to be acquired, offers great potential for the synergetic development of both senior and middle managers. Many headteachers have realised this and are engaged in development programmes with their management staff. In the experience of the writers of this chapter, this is the first, often painful, step in creating the learning organisation. Those heads who take this on board and focus on opening up the debate to unlock all the learning power of all the staff are finding huge benefits in directions which they could not have known at the outset. However, some are finding the presence of upskilled effective and dynamic middle managers rather challenging and sometimes uncomfortable!

DEVELOPING MIDDLE MANAGEMENT

For many years Hereford and Worcester LEA has been committed to a strategy for management development which supports increasingly self-developing schools and which incorporates the following principles:

- participation in management development by all teachers;
- the notion of continuous development;
- the vital importance of school-based learning;
- action orientated development;
- continuous check on the quality of provision.

It has also attempted to embrace a key principle from the report of the School Management Task Force, which stated that 'At the practical level of the school, management development must be integrated with the professional development of the whole staff in a collective effort to improve the quality of learning' (School Management Task Force, 1990, p. 22) To this end the LEA's Inspection, Advice and Training Service has started to examine the potential of supporting whole-school staff development, including non-teaching support staff, via the medium of National Vocational Qualifications (NVQ). Since the Inspection, Advice and Training Service already fully supports the professional development of teaching staff through a range of activities including INSET and qualification routes, the NVQ qualification route provides all colleagues with accessible steps to life-long learning. For many colleagues, an approach which enables staff to obtain credit for undertaking their everyday work and to gain an appreciation of the competency levels associated with their role in support of the school and its development is most attractive.

Delivering a school-based CPD programme

Blessed Edward Oldcorne Roman Catholic High School is a co-educational, Voluntary Aided Comprehensive Day School. It serves the area of Worcester City, Droitwich, Pershore, Evesham, Malvern and the neighbouring parts of south Worcestershire. It primarily admits pupils aged 11–16 with a denominational preference, but pupils other than those of the R.C. faith whose parents wish them to receive a Christian based education, are welcomed. There are approximately 890 pupils on roll. The school is staffed with a Principal, Deputy Principal, two assistant Principals and forty seven teachers, eight of whom are employed on a part-time basis. Several members of staff are given specific areas of responsibility within the School. The Deputy Principal is in charge of curriculum development and related matters, and there is an Assistant Principal responsible for the pastoral care of pupils. The pastoral system is organised in Year Groups with each year having a Year Head responsible, through form tutors, for the welfare and progress of pupils.

The school has a training programme for its staff based on a school development plan in which training needs are identified. The school makes use of a variety of training agencies and providers and was commended for its quality of education in a recent OFSTED report. It is a school which is solidly committed to high quality training for all its staff.

Having identified the need to make available to staff, and especially middle managers, opportunities for management training, the Principal approached the Inspection, Advice and Training Service in September 1995 to provide a programme of management training. The intention was to make this training available to middle and senior managers in the first instance – a total of 14 staff.

The school had in mind a programme of training which would help

- develop and accredit the competence of the staff involved;
- ensure that the staff possessed the necessary underpinning knowledge and understanding;
- support staff in applying the above in the performance of their managerial function.

Negotiation between the school's Senior Management Team and the LEA's representative resulted in the adoption of the National Vocational Qualification in Management at Levels 4 and 5.

The LEA and the school attempted to summarise the potential benefits of the programme for both the organisation and individual staff in the following way:

Potential benefits for individuals

- recognise and gain confidence for their own management achievements and learning;
- take a more active role in their own professional development;
- perform more effectively as managers of children's learning.

Potential benefits for the school

- promotes a development culture and enhances quality management;
- provides a coherent, common framework and language for management development;
- provides cost-effective solution to staff development and training needs;
- reveals the managerial capacity and potential of staff.

Aims of the programme

The aims of the programme are to help colleagues develop or confirm competence in aspects of their managerial role and to demonstrate this competence to an assessor. This they do by developing or reflecting on the skills and knowledge that the role contains. Skills and knowledge owned or acquired through training are assessed against national benchmarks and accredited and certificated. Candidates are required to prove that they can perform their work to the required standard consistently and that they have the necessary knowledge and understanding. It is competence in the real work situation which is being assessed not their ability to pass exams, write assignments or skill tests.

Programme content

The standards at each level share a common structure with a defined key purpose from which the standards are derived. The key purpose for managers is 'to achieve the organisation's objectives and continuously improve its perfor-mance'. The management activities have been grouped into four functional areas:

- managing operations (planning, quality and change);
- managing resources (equipment, accommodation and finance);
- managing people (personnel, human resource management, conflict);
- managing information (information systems, communication and decision-making).

Each function is made up of a number of units of competence which describe what is expected of a competent manager in particular aspects of the job. Each unit consists of a number of elements of competence together with perfor-mance criteria and range indicators. Qualifications are made up of units which can be separately credited or accumulated to gain a whole NVQ. The content of the Level 4 Programme is as follows:

a) Management Standards and their use in the Management of Education.
b) Review of NVQ/MCI/RSA system. Qualifications and certification. APL, evidence and assessment. Quality assurance.
c) Personal Action Plans.

d) Finance management, including financial analysis, schools' budget management, forecasting and financial aspects of resource management.

e) Management processes including objective setting, planning, directing, co-ordinating, decision-making and delegating.

f) Principles of effective management including planning, organising, prioritising, coordinating the work of others, problem solving, directing and re-directing situations.

g) Managerial enterprise including innovation, creativity, change management, making change work, strategies for overcoming resistance, implementation management and risk assessment.

h) Project management including feasibility studies, critical path analysis, monitoring and evaluation.

i) Total Quality Management, including quality improvement techniques, quality implementation, costing quality, customer care/pupil delight.

j) Managing people including management by control and commitment, persuasion, delegation, support and counselling staff training and development, performance appraisal.

k) Communications skills review and skills honing in relation to meetings management, teams management and time management.

l) Personnel requirements in relation to recruitment and selection, academic and support staff planning, conditions of service, disciplinary and grievance procedures.

m) Legal aspects of the manager's role in school. Health and Safety dimensions.

n) Systems management including analysis methodology, systems analysis, work method, monitoring and evaluation.

Underpinning knowledge and content suitable for Levels 4 and 5 form the topics for workshops and school-based study and assignments. The study topics are discussed with colleagues and contextualised as appropriate.

Given that personal effectiveness underpins all successful managerial competence, alongside the management standards has developed a model of personal competence which defines behaviour in competent managers. This embraces how managers do their jobs and the individual style employed. The personal competences include:

- planning to optimise the achievement of results;
- managing others to optimise results;
- managing oneself to optimise results;
- using intellect to optimise results.

The Process

The programme is needs based and therefore flexible to allow individual choice within the context of the school's objectives and the framework for national standards. This aims to support individuals in the development of skills and knowledge and to design and develop an appropriate process of collaborative training, accreditation, research and evaluation. The key features of such a programme are:

- *academic study*: access to theory, research findings, current policy, accounts of good practice;
- *action learning*: review, action research and development of self, team and school;
- *support*: from distance learning materials; fellow management learners in the school; senior management who may 'commission' projects; external facilitators/tutors from the LEA, University or other management development providers.

Assessment of competence

The NVQ assessment process involves making judgements about candidates' competence by measuring their performance against the standards. For the purpose of assessment, the cohort is divided into three, with each group being allocated to one of three assessor/advisers. The three assessors are members of the LEA's schools' inspectorate and opportunities are scheduled for the assessors to meet with candidates at regular intervals to discuss portfolio development.

In some cases, the candidate simply arranges for the assessor to observe and assess the candidate undertaking normal work activities e.g. conducting a departmental meeting. Competence of candidates can also be proved by collecting evidence which demonstrates the level of performance achieved and which meets all the requirements described in the standards. Examples include:

- assessor report of observations carried out
- candidate reports authenticated by the assessor or another recognised authority
- reports by previous employers/colleagues
- products of the work of the candidate produced through everyday activities at work or in other relevant environments
- video and/or audio recordings
- minutes of meetings
- endorsed photographs
- notes of discussion with assessors including details of specific questions
- project reports
- case studies
- assignments
- outcomes of other written questions or knowledge tests

Evidence collection is ongoing and candidates are encouraged to build a portfolio of evidence which allows the candidate and the assessor to cross-reference the evidence against all aspects of the standards in order to ensure that sufficient evidence has been identified.

In order to cater for varying experience and rates of progress in gathering evidence, candidates can claim accreditation of prior achievement for any units or elements of the NVQ, providing the evidence collected meets the standards laid down in the performance criteria. The assessment process is further supported by an:

- *internal verifier* who checks that both candidates and assessor(s) clearly understand what is required by the standards and ensures that all assessors' judgements are valid and consistent;
- *external verifier* appointed by the accrediting body e.g. RSA, BTEC to visit the approved centre to ensure that its judgements are to the same level as other centres and thus the national standard is maintained.

There is no specific period of time required to complete the units or the NVQ but, having taken account of the level of expertise of group members, the pace at which members of the group can progress and accumulate evidence given the pressurised nature of the work, the school has set itself an 18 month limit.

The total learning programme is structured to cover all units in a holistic way. Individualised programmes negotiated with candidates allow for flexibility in balancing and tutorial inputs. Flexible and open learning approaches are often appropriate. Assessment on demand in the form of readily available access to intermediate unit assessment and accreditation is envisaged.

Preliminary outcomes

The key question for both the school and the LEA is whether the initiative is having a beneficial effect on the quality of teaching and learning and the standards achieved by pupils. It is unlikely that the question could be answered with any great degree of confidence for some time yet. However, it seems reasonable, at this stage, to ask how far the management development process is facilitating improvements in school-based management at the levels of the individual, the team and the whole school.

As a further example of collaboration, the school, the LEA and the University of Humberside and Lincoln have embarked on an evaluation of the initiative, in particular the impact of a school-based management development programme on education provision.

Feedback received to date via ongoing monitoring carried out by the planning team and informal evaluation provided by the group have indicated that, in general:

- members of the group are already deriving the benefits set out in the programme;
  'I've already learnt a great deal about how to manage my department'.
  'Not everything we've heard is new, but it's helped me consolidate my current understanding.'
  'I much prefer to get a qualification this way . . . I can't write essays to save my life'

- the lead sessions have introduced them to new ideas which have enhanced their knowledge, skills and understanding;

  'I have never thought of schools as providers of a service for customers but it has made me think differently about the quality of our product. I'm still uncomfortable with the terminology, though'.

  'The TQM techniques . . . were really interesting. I've started to use some of them already'.

- the lead sessions have also encouraged an openness which has meant that colleagues have been prepared to confess to uncertainties, even errors of interpretation;

  'There is far more of a team feeling now'.

  'Working alongside the senior management team has meant that we can clarify things even make some constructive criticisms'.

  'The sessions have quite nicely reduced the hierarchical feel which means less of a "them and us" attitude'.

- the group feel valued;

  'I was a little apprehensive at first but I then began to realise the investment being made in me by the school – it can't be cheap to put this kind of programme on'.

  'For once I actually feel that my views count for something.'.

  'I began to realise after a while that I had never had the opportunity of hearing the views of my colleagues on a range of school issues. I was so impressed by what they were doing. I also felt reassured by much of what I'd heard'.

- the group feel more confident about dealing with their teams;

  'I feel quite confident about relaying some of the things I've found out to members of my department'.

  'I'm going to try some of the TQM techniques within my department'.

  'I've been reassured by what I've heard from the course tutor and my colleagues. This helps my confidence as a newcomer'.

- more aware of what it means to be an effective manager;

  'I thought I was quite good as a manager, but when you read some of the competences it makes you realise that there is more to it. This doesn't worry me. It gives me something to work for'.

  'I wish I'd come across these competences earlier. They are a good checklist'.

- pleasantly surprised by the quantity of evidence already available;

  'I was very sceptical about the NVQ. I had got the impression that it was a paper chase which, to a certain extent it is, but I've been amazed at the amount of evidence I could submit. The main problem is putting my hands on it and organising it for the portfolio'.

- concern about extra work;

  'I understand the intention behind it but it still puts pressure on me which I don't want and don't need'.

ISSUES FOR THE FUTURE

The role of middle managers in promoting the quality of education in schools will continue to attract the attention of policy makers and researchers for some time to come. It may be the result of a belated recognition of their pivotal role in bringing about improvement in schools or a knee-jerk reaction to the need to maximise human resources at a time when resources generally are squeezed. Whatever the reason, the crucial thing is that the debate about the function, competence and development of middle managers is underway.

It seems clear that whatever direction the debate takes schools will rely heavily on skilled personnel to occupy these key management roles. Research into effective middle management practice will need to inform the debate. It is hoped that the content of this chapter has made some contribution.

There is a strong case for basing a management development programme for middle managers on national standards. After all, this is the first time that definitions of the functions expected of managers in the work place and criteria for competent performance of these functions have been made explicit. Competency approaches for managers have the advantage of encouraging flexible, work based learning and individualised programmes. They recognise achievement, wherever it takes place, in the form of national qualifications or units towards them. The national standards help to clarify the relationship between different management roles within a school and also provide a coherent framework for job descriptions and the recruitment and selection of managers.

Competency based approaches are not a panacea but they do offer a way forward for management development in schools and unlocking the potential of some of the key players.

Questions for discussion

Does the new National Professional Qualification for Subject Leaders address the issues raised in this chapter?

How do the megatrends impact on CPD in education?

How do you evaluate the success of the Hereford and Worcester case study?

9

The Introduction of the National Professional Qualification for Headship

TERRY CREISSEN

The formation of the Teacher Training Agency (TTA) in October 1994 has had a profound impact on the development of higher standards for teacher education. From initial training through to classroom practice and managerial posts, the TTA has created a framework for the continuing professional development (CPD) of teachers.

As part of this work, the Agency was asked to develop a professional qualification for aspiring headteachers, which is now beginning a pilot phase across England and Wales. This was not to be a re-vamped masters degree, or similar academic qualification, nor a tick-box skills ability profile but something rather better geared to the practical application of the skills and abilities required by headteachers.

The qualification is also intended to be a high quality measure for school governors as an assurance that those with the qualification have the levels of knowledge, understanding, skills and abilities needed for the good leadership of today's schools. Thus, the National Professional Qualification for Headship (NPQH) looks to be setting the way for a series of measures throughout the teaching profession to train and test teachers with the intention of improving the quality of the educational process in our schools.

In *Ten Good Schools*, Her Majesty's Inspectors noted that 'without exception, the most important single factor in the success of these schools is the quality of leadership of the head' (DES, 1977, p. 36). Heads must be prepared to lead the school in improvement and demonstrate ability to lead the school for effectiveness.

Fullan (1985) argues that heads must address four issues of process to give meaning to effective school needs. These, he claims, are designed to enhance the ethos and image of the school and are fundamental in bringing about purposeful and effective change. He lists them as '(1) a feel for the process on the part of leadership, (2) a guiding value system, (3) intense interaction and communication and, (4) collaborative planning and implementation' (Fullan, 1985, p. 400). His terminology of having a 'feel' for the process emphasises the intangible measurement of effective leadership in a conventional and formal system. Conventional models of academic assessment are inappropriate to measure the current ability or potential of the NPQH candidate in this respect. Yet, leadership of the school for continuous improvement is at the heart of this qualification. It has to be measured by its impact and effect on others as does the overall effectiveness of the candidate in bringing about the right culture to promote improvement. In essence the NPQH reflects the view that 'success in leadership . . . refers to the way in which followers behave. Effectiveness refers to the motivational state of followers' (Owens, 1987, p. 136). The writing of assessment criteria in this domain will certainly be one of the most difficult tasks of the NPQH development.

Several researchers have outlined the characteristics and qualities of successful heads. Bolam, McMahon, Pocklington and Weindling (1993) produced a list summarising the managerial qualities, attributes and competencies most often displayed by heads who are considered to be effective school leaders. It is not the purpose of this chapter to compare the various listings, suffice it to say that there are many such descriptions (see Lyons, 1976; Morgan, Hall and Mackay, 1983; Evetts, 1994; Jirasinghe and Lyons, 1995) and the list of skills, knowledge and abilities presented in the NPQH framework draws on many of those analyses.

The way that heads display their competencies, the style they adopt in their leadership has a profound impact on their effectiveness and the way they are viewed by colleagues, parents, pupils and the wider community. Not only do heads need to be task focused, they need to be sensitive to the development of positive relationships within and beyond the school. The balance between these two, often conflicting demands is a fine one (see Beare, Caldwell and Millikan, 1989).

The work of McHugh and McMullan (1995) in Northern Ireland looked at the multifarious role of the head and the training taken by 8 headteachers to meet the ever-changing demands of their roles in school. With the changes under the Education Reform Act, they noted that 'the headteacher's job is now widely regarded as being primarily a managerial post' (McHugh and McMullan, 1995, p. 24). They assert that such a change requires 'the acquisition and development of a range of skills hitherto ignored by those concerned with teacher training' (McHugh and McMullan, 1995, p. 24).

A similar plea for effective preparation of headteachers is made by the National Commission on Education which noted 'a rather *ad hoc* system of headteacher preparation' and 'haphazard practices in the selection of headteachers in this country' (National Commission on Education, 1993, p. 230).

Since the advent of GMS and LMS, it has become increasingly clear that the competencies of business management through strategic planning, target setting and performance management are equally applicable to schools. Throughout the 1980s a number of initiatives were established to encourage the transfer of these skills. The work by the TTA on the NPQH set out to tap the non-educational sectors in the preliminary stages of the standards for the qualification. This is not a new concept. In an Education Journal Digest of 1984, it is noted that 'there has been a continuing debate about the value to providers and users of educational management training or experience from fields outside education – industry and commerce, public services, the armed forces' (Education Digest, 1984, p. ii). This was written at the time the National Development Centre for school management training had been in operation for a year, when research on the changing role of the headteacher was being sponsored by the Leverhulme Trust and significant research had been carried out into the selection of headteachers for appointment (see Morgan, Hall and Mackay, 1983).

Measuring potential is complicated by the cultural context of the headteacher's job within the school environment. This forms an important dimension to the understanding of the application of the standards set out in the qualification. As such, careful recognition of the impact of school culture must be a significant feature of the work of the assessment of the aspirant headteacher in the management of their level of competence within the system.

If culture is about 'the way we do things around here' (Deal, 1988, p. 203), then the head's ability to affect that culture will impact on the quality of the output of the school. Conversely, if a head cannot control the culture then he/she cannot change the workings of the staff in the school for improvement or otherwise. Whilst Morgan (1986) argues that 'managers can influence the evolution of culture . . . but they can never control culture' (p. 139), this new qualification attempts to identify the candidate's ability to manage the cultural development of the school through the contextualisation of the processes of school management within the candidate's current post.

Changing and moulding the culture takes time and the individual influence of the head is hard to measure as schools become more and more team focused. The determination of the cultural context of the school and its subsequent effectiveness as an educational organisation is difficult to ascribe to the effect of one individual. A flexible assessment process to enable prior performance to be taken into account and validated for the qualification is an essential feature of the NPQH.

The NPQH offers something more than a competency model, recognising the limitations of such a qualification. With the NPQH placing emphasis on the assessment of potential within the context of school improvement, it attempts to go beyond the competence approach to focus on evidence-based criteria. This fundamental difference makes the qualification stand out from others because it is aiming to assess potential rather than actual performance.

Measuring an individual's potential against the generally accepted demands of the job through a careful analysis of the headteacher's role must lead us to a better state of affairs than a declaration that the task is not possible. The measurement of competence potential can form a very useful and important guide towards the required levels of skills, knowledge and abilities for the improved leadership of schools. It is in this context that the qualification is framed.

With the advent of Local Management of Schools (LMS) and Grant Maintained Status (GMS), the role of the head has grown more complex, thereby intensifying the need for a comprehensive and consistent training and development programme. HEADLAMP was the first initiative to address this issue on a national scale. The impetus for a national training and development programme, tied into a full assessment of potential prior to being selected for a headship, is a natural extension of this work. We need better trained leaders in our schools and we need to prepare those aspiring to such positions in the most effective and objective manner possible. Teachers cannot be trained once and for all. They need constant updating in new technology, pedagogic improvements and personal leadership development. The Secretary of State for Education and Employment has echoed the importance of this view and has asked the TTA to develop a national framework for the professional development of teachers within which we can secure a co-ordinated and targeted approach. Similar developments are occurring overseas in the United States with the National Board for Standards in Education and in Australia with the Professional Recognition Programme. However, such developments on an international level are not the focus of this chapter.

In the Seventies, from the James Report (DES, 1972a) to the raising of the importance of the continuous professional development (CPD) of staff as a continuum by HMI (DES, 1979, p. 268), too much emphasis was placed on initial and induction training and it was not until the early 1980s that the inservice training of teachers in its widest sense was fully accepted amongst the profession. It became increasingly clear that a consistent and contextualised approach to headteacher training should focus on the values and principles of the head as leader within a democratic management team (see White, 1982).

The notion of continuous staff development is supported by Barber (1994) who states that teachers should be 'required periodically to discuss with peers what they have done in terms of career and professional development and indeed the development of their pedagogical and other professional skills . . . the profession itself should lay down minimum expectations for involvement in professional development over the five year period' (Barber, 1994, p. 14). Perhaps this signals the arrival of short-term contracts for senior school managers, required to meet predetermined targets and undertake regular training for their managerial and professional expertise.

In terms of CPD for school leadership, a number of government-sponsored national strategies to support senior management training programmes were outlined in circulars 3/83 (England) and 24/83 (Wales). From this came the One-Term Training Opportunities (OTTO) as well as basic 20-day courses. An evaluation of one of the first cohorts of 'OTTO' heads was carried out by Hellawell (1988) and concluded that such an opportunity gave heads the chance to reflect 'on the particular nature of the job of headteacher and the individual's particular ways of carrying out that job' (Hellawell, 1988, p. 229).

He concludes that the OTTO experience considerably aided the heads to manage themselves and others better.

One term secondments may be beneficial for existing heads but preparation for headship requires an on-going commitment to managerial skills development within a school setting. Maw (1984) highlights concern over the 'centralised pronouncements on preparation for headship' which 'have concentrated more on the professional than the managerial aspects of the role' (Maw, 1984, p. 8). The NPQH aims to counter such criticism by focusing on leadership and management standards related to the key tasks of school improvement. This is not made easy by senior educationalists in schools who hold firm to their educational role. This has prohibited their wholesale acceptance of good management practice outside education. Holmes and Neilson (1988) refer to this as a cultural issue which needs to be resolved in order for a training programme for school headteachers to be effective in meeting the competencies of the post. They claim that heads 'have to recognise that the behaviours that they need to master may be perceived by themselves, and their staff, as the antithesis of the values that led them to become educationalists in the first place' (Holmes and Neilson, 1988, pp. 24–5).

Investigating methods within and outside education, the POST project looked at the selection of secondary school headteachers. Whilst many of the LEA respondents described the process of headteacher selection as 'the most important thing we do' (Education Digest, 1983, p. i), they seemingly had little detailed understanding of the head's job and the researchers 'found no two LEAs with exactly the same procedures and no two selectors looking at exactly the same thing when dealing with the same appointment' (Education Digest, 1983, p. ii).

The lack of consistency in appointments and the seemingly hit and miss approach to the selection of headteachers, based on individual perceptions of who might best fit an individual's view of what constitutes a good head, leaves governing bodies little chance of rational decision-making in selecting a candidate who has the greatest potential for creating or maintaining the success of a school.

For such a crucial post and one which is regarded as the major influence on the success of the school, the selection procedures described in the POST project exemplify the need for a clear view of the role of the head and a full understanding of the criteria which heads should be able to demonstrate and be measured against. Whilst the NPQH cannot replace the interview, the qualification aims to assure governing bodies that the candidates before them have the potential to meet the standards for headship. The task for selectors can then focus on such aspects as the candidate's personality traits, values, experience and achievements, matched to the needs of the school. The qualification also sets out clear criteria to demonstrate to governors the sorts of aptitudes, skills, knowledge and abilities that headteachers ought to possess if they are to lead the school. Such a written measure is a positive response to the many criticisms levelled through the POST project.

The introduction of competency-based assessments evolved through the Youth Training Schemes of the 1980s and was supported by the Manpower Services Commission and the Further Education Unit. These then led to the creation of NVQs (National Vocational Qualifications) and subsequently, the GNVQ (General National Vocational Qualification) and the work of the Management Charter Initiative (MCI) (see Trotter, 1994, p. 5). It is clear that the NPQH sets out to measure the competence of aspirant headteachers in terms of their ability to demonstrate the competencies identified for the post to which they aspire.

The use of a set of competencies for the development of individuals is accepted as a meaningful and useful method of identifying individual strengths and weaknesses (Esp, 1993; Schroder, 1989; Lyons and Jirasinghe, 1992). The McBer approach reported by Boyatzis (1982) demonstrates the interactive nature of individual competencies to the demands of the job and the context of the organisation. Other approaches focus on the outcomes which have to be achieved for the individual to be recognised as competent. In this sense, competence is defined as 'the ability to perform the activities within an occupation or function to the standards expected in employment' (Jirasinghe and Lyons, 1996, p. 22).

As a follow up to MCI competency models for senior managers, School Management South (Earley, 1992) set out to develop a key purpose, key roles and units of competence for school managers. The measurement of individuals against an agreed expected standard stems from the greater drive for accountability in the profession. Greenfield (1989) reminds us that the health of an organisation rests with the competence of the people within it and we have to acknowledge that 'organisational goals are ideas held in the human mind rather than the property of an abstraction – the organisation itself' (Greenfield, 1989, p. 85). It is for this reason that the government and the TTA have focused their efforts on establishing a training and development model for the people newly appointed to headship (through HEADLAMP) and those aspiring to the most significant leadership role in the school.

It is also important to recognise that the competencies required of headteachers will alter over time. The role of headteachers has changed significantly over the past decade in terms of the varying influences and increased accountability placed in their hands. It is recognised that 'school administration now takes place in an increasingly turbulent, politically-charged environment; bluntly, running schools has become a tough job which involves more knowledge and skill than it did even a decade ago' (Beare, Caldwell and Millikan, 1989, p. xi). As schools and their social and political contexts grow and develop, so the qualification itself will have to evolve and transform to meet changing demands. Jenkins (1991) recognises that changes have already occurred and that there is a demand for a new set of competencies for headship. The NPQH is a genuine attempt to redefine the competencies relevant to modern day headship through open, national debate.

The NPQH must ensure that candidates cannot simply present a 'public performance of competence' (Ball, 1987, p. 173) but must truly be able to demonstrate their ability to achieve the skills levels required of the qualification, either through past performance, or through simulations designed to test potential.

The new qualification sets out to keep a clear focus on the core purpose of headship which involves establishing the strategic direction and leadership for the organisation for the improvement of pupil achievement. In this respect, it plans to assess the potential of the candidate in bringing about this aspect of a headteacher's role against the demonstration of the application of theoretical concepts to the practical situation. It has been shown above that the complexity of the task is not made easier by cultural and contextual issues. This takes it beyond the limits of academic, theoretical-based programmes and beyond the competency based assessments of NVQ to a qualification which tries to pull out the best of both, in that it focuses on the application and the potential application of the necessary skills and abilities required for headship in the school setting. This is not a simple qualification in management, it is a qualification in leadership. Leading the school is a fundamental part of the head's work.

When looking at candidates for selection, Morgan, Hall and Mackay (1983) suggest that candidates be assessed on: problem analysis and judgement; organisational ability; leadership; sensitivity; written communication; and, oral communication. Comparing this to the competencies assessed through the National Education Assessment Centre model, certain similarities are immediately apparent. This suggests the formulation of a consensus in the role of the head. When cross referenced to the framework of the NPQH with the five areas for development and assessment (see TTA, 1996c, p. 5), it can clearly be seen that there has been progress in acknowledging that the head's job has changed and that it can be assessed.

Leadership, then, is at the heart of the competencies and the qualification rightly emphasises this. This is echoed by the National Commission on Education:

> Good leadership is one of the key features of successful schools . . . It has always been the case, particularly in Britain where heads have a powerful role, but the major changes which are affecting schools will make even more significant demands. Such changes increase the importance of adaptability and place a premium on the ability to manage change.
>
> (National Commission on Education, 1993, p. 229)

The important factor for the NPQH must be to see through the stylistic traits of potential heads and focus on the candidate's ability to demonstrate the leadership and management tasks, skills and abilities themselves. In doing this, any recognition of prior experience will only be valid if relevant achievements can be demonstrated in the process. In this respect, the assessment of the qualification must be rigorous and clearly focused on the standards for headship.

There are four key issues to be addressed by the new qualification. Firstly, headship requires strong leadership and sound management qualities which need to be developed through training. Secondly, the training aspect must focus on the needs of the individual with each candidate viewed in the context within which they are operating if the qualification is to predict potential in an equitable and meaningful manner. Thirdly, it is important to recognise that there are often contexts which are inappropriate for the good preparation of potential headteachers – namely, poor schools or those with unsupportive heads. Means to overcome such hurdles will be required through the flexible application of the qualification if those candidates are not to be denied access to the NPQH. Finally, assessing the leadership and management tasks, skills and abilities must be undertaken in a cost-effective manner so that there is no bias in favour of the funding of the assessment process to the detriment of the training and development needs of aspiring headteachers.

The TTA initially sought views on the standards which candidates should have prior to seeking promotion to headship. From this, a series of issues were raised and some guidance about essential aspects of the qualification were suggested. These were then considered by the National Advisory Group for the National Professional Qualification for Headship before the set of draft standards was sent out for formal consultation.

The level of support for the NPQH was widespread with a strong view for a high quality qualification. Several initial responses highlighted the link between the professional and the personal qualities required in successful headship, urging that the competency model consider the personal attributes that an individual brings to the contextual nature of the post. Issues of access to the assessment for the qualification were also discussed in depth through the Advisory Group.

There was a great deal of anxiety about setting up a standard which was unattainable, as well as missing out a key aspect of headship potential which would remain uncovered by the new scheme. It was, therefore, felt vital that a managed pilot programme be established.

One important development from the initial request for views was an increased emphasis in the final consultation document on the relationship between the governing body and the headteacher. Candidates ought to have a good knowledge of the workings of governing bodies and be able to demonstrate that they can work effectively with their governors. In the final consultation document, the additional references to the governing body are particularly noticeable in sections 1 and 2 of the consultation paper (TTA, 1996c). Apart from the content of the qualification in terms of the competencies to be assessed, further concerns focused on the funding arrangements, access for candidates and the context of this qualification in the range of professional development activities for the teaching profession.

The issue of access was clearly linked to the pattern of funding and, in the light of comments from the initial stage of the debate, a section on funding and eligibility issues was added. The debate on access and entry requirements was to become a significant one about which there are still concerns which will need to be tested in the pilot of the NPQH. A consensus began to evolve in which candidates considering the NPQH from the Independent and the Grant Maintained sectors would apply direct to an assessment centre. For candidates in LEA maintained schools, the LEA would be the 'gatekeepers' whilst anyone would be able to apply direct to the Assessment Centre of their region if funded through independent means (self-funding). A minority believe that the qualification entry point must be upheld by 'gatekeepers' if it is to retain its credibility. It became clear after the national consultation that most respondents preferred a central grant system similar to that provided for HEADLAMP but with safeguards to ensure that entry requirements were established to prevent unsuitable candidates from gaining access to the qualification.

Further concerns raised issues on the balance between training and assessment, in terms of both time and funding, with one secondary school headteacher respondent stating: 'I do believe that the NPQH was formed . . . to measure how fit people were for the purpose of headship. Therefore, I would suggest that the consultation needs to have a bigger sway towards assessment and award of the qualification rather than training and development issues.'

Part of the concern on assessment was the desire to make a rigorous process neither excessively demanding on finances nor on time. One solution was to develop high quality self-assessment exercises which would short-cut the lengthy and time-consuming nature of this necessary work.

Finally, there was a clear view that the head, as professional leader of the pedagogy as well as manager in terms of Chief Executive, should maintain the fine balance between these two roles. This view echoed that of the National Commission on Education which stated that 'the increase in management tasks has not reduced the need for senior staff to provide curriculum leadership and to maintain concern for the development of professional skills throughout the school' (National Commission on Education, 1993, p. 229).

Emphasis is placed on the leadership role and the importance of the head to make sure that 'the school development plan identifies appropriate priorities and targets for improvement and relates to overall financial planning' (TTA, 1996a, p. 6). It recognised the need for teamwork and working with the governing body. It was pointed out that in the section on skills and abilities, the listing failed to include 'teaching' amongst the competencies. This omission was raised as a concern by many respondents and demonstrated the desire for balance between the managerial and the professional, pedagogic aspects of the headteacher's role. One respondent from Higher Education remarked that 'at the heart of the organisation . . . are the dynamic interactions between teaching and learning . . . research suggests that heads of schools that achieve excellent results . . . are almost obsessed by issues of teaching and learning'. The argument for strong pedagogic leadership in the primary school was felt to be a particular requirement of heads in the primary sector. This is echoed in the work of Jirasinghe and Lyons where they note a difference in the amount of direct contact between the secondary and the primary headteacher with pupils (see Jirasinghe and Lyons, 1996, p. 73).

The issue of access focused on the size and type of school. Candidates working in smaller schools were deemed to be most at risk where reservations included 'the need to make more explicit the principle of access, in terms of race, sex and age and size, type and location of school' (TTA, 1996b, paragraph 6). Rural schools were also felt to be in this category where 'the isolation of rural schools was especially mentioned' (TTA, 1996b, paragraph 22).

In the initial stages of the development of the work on the new qualification, there was a lack of consensus on the award's applicability to the different phases of education. The views from the consultation reflected those of Jirasinghe and Lyons (1996) who were unable to find strong evidence for a difference in the leadership style between different sizes and types of school. It was accepted that 'the implications of the standards in practice would be very different for the two-teacher primary school and the 80 teacher 11–18 school' (TTA, 1996b, paragraph 37). Instead, it was accepted that different aspects of the standards should be given different weighting according to these variables in type, phase and size. The context in which the candidate undertook the qualification, it was felt, would be signal enough as to the type of headship with which the aspirant head would be likely to be able to cope. This was regarded as a difference 'in emphasis, prioritization or urgency to a specified set of generic competencies for headteachers, rather than altering the set of competencies *per se*' (Jirasinghe and Lyons, 1996, p. 38).

Strong recommendations about demonstrating improvement within the candidate's own work situation were made to ensure that the practical application of the theoretical work was carried through. This reinforces the Secretary of State's desire for the qualification to be rooted in school improvement and is echoed in the words of a secondary headteacher who pointed out that 'whilst theory is essential, it is vital that actual management skills and skills training take a high priority in training'.

Part of the development of the new qualification was to recognise the work of areas outside education so, consequently, it was not surprising to see the TTA taking a strong line on this in the establishment of the Regional Centres making it clear that 'it will be a condition of contract that the provision at the NPQH Training and Development Centres draws on the best practice from outside education as well as from inside the profession' (TTA, 1996b, paragraph 36). The qualification has, in response to these views, made changes to the tone and nature of the standards and the manner in which they are to be assessed.

Following the consultation, the TTA agreed to establish a set of 10 regional centres in England: one for Assessment and another for Training and Development. Each centre will be under the control of the TTA and accountable to the Board. In addition to this, a series of distance learning materials will be developed so that issues of access are not a prohibitive aspect for candidates. The compulsory core will focus on 'strategic direction and development . . . implementation, monitoring and reviewing of policies and practices' (TTA, 1996b, page 11). The qualification will be gained within one to three years with funding 'channelled as a grant to the successful candidates through LEAs for those in LEA-maintained schools and through the NPQH Assessment Centres for those in grant-maintained schools' (TTA, 1996b, page 14).

It is important to maintain a high quality qualification in order to create confidence in the value of the NPQH and in the ability of candidates who possess it. It was also felt that whilst it should support the candidate, the qualification must not be able to be achieved by those clearly unable to take on the demands of headship. For its aim of providing a guide for headteacher appointing panels, the new qualification, in addition to the normal selection procedures for new heads – interviews, in-tray exercises, psychometric testing amongst others – will enhance the selectors' knowledge of their candidates and give them reliable information upon which they will be making judgements according to their needs. There are aspects of the head's job which are hard to assess through the NPQH and which have to be measured through confidential references and the interview process. Such issues are about styles of leadership, the individual's notion of 'power' and personal traits. There is also an intuitive nature to headship which is a problematic issue for assessment.

If the qualification is to be a useful developmental tool for candidates, there must be a supportive framework to help the aspirant head to learn from experiences and access training to meet their particular needs. It is, therefore, a prerequisite to starting on the NPQH that the candidate will attend one of the Regional Assessment Centres for a needs assessment in order to identify their training and development requirements.

Recognition has been given to the changing role of the head and the increasing demands on this complex role of professional, educational leader and executive manager. This has to draw on the experiences within and outside education if it is not to ignore the positive developments through the competence framework of NVQ, the work of MCI and the traditional academic studies of Higher Education Institutions.

It remains unclear as to whether or not a headteacher has to be an 'expert' classroom teacher or indeed, whether a head has to hold Qualified Teacher Status. This is an aspect of headship which might well be explored in the future.

The NPQH now moves into a new dimension of development with the establishment of a Management and Development group for the NPQH as well as the Headship Training Advisory Group. This structure has the potential to maximise the validity and effectiveness of professional qualifications within the teaching profession at all levels of management and competence. The work of the Management and Development Group will be to finalise the standards, draw up detailed assessment objectives, set the selection criteria, develop materials for use in the qualification and establish the assessment procedures for the final award.

With the introduction of the NPQH, supported by the government and developed collaboratively through the educational sector by the TTA, we may have plugged the gap in training our school leaders. All that now remains is for the qualification to be a rigorous measure of potential in aspirant headteachers as a sure guide to governors and a clear programme for the development of future school leaders.

The qualification is not intended to replace the need for mentor training after appointment nor does it replace the need for further training in the early years of taking up a first headship which is currently supported by the HEAD-LAMP scheme. However, for the first time, colleagues looking to headship as a career progression have a clear set of guidelines outlining the competencies they will be expected to demonstrate prior to taking up headship. Whilst the qualification is not compulsory, it is anticipated that most people seeking their first headship will look to the qualification as a sensible preparation for the demands of the job.

National standards, national guidelines and national expectations for the school head need to be developed and evaluated carefully to enable the award of the NPQH to be a high quality qualification, holding credibility with the profession and with governing bodies on the selection panels at interviews. The impact on parents, teachers and students will derive from governors appointing good quality headteachers to lead schools in the future.

If this qualification is to be manageable and realistic then it must acknowledge that no one person can meet the requirements for 'super-head' and individuals will have strengths and weaknesses which need to be matched to the school to which they apply for headship followed by professional development to enable them to continue to meet the demands of the job. The NPQH supports the training and development of potential school leaders through a flexible yet rigorous assessment procedure. Unless it can fulfil these demands, it will lack credibility with the profession, with the selection panels for headship but, most importantly, with the candidates themselves.

Questions for discussion

What are the qualities of successful headteachers?

How do you evaluate the NPQH standards model?

How would you characterise the differences between the level of performance required for the NPQH and for an expert headteacher?

10

HEADLAMP – A Local Experience in Partnership

HUGH BUSHER[1] AND LIZ PAXTON

GENESIS

The definition by the Teacher Training Agency (TTA) of Headteacher tasks and abilities (TTA, 1995c) and the emergence of headteacher training programmes (Headteacher Leadership and Management Programmes: HEADLAMP) was the culmination of considerable research and development in the late 1980s and early 1990s related to headteacher training. It not only created a visible framework for headteacher development but also created an implicit model for professional development at all levels. This began to be made explicit in 1996 as the TTA started work on the definition of standards for teachers at four career stages (TTA, 1996c), including the National Professional Qualification for Headship (NPQH). Teachers were to be assessed for their competence at these levels and then given training through local consortia of LEA, business and HEI leading to a competence-based National Vocational Qualification which might or might not have equivalent accreditation through a route of academic study, such as a Master's degree.

Under the auspices of the DES, the School Management Task Force produced a report (1990) making recommendations on how existing training provision for headteachers could be improved. They suggested:

- helping people to analyse their needs;
- more accurately targeting training and development requirements;
- examining the most appropriate delivery mechanisms;
- monitoring and evaluating effectiveness in the work place.

The report urged LEAs to promote partnerships with schools and external bodies, including higher education, to develop high quality management. It suggested that higher education institutions should work both in conjunction with LEAs and together in regional consortia to:

- meet the requirements for management development;
- develop appropriate modules and programmes;
- give accreditation to prior learning.

The authors of the report warned against the danger of creating a managerial cadre of headteachers distanced from other teachers through their having training and development activities to which other staff did not have access.

In 1994 the DfE and OFSTED commissioned, and the Confederation of British Industry (CBI) through its public relations agency Understanding British Industry (UBI) supported, a research project into the training and development needs of headteachers, their deputies and those of chairpersons of governors in secondary schools. It identified several training priorities (DfE, 1995):

- Strategic management.
- Monitoring, evaluation and review.
- School development and business planning.
- The policy, development and implementation process.
- The development of middle managers.
- The delegation and accountability of management roles.
- Leadership.

Worryingly it also reported that headteachers not only felt there were few schemes for their own professional development but that they seemed to consider their own needs last, if at all, and failed to reflect their own development needs in staff development plans. This view was borne out by a survey carried out for the Education Management Information Exchange (Baker, 1996) which found that a significant number of headteachers neglected their own professional development or did not perceive the need for it. It found that LEAs were reporting that headteachers were looking for a 'quick fix, everything at once culture' since it was difficult for headteachers to get out of school for more than half a day at a time.

To promote better headteacher training, in 1994 the TTA introduced the HEADLAMP programme. They offered £2,500 to school governors to spend on training newly appointed headteachers over a two year period from the time of their appointment. To try to ensure that the money was well spent, the TTA set up a scheme for franchising providers, only allowing school governors to spend the HEADLAMP money on TTA approved courses. This legitimised training and development for new headteachers and the time needed for it. By 1996 more than 200 HEADLAMP providers had been licensed, though some only provided training in one or two aspects of management.

The task for Headlamp providers was to structure their programmes in such a way as to make them appropriate to TTA requirements and accessible and manageable for busy headteachers, especially those with teaching commitments. To meet the former, programmes had to focus on the generic needs of headteachers, identified by the TTA through a list of tasks and abilities for headteachers (TTA, 1995c), while also maintaining the flexibility to respond to the needs of individual headteachers and the contexts of their schools.

The introduction of the HEADLAMP programme coincided with the marketisation of LEA services. By the early 1990s all schools had delegated budgets, the powers and responsibilities of local management and a high level of devolution of funds for professional development through GEST. To meet this challenge, in 1993

Leicestershire LEA had been restructured into a small core of officers with strategic responsibilities and a series of trading units such as an Inspection and Advice unit. The advent of HEADLAMP therefore created tensions within the LEA as trading units saw a market opportunity but those responsible for strategic planning saw the potential value that could be added by offering provision in partnership with a university.

THE BASES FOR A HOLISTIC HEADLAMP PROGRAMME

The programme described in this chapter was designed on the basis of partnership between a university (Loughborough University), an LEA (Leicestershire) and headteachers within that LEA to meet and support the needs of new headteachers. We make no claims to it being unique. It does, however, offer an integrated programme for those new headteachers who want it, covering all aspects of the tasks and abilities specified by the TTA as well as giving them a Masters degree from Loughborough University when they complete it. The programme enshrines a holistic model of professional enrichment to support school improvement rather than an assessment/competence model for auditing and honing headteacher performance.

In this model it is assumed, on the evidence of existing sound professional practice in schools and LEA, that many teachers are competent to diagnose their own problems and develop effective solutions for them. What new head teachers in particular need from external agencies be they LEA, experienced headteachers or Higher Education Institutions (HEI), is a diagnostic framework to help them make adequate analysis of their institutional contexts and professional needs, and support to develop those personal and professional skills they require to implement change to resolve the needs and tensions they have identified.

As each headteacher's professional history and that of their institution is different, it is difficult to apply fixed solutions to particular situations in all schools. Indeed, we would argue that an important part of the construction of a solution to an identified problem lies through a headteacher working with colleagues in a school to develop a solution which fits the school's specific educational and social contexts, i.e. is itself a holistic process. Prescriptive processes of managing change and context-free practices for developing personal skills are likely to be less effective because they will not encourage new headteachers to recognise the importance, to bringing about successful change, of developing collaborative working with their colleagues: the staff and governors of their new schools. In such circumstances, becoming a competent management marionette making set moves in line with the grand designs of a renowned management guru might even be counter-productive, given the hostility to rational approaches to management found in the professional cultures of many school staffrooms.

A holistic approach to professional enrichment and institutional improvement leaves control of the processes with the practitioners, encouraging autonomy based on sound knowledge and ethical guidelines for professional practice rather than dependency based externally validated and prescribed frameworks of action. To ensure that autonomous decision-making is soundly based, the practitioners have to have access to rigorously gathered evidence and information and to sophisticated personal and professional knowledge when they need it. Part of the aim of this programme, then, was to create a 'toolkit' of analytical instruments which programme participants could use in their own schools. To ensure the validity of these they were derived from what was currently known to be effective practice and from theory based on recent soundly constructed research.

The list of tasks and abilities which the Teacher Training Agency (TTA, 1995c) required providers of HEADLAMP training programmes to offer new headteachers fitted well with this holistic approach since these seemed to match closely the findings of much of the recent research on effective leadership and school improvement. These offered, then, a useful framework against which to check the knowledge base the programme provided (see Figure 10.1 – The headteacher training programme in outline), while leaving the programme leaders free to help the new headteachers to become familiar with and apply to their own schools the knowledge required to develop those abilities and tackle such tasks once need had been identified. Thus although the programme paid attention to the emerging UK national definitions of headteacher competencies, the programme was designed to support the development of judgement and autonomous decision-making rather than to be competency driven i.e. to train participants to behave in certain ways such as those outlined by the performance criteria and range statements of the School Management South Project (e.g. Earley, 1993).

The late 1980s and early 1990s have seen the development of the competency approach to management development. It was noticeable that the TTA consultation document on HEADLAMP referred to headteacher competences, whereas the final scheme detailed a range of tasks and abilities. Like attempts to specify competences in other fields of work, the attempt to specify teacher and headteacher competences is based on defining what are thought to be the most appropriate behaviours or outcomes for an operative in particular circumstances. By implication it is assumed first, that it is the action rather than how the action is carried out which is crucial to a continuing effective operation, and second that an appropriate behaviour can be defined without regard to the particular social or institutional context in which it is needed.

Whilst the value and applicability of this simple rational model of human behaviour has a certain common sense logic when focused on tasks requiring mechanical or technical skills, there has been considerable debate about its efficacy when applied to complex non-mechanical situations such as teaching (e.g. Whitty and Willmot, 1991). Bound up with such debates are competing claims to professional identities and job demarcations between professional, technical and manual work. On the other hand, Everard (1995) estimated that by the mid 1990s competence based standards of performance validated by National Vocational Qualifications (NVQs) up to level four (i.e. roughly

Element	Process	Tasks and abilities addressed
1. Professional Enrichment for School Improvement	Professional Development Centre A 2-day block of seminars, workshops and in-depth individual professional development interviews. Conference on organisational audit One day of participant presentations to colleagues, mentors and tutors.	Institutional Defining aims and objectives of a school. Reviewing policies for all aspects of a school. Reviewing standards of pupils' achievements. Reviewing the quality of teaching and learning. Anticipating problems, making judgements. Analysing a school's changing circumstances. Considering and giving priority to solving problems. Individual Audit of prior professional experiences. Help participants assess future training needs.
2. Managing Schools	Lectures, seminars and workshops on: vision and values; the role of headship; human resource management; financial management; working with governors; managing the external environment. (A 2-day block plus one other day.)	Institutional Defining the aim and objectives of the school. Planning and managing resource provision. Solving problems. Liaising with parents, the local community and other organisations. Giving a clear sense of direction and purpose to a school so it will achieve its mission. Individual Negotiates, delegates, consults and co-ordinates the work of other people. Communicates effectively with staff, pupils, parents and governors. Keeps up to date with current relevant educational and management ideas.
3. Evaluating school performance	Research methods A 2-day block of seminars. Evaluating an aspect of school A 1-day conference when participants present their evaluations.	Institutional Assessing and reviewing standards of pupil achievement. Assessing the quality of teaching and learning. Liaising with parents, the local community and other organisations. Individual Anticipate problems and make judgements. Monitor and review the effectiveness of policies in practice. Communicate effectively with staff at all levels, parents, governors and the wider community.

Element	Process	Tasks and abilities addressed
4. *Managing a quality learning institution: leading schools today*	Seminars and workshops focusing on: leadership; collaboration, consultation and collegiality; developing policy; managing staff development; internal review and external inspection. (A 2-day block plus one other day)	*Institutional* Developing and implementing a school assessment policy. Selecting, managing and appraising staff. Reviewing standards of pupils' achievements and the quality of teaching and learning. *Individual* Giving a clear sense of direction and mission to a school. Anticipating problems and making judgements. Adapting to changing circumstances and new ideas. Pursuing policies to implementation.
5&6. *Professional Development Portfolio*	Must be the equivalent of at least 15,000 words long; must include: corroborated reflection on professional and school development; a strategic plan for the school for the next three years; evidence of study of and reflection on a major management text.	*Institutional* Define the aims of a school review and develop policies. Plan and manage resource provision. Assess and review standard of pupil achievements. *Individual* Give a clear sense of direction and purpose to a school. Adapt to changing circumstances. Anticipate problems and offer solutions. Monitor and review the effectiveness of policies. Understanding and keeping up to date with relevant current educational and management ideas.

Figure 10.1   The headteacher training programme in outline

equivalent to a higher national training qualification) were available for 85 per cent of the UK working population.

At the level of professional activity (level five NVQ) such as that of occupations like pharmacy and accountancy, the most successful development of competences to define action has been in management, particularly through the work of the Managment Charter Initiative (e.g. MCI, 1994). The major attempt to draw up occupational standards for school managers was that undertaken by School Management South (e.g. Earley, 1993, p. 136) Their key purpose was 'to create, maintain, review and develop the conditions which enable teachers and pupils to achieve effective learning'. The four key functions which these standards identified were managing policy, managing learning, managing people and managing resources. These are reflected in the elements of the programme discussed here.

At East London University and at Oxford Brookes University, considerable progress has been made in developing batteries of tests, based on competences, to assess the readiness of managers for promotion. Lyons (1993) claims these are successful in identifying which people, including senior teachers should be promoted, in some cases after appropriate training. Issacs (1992) presents an interesting analysis of the success of the Florida competence programme in sifting and preparing teachers for promotion. Such assessment processes are based on trained observers watching and analysing participants perform in simulated situations. This appears to deny the ability of participants to evaluate their own performance, assuming that the most powerful knowledge (the coercive power of pass or fail) is held by experts outside the decision-making situation.

Our programme assumed that participants were able to analyse their own performance effectively so long as they were shown how to do so and given the knowledge to do so if they needed it. We did not run an assessment centre for the new headteachers joining our programme, but offered them a series of semi-structured interviews with experienced practitioners to help them reflect on their professional experiences and begin to map out the next steps for their personal and institutional development. This approach delegated power to participants rather than divorcing them from it. We have referred earlier to the way in which this programme developed evaluation tools for new headteachers to apply to and in their own situations.

The programme was designed using the five types of staff development activity which the research of Joyce and Showers (1980) suggests has an impact on student achievement:

- providing information and theory;
- demonstration;
- practice;
- feedback
- coaching on performance.

It aimed to develop the four learning outcomes they suggest in-service courses should try to achieve:

- increased knowledge and awareness of educational theory, practices and policies;
- changes in attitude to (curriculum) content or their own identity as a teacher;
- development of a skill;
- transfer – consistent and appropriate use of new skills and strategies (for classroom teaching).

The process of evaluating the programme was designed as the programme was being constructed, although this was carried out later than the construction of the modules. It sought to combine elements of internal and external evaluation, drawing on Thomas (1985), which focused on both course processes and course outcomes, the latter being differentiated into immediate (end of course) outcomes and longer term application of learning in the workplace, drawing on the work of Lomax (1987). Some early findings from this process of evaluation are reported later in this chapter.

DEVELOPING THE PROGRAMME

The publication by the TTA of their consultation document on HEADLAMP in the Autumn of 1994 prompted informal discussion between a university lecturer and a local authority officer about possible partnership in providing training and development for newly appointed headteachers.

Leicestershire headteachers and schools have a long tradition of autonomy with the LEA enabling and supporting rather than directing and controlling; local management has enhanced this autonomy. This, and the cultural shift in the restructuring of the LEA onto a purchaser/provider basis strengthened the already strong and influential headteacher groups within the county. The authority already had in place a representative group of headteachers appointed by primary and secondary heads groups to work with LEA officers in planning support and development programmes for headteachers and senior staff in schools.

Within weeks of the announcement of HEADLAMP and the informal discussions between the LEA and university, this headteacher planning group and representatives of the teachers' associations were consulted on the desirability of a partnership programme which they fully endorsed. Subsequently this approach was endorsed by the senior management team of the Education Department at the LEA.

Four experienced headteachers trained under the DES GEST Mentor Training Scheme were recruited to form a core team along with the LEA officer and the university tutor. Their role was to be multifaceted. They provided a measure of quality assurance that the programme modules (called 'elements' to avoid too academic a flavour to the programme) and their support materials would meet the needs of new headteachers i.e. that abstract knowledge presented in a particular form would, in their view, help new headteachers to reflect on practice. When the programme started, they were attached to new headteachers to provide mentor support in school. But they also played a role as quasi-tutors, attending programme sessions, counselling participants, acting as critical audience when students made public presentations about their work in some programme sessions. One also acted as a lead speaker on a topic during the programme.

A similar process of negotiation and legitimation took place within the university at the same time as in the LEA. Here there was considerable interest in the possibilities of working in partnership with the LEA to provide programmes which would both meet the needs of teachers and attract people onto existing higher degrees programmes. A combination of altruism and self-interest proved a potent fuel, as usual. Since recruitment to weekday higher degree courses had slumped, and HEADLAMP offered a potential source of students amongst other successful initiatives in the MA programme at Loughborough. Altruistically, there was the challenge of shaping existing higher degree modules to meet teachers' needs and in doing so constructing a complete course out of apparently disparate modules. There was also the intellectual challenge of seeing how and how far TTA defined headteacher tasks and competences could be matched to existing higher degree modules in education management and what knowledge and pedagogical processes could be developed to help new headteachers achieve these.

By early 1995, all three parties – headteachers, LEA, university – were involved in programme development, but the TTA had not yet published its final version of the HEADLAMP scheme. All that was known was the head-teacher competences outlined in the original consultation document, the need for providers to gain recognition from the TTA before they could run courses for which new headteachers could reclaim government funding, and the intention for HEADLAMP programmes to start no later than September 1995. The timescale for development was somewhat short!

In the process of programme development there was excitement in trying to apply in practice what was much discussed in the literature on education management as a key element of effective management, the creation of partnership through coopera-tive working to solve identified institutional needs. In this sense, the working pro-cesses for developing the HEADLAMP programme began to mirror the kinds of practice that the programme would be recommending eventually to participants for promoting professional and institutional development. Throughout the planning stage, then, there was emphasis on:

- the notion of a federation within which each partner was able to make a distinct contribution;
- principled negotiation between partners whose contribution to the develop-ment and to the programme was of equal value;
- the creation of a professional network involving new headteachers, existing headteachers, LEA officers and university lecturers to enhance the profes-sional learning of all;
- mutual benefit in terms of professional stimulus, development and satisfac-tion that was also soundly based financially.

A collection of materials was developed to support organisational analysis and per-sonal review/development planning – the 'toolkit'. These were developed for two purposes: initially to help participants analyse their existing professional knowledge and the exisiting situation in their new school, but eventually to help them create a personal development portfolio. This last constitutes one-third of the accreditation of the overall programme and is equivalent to the dissertation on other MA pro-grammes. The language used in these materials was chosen with great care in order to sustain the notion of professional partnership. As we developed the programme we became increasingly aware that what we were creating could be appropriate not only for new headteachers but also for existing heads and other senior managers in schools, and we considered how, at a later date such people could be incorporated into the programmes. We also became aware that there could be a demand for the programme outside our own parish and wondered how these people might be reached, too.

At the same time materials had to be prepared for advertising the programme and the programme had to be costed. The latter raised some interesting questions as the core team wanted to build in the process of mentor support to all six modules of the programme, creating a programme which had a sense of entity to it, while still providing for those people who only wanted to take the occasional module. The last was a TTA requirement for provider recognition. Although participants would be encouraged to register for the whole programme it was planned and costed in such a way that new headteachers (or other heads/senior managers) could access individual elements.

The publication by the TTA of the actual HEADLAMP scheme in May 1995 came as a great relief, not least because it only required minor modifications to the planned programme. We were then able to advertise the programme as soon as we gained provider recognition from the TTA.

THE STRUCTURE OF THE PROGRAMME

Detailed planning began early in 1995. The aims and structure of the programme were agreed fairly quickly which meant that attention could focus on the processes to be employed within the programme.

This programme is rooted in the needs of individuals and their schools. It has been designed to be school focused so as not to distance headteachers from their staff but to involve them fully in working with staff and other stake-holders. As can be seen in Figure 10.1 the programme has a six module/element structure, similar to Loughborough University Masters degrees in Education. It uses four taught elements which were already accredited by the university, so avoiding having to gain accreditation of new elements, a potentially slow process. The remaining two elements, which form the professional development portfolio, are a variation on a Masters degree dissertation which is recognised under university regulations. The portfolio also allows participants to demonstrate the competence they have achieved so, again, helping to link professional control with quasi-objective understandings of effective practice.

The initial element *Professional Enrichment for School Improvement* involves supported self-assessment of school and individual needs. It is focused round the 'toolkit' which has already been discussed. It is deliberately linked to the second element on *Managing Schools* since it was thought by the core team to be pointless to discover needs without offering some means of addressing them. The third element focuses on institutional evaluation. OFSTED pointed out (1994) that a key need for senior staff is to find out what is being achieved in a school and how effectively a school is meeting the needs of its students. A more detailed analysis of these modules, to be found in Figure 10.1 also shows how each element is linked to some of the headteacher tasks and abilities prescribed by the TTA for a recognised HEADLAMP programme, all the tasks and abilities being covered at least once in one of the modules.

Each of the elements is taught in a pattern of a two day block plus one other day (see Table 10.1). This pattern was developed for practical and academic reasons. The core team thought that headteachers would have difficulty gaining more than

Table 10.1   Headlamp schedule

	Cohort 1	Cohort 2	Cohort 3
1995			
November	Element 1 2 days		
1996			
January	Element 2 2 days		
February	Element 2 1 day		
March	Element 1 1 day		
May	Element 3 2 days	Element 1 2 days	
September	Element 3 1 day		
October	Element 4 2 days	Element 1 1 day	
		Element 2 2 days	
November			Element 1 2 days
December		Element 2 1 day	
1997			
January	Element 4 1 day	Element 3 2 days	Element 2 2 days
February	Start Elements 5/6		Element 2 1 day
March/April		Element 3 1 day	Element 1 1 day
May			Element 3 2 days
September		Element 4 2 days	Element 3 1 day
November		Element 4 1 day	Element 4 2 days
December	End Elements 5/6	Start Elements 5/6	
1998		(2 terms)	
January			
April			Element 4 1 day
			Start Elements 5/6
			(2 terms)

two days out of school in any one week, especially in their early years in post. Academically, the gap between the two parts of each element gives time for participants to reflect on what they have discussed, apply it to their schools and consider it with their mentors. This draws on the theory of Donald Schon (1987) on how to help professionals develop reflection on practice. For two elements, the first and the third, this gap is used to give participants time to create a presentation, given during the second part of the element, analysing some of their schools' processes. In the first element, for the first cohort of participants, the whole of the second element was intercalated to give them learning support for their presentations – an organisational audit of their new school.

Integral to each element is the support of a trained mentor for each participant. Each mentor works with two new headteachers during some of the university-based days and in the new headteachers' schools. There is therefore the potential for one-to-one activities, paired activities, or for a trio to operate. Mentors assist new headteachers in analysing their professional development needs and in developing their personal development plans. The latter is subsequently reviewed jointly by headteacher and mentor, drawing on relevant evidence. They support the new heads in undertaking an organisational analysis of their new school and in element three in evaluating the performance of their school. Mentors also conduct a formal review session with their new headteachers at the end of their first year in post and jointly supervise with a university tutor the compilation of the new headteachers' professional development portfolio.

The university-based elements of the programme are tutored by university lecturers, LEA officers, headteachers and visiting professionals. This ensures access by the new headteachers to a wide range of expertise. It also helps to give legitimacy to practice as a source of knowledge on which to base abstraction and reflection, encouraging new headteachers not to underrate their own theorising, i.e. constructing patterns and meanings out of their own experiences on the basis of sound evidence. The pedagogic style of these sessions is inter-active rather than didactic, allowing participants to share practice as well as to engage with theory, although each session is related to a core theoretical point as well as to a TTA task or headteacher ability. Each element is assessed through an assignment (called a 'professional development project' in the programme) to gain credit as a higher degree module. The research focus of each project, chosen by each new headteacher, is an aspect of school practice which needs to be reviewed as part of their everyday process of being a headteacher.

EARLY OUTCOMES

The first cohort of new headteachers drawn from primary, secondary and special schools started the programme in November 1995. The second cohort also of eight new headteachers but only from primary schools started in May 1996. At the time of writing only elements one and two have been evaluated.

At present evidence is being gathered of programme processes and immediate and long term outcomes through a variety of internal means. These are:

- end of element evaluation forms;
- an examination of assignments for evidence of achievement of the objectives of each element and of development related to the tasks and abilities specified by the TTA;
- participant contributions to the mini-conferences which form part of elements one and three;
- mentor/ new headteacher review at the end of the first year;
- evidence of personal and school development presented in the new headteacher's portfolio.

Plans are also in place to commission external evaluation by a recently retired headteacher during the second and third years of the programme.

Participants claim that the structure of the programme corresponds well to their needs over a period of time, to their own state of readiness for particular foci and for developing a more academic approach to these. Although some had not originally intended to use the programme to attain a Masters degree all participants in the first cohort have now decided to pursue a higher degree and feel that this is manageable given the school-focused nature of the assignment for each element.

In commenting on the learning outcomes from element one – audit of current professional experience and school's organisation needs; programme for professional and organisational development – participants indicated that the most useful parts were the individual review and mentor discussions, which focused reflection on a range of issues, and the provision of the 'toolkit' and guidance on organisational audit. Participants found that the element assisted them in clarifying their role as headteacher, helped them to identify priorities for development and increased their awareness of the importance of collaborative planning and of basing decision-making on evidence.

In element two – managing schools – participants particularly valued work on vision and values, the politics and micropolitics of schools and on human resource management. After element two, the range of learning and action points which participants identified was more extensive than after element one, reflecting perhaps the new headteachers' appreciation of the individuality of their school contexts and of their own skills and abilities. Participants felt that this element made a particular contribution to their understanding of management styles, including their personal management style, and helped them to appreciate and manage groups and conflict. They also reported that the element helped them further to improve planning and prioritisation and to focus on the positive aspects of their schools. This was perceived as a means of building on achievement to develop the weaker aspects of a school.

Although evaluative evidence is limited there seems to be some early evidence of double loop learning (Argyris and Schon, 1974). Participants were claiming that they knew better how to think about undertaking their tasks as well as being better able to do them.

In commenting on the learning processes, participants reported their appreciation of the blend of academic study/theory with discussions about practice. They valued the support and advice offered by their peers when the group discussed problems which they faced in school. The group of new headteachers was augmented at times by experienced headteachers as well as tutors. This allowed them to discuss practice, good and bad experiences, mistakes and failures in a positive atmosphere that was sometimes challenging but always non-threatening. In all the evaluations to date and in informal feedback, mentor support in school has been very highly rated, particularly the ability of mentors to listen, advise and share experiences in a non-judgmental way.

CONCLUSIONS

HEADLAMP programmes are now entering their second year. All the participants to date on the Loughborough/Leicestershire programme have enrolled for the full programme but a number of heads now entering their second year of headship have enquired about gaining access to individual modules. There may also be scope and a need to develop this programme over time to meet the requirements of the new Professional Qualification for Headship. The first cohort will complete their programme in the summer of 1997 at which time it will be possible to evaluate the programme as a whole, although full evaluation of its impact is likely to require longitudinal study.

Despite the small amount of evidence available at the time of writing, certain themes seem to be emerging from the programme:

- The success of a holistic approach to teacher professional development through which practitioners are empowered as partners with administrators and academics in a process of professional and institutional development.
- The importance of federalism and its companion, subsidarity – see Busher and Hodgkinson 1996 – as principles for guiding partners collaborating in a common project. Each may have their own personal and professional agenda, but much of the resulting multilayered agenda can be achieved as long as the agenda of all the parties are recognised as legitimate.
- That the key aspect of federalism is trust (see Locke, 1992) together with mutual recognition of and support for individual agendas as well as for a common purpose; job specification is less important.
- That teachers are able themselves to develop rigorous internal audit procedures. In this case instruments for analysing practice were constructed on the basis of known, sound, practice and research-based theory.
- That there is validity both in school-based research and in the application of educational theory to practice (cf. Hargreaves, 1996).
- That evidence of practice can be validated by cross-referencing the views and experiences of individual participants with those of other participants and of an experienced mentor, thereby creating a qualitative process of review.
- It is possible for teachers to develop and operate a rigorous model of validated self-audit and development for demonstrating practitioner competence.
- That senior staff in schools act as extended professionals (Hoyle, 1981), concerning themselves with issues to do with people, curriculum, operations and financial and physical resources. It raises questions about whether a new understanding of professionality is emerging for senior teachers in schools. To what extent do they perceive themselves as teachers, and in whose interests are they managing?

NOTES

1. Hugh Busher was a lecturer at Loughborough University when the HEADLAMP course was being established.

Questions for discussion

What seem to be the strengths and weaknesses of Local Authority/University partnership programmes in developing headteacher training?

How would you evaluate the success of a HEADLAMP programme or any other process of teacher professional development?

To what extent are particular views of professionalism disseminated through the processes by which professional development courses are constructed and run?

11

Continuing Professional Development for School Leaders: the UK and North American Experience

GARY HOLMES AND AUSTIN HARDING

The role, performance and effectiveness of school leaders have been under close critical scrutiny from all points of the international educational compass in recent years. In those educational cultures which are broadly cognate with our own, this scrutiny has been accompanied by a particular focus on those policies, mechanisms and indeed philosophies which purport to refine the business of selecting, developing and further enhancing our school leaders. The purpose of this chapter is to examine the preparation and development of Heads (Principals) in two contrasting cultures, the UK and the North American. This examination then uses the resulting trends and themes to consider the potential impact of current policy initiatives in the UK in particular.

A growing wealth of research evidence demonstrates the significant influences which skilled principals have on the effectiveness of their schools. It is also the case, however, that the role of the school principal is subject to an expanding array of demands from societal pressures outside of the school (including major external policy initiatives), curricular and pedagogic pressures from within the school and, of course, the ever changing needs of the students served by the school. In both the UK and North America, the developmental needs which this new complexity has aroused were only partially met for some time. Buckley (1985) described how this increase in the complexity and scope of the principal's role generates not only a massively increased workload but all too often also leads to feelings of isolation, loneliness and personal stress. Faced with numerous conflicting and confusing demands the principal, often without appropriate training, can suffer from the 'present–future dilemma' a debilitating need to cope with the stream of 'today's' problems whilst seeking to anticipate and prepare for those of 'tomorrow'. In both the UK and North America this has led to a growing acceptance of, and recognition for, the need for new models of management and leadership training. In accepting this need, however, both cultures have had to face the implications of such models for the traditional role of those school leaders. For example, in updating both the technology and the content of leadership training are we refining a fundamentally 'educationalist' model of the school leader or are we imperceptibly assuming a new 'managerialist' model of leadership?

Of course the training needs of school principals have been embodied in appropriate CPD provision for some considerable time in both cultures. Until quite recently however such provision has been subjected to considerable criticism. Wilson and Macintosh (1991), reviewing some of the criticisms of preparation programmes for school principals in North America decried the mandatory preparation (certification requirements) imposed by some states and provinces. Citing the work of Griffiths (1988) they saw many programmes as a mixed bag of weekend 'how to do it' courses at worst and, at best, unpopular, heavily criticised traditional university based graduate courses. Many of the former were seen as superficial, badly planned and organised with little developed rationale. Many of the latter were viewed with equal criticism as having little integrity, being customised to attract, and to suit the convenience of, part-time students. These courses it was claimed, frequently lacked logical structure and the orderly sequencing of content. Low standards characterised student performance at entry and exit points in many programmes. The most consistent criticism was of the discontinuities between the formal study of educational administration and its day to day implementation and practice by course members in their workplace. Even earlier, Bridges (1977) saw graduate training as too frequently resulting in 'trained incapacity'. He argued that the academic study setting is too dissimilar to that of the workplace and that formal training was consequently dysfunctional.

Until very recent times, these critiques were echoed in examinations of UK provision. Poster (1987), for example, described how there had been a historical absence of a national concern for management training both within the profession and also in national and local provision. He described how, though there had been considerable expansion in the provision of courses in educational management both nationally by the then DES and bodies like the College of Preceptors, as well as regionally through universities and LEAs, such courses were very poorly co-ordinated with each other, had little consensus about what constituted educational management, paid scant heed to the 'felt needs' of practising principals, were insufficiently focused on the work of senior teachers and were not backed up and informed by research findings and experimentation.

FRAMING THE DEBATE

Any discussion of the UK and North American experiences of continuing professional development for school principals requires an organising framework. Sparks (1993) suggested such a framework from his synthesis of research projects and studies into the effectiveness of programmes aimed at increasing the effectiveness of senior school staff. He suggested three broad categories within which the experiences on both sides of the Atlantic can be located and discussed. These are:

a) the context – the environments(s) within which the training process occurs;
b) the training process – the usually overt actions taken to accomplish some set of goals;
c) the goals and content – the ends to which such actions are aimed and the vehicles and content within which these ends have meaning.

These 3 foci will be used to facilitate the subsequent discussion of UK and North American initiatives within the field of school principal development.

THE CONTEXT OF TRAINING

For some considerable time in management development training has been seen as a process of acquiring knowledge and skills at a site away from the workplace. In both cultures (UK and North America) training has been provided by an uneven and unstable patchwork of formats (short and long term, full and part time etc.), locations (universities, LEAs, other agencies), outcomes (award and non-award bearing) and orientations (academic and theoretical or practical 'how to' courses). Those occurring in academic institutions, often physically and ideologically distant from the work place, were award bearing and were considered the most prestigious though not necessarily the most effective. Indeed there has been a strengthening recognition of the gaps between the formal, academic study of educational management and the day to day work of practitioners. Such a recognition has called the universities near monopoly of prestigious courses seriously into question. Stout (1989) summarised the growing criticisms of an over-reliance on off-site university based training in North America. He argued that the universities had to deal, for the most part, with students of poor academic quality (teachers being the least academically able of college students!) The process of 'sponsored mobility' in turn encouraged the promotion of more passive, accepting, candidates and discriminated against the more assertive, sceptical and independently minded students. Such candidates, frequently pragmatic in outlook, often treated the course as a 'ticket' to upward mobility. With few careful and deliberate selection procedures, admission was often quite perfunctory. Few students failed such courses and, in many cases, persistence seemed to be sufficient for eventual completion. Typically, instruction was faculty-dominated in the definition of both what was taught and how it was taught; faculty were perceived by the students as being out of touch with the important issues of school life; and as being dysfunctional in preparing effective school leaders. In brief, the training was seen to provide little or no opportunity to learn and to practise the necessary skills for effective school leadership (Thomas, 1982; Earthman, 1989).

A similarly patchy pattern of provision had also existed in the UK for quite some time. Indeed Poster (1987) described how until quite recently educational management was quite separate from mainstream industrial and commercial management with educators frequently adopting a kind of 'holier than thou' isolation and, out of perversion and/or ignorance, cutting themselves of from a whole range of skills, techniques, processes and management theory which might have contributed considerably to school improvement. The need to identify and promote education for school management in this country has been a long time coming; only in 1967 was the first significant step taken by the DES with the establishment of COSMOS (Committee on the Organisation, Staffing and Management of Schools).

During the 1970s there was considerable expansion of courses in educational management, both at a national level through the DES and agencies like the College of Preceptors, and at regional level through universities, polytechnics and LEAs. Despite such expansion, however, there was little coordination, no real consensus about the nature of educational management, insufficient places on courses for those who wanted them (let alone those who needed them), insufficient focus on the case of 'senior' teachers and an almost total lack of a research and experimentation base from which future developments might be guided and sustained.

In 1972 Glatter argued a concise, well researched and powerful case for the establishment of development centres for educational management in order to research administration in education, examine the applicability to educational organisations of non-education sector management systems and techniques, develop more effective training methods, disseminate research findings and training materials and direct the promotion of courses, workshops and training activities. Only by 1977, however, was the DES beginning to recognise the need for 'training of senior teachers for the complex tasks of school organisation and management. A grant was given to the University of Birmingham 'to obtain a clearer picture of provision . . . and thereby have a firmer basis for policy making by central and local government'. The report (Hughes 1981) surveyed both award bearing and non-award bearing courses (these latter were found to be especially varied, confused and ill-planned). It argued for a 'more coherent approach and some degree of consultation amongst providers'. It went further in seeking 'the creation of an executive agency . . . (with) specific responsibility for promoting the expansion and improvement of professional development provision in England and Wales'.

The situation revealed by the Hughes Report was far from satisfactory; much was available but it was badly coordinated and of variable quality. In 1980, 24 universities, 13 polytechnic and 21 other Colleges of Higher Education accounted for the graduation of 1,600 students. Of the short non-award bearing courses, the provision of which was found to be especially patchy and uneven, some were found to be good though many were not. In 1980, 696 such courses were provided by LEAs (although 170 of the courses were provided by 4 LEAs) and they accounted for 20,000 student registrations.

The publication of the report prompted two decisive DES initiatives. Circular 3/83 provided funding for two types of courses; OTTO courses (One Term Training Opportunities) for experienced school managers and Twenty Day Courses for senior staff with the improvement of participants' schools as their main aim. The other DES initiative was the funding of a National Development Centre for School Management project in Bristol. This centre was to provide a national focus for management training in schools. Its task was to evaluate existing courses, develop new materials, set up a research bank and disseminate information as well as fostering the establishment of new regional training centres.

The situation in the UK was further compounded by the demands placed upon funds to pay for the 'tooling up' of teachers to help them cope with the demands of the National Curriculum, its assessment and other central initiatives.

The vast majority of the UK initiatives described above resulted in off-site training experiences. The match between training and the actual demands inherent in running a school is clearly problematic. Despite improvements and some shifts in the rhetoric of educational management discourse Murphy and Hallinger (1992) consider the situation in America as still 'seriously flawed and wanting in nearly every respect', and NASSP (1992) have lamented students being inundated with theory whilst having few opportunities to apply it to their specific professional problems and challenges.

As long ago as 1975 Lortie was arguing for a 'division of labour' between the academics in the universities and practising teachers. Bridges (1977) whilst highly critical of off-site university-based training warned against the potential dangers of a totally ill-judged replacement of academic study with what could be an atheoretical, shallow, trial-and-error pragmatism via on-the-job training. NASSP (1985) argued that the best study programmes were likely to be those which achieved a well articulated continuum of activities throughout the academic and the workplace settings. In the UK there has been a growing recognition that individual development is directly related to the structure and quality of the everyday working experiences far more than to off-site training. Management training is thus seen, more and more, as a school based activity (DES 1990). The theory–practice, on-site off-site tension still remains however. Whilst an increased concern with the everyday practicalities of school life must be unequivocally welcomed the universities, equally, need to hold on to what they do best – help students develop imagination, objectivity, critical awareness, and reflexivity.

THE TRAINING PROCESS

Traditionally, then, the study of educational management has involved principals in being removed from their work place to receive instruction and teaching in off-site locations, frequently universities, from 'experts' often academics with little or no experience in the field. Course content and methodology have been directed by tutors in an essentially didactic manner with course members being placed in largely passive roles as learners. The growing concern about the effectiveness of such courses and the growing interests in off-site learning, collaborative approaches, and the rooting of learning in real life or well simulated situations have all contributed to a re-assessment of how and where head teachers will learn best. Whilst there appears to be an absence of good reliable data on the effectiveness of which modes and formats can best develop the capabilities of school principals, there have been a number of interesting developments in pedagogy which reflect the theory-practice debate. The NASSP (1985), in seeking to draw together the best of the theoretical and the practical, raised the issue of practical experiences in the form of internships as a mechanism through which valuable administrative skills might be developed, demonstrated and evaluated within a 'real life' situation where the student would have regular support and feedback as well as being able to share the experiences with fellow students. Internships certainly have a long history dating back to the Ford Foundation projects of the 1960s but as Hickcox and House (1991) reported neither the universities nor school systems, in Canada at least, had developed internship as part of the professional training of school principals. Their examination of 27 such studies revealed little other than that they were full or part time, lasted from 2 days to 2 years (those most acclaimed lasted a full year), occasionally carried a stipend, were based upon poor selection procedures and mechanisms and usually involved a combination of school placement and university seminar situations. They were usually run jointly between the universities and the school system and little information was available about the actual content of the experience. Whilst acknowledging the attractiveness of the idea of internships the authors bemoan the lack of hard evidence about their effectiveness. They cite the work, for example, of Sweeney, Huth and Engle (Hickcox and House 1991) in which no significant differences were found in the administrative skills of 60 principals who had experienced an internship and 60 who had not. In their own survey of Canadian universities with masters or doctoral programmes in Educational Administration they discovered that of the 11 who replied only the Ontario Institute for Studies in Education (OISE) made internship central to their programmes; the use of internships in the remaining programmes was only partial. At OISE, students have a 10–12 week placement during the residence year of the EdD programme. They have a university supervisor and an on-site supervisor who together with the student negotiate the exploration of an administrative task. All interns meet once per week at the university where experiences are pooled and shared. The terminal assessment of the internship is jointly shared between the university and the school supervisor. No school districts reported having developed in-house internship experiences. The authors concluded that there seemed to be little activity and interest in internships amongst departments of Educational Administration in Canada. This contrasts strongly with the situation described by Earthman (1989) in Virginia, USA where the principal training programme was jointly restructured by the university and the local school system. The selection of students, course content and methodology and evaluation were the joint responsibility of the university and the school system. Internship was a strong feature of the course in Virginia where each intern undertook a minimum of 90 days in a school during a 2 year period. Each intern was assigned a mentor who was the first line supervisor of activities in school. The mentor helped the intern identify and achieve objectives and might provide direct instruction. Mentors were chosen for their exceptional leadership qualities in the local school system. The intern actually administered portions of a school programme (e.g. organise and conduct staff development) under the watchful eye of the mentor just as a medical intern practices under the supervision of a fully licensed physician.

Another initiative which is now appearing in the mainstream of principal preparation in the USA is Problem Based Learning (PBL). Students are presented with a hypothetical situation that is likely to confront an in-post principal. After exposure to theory and research on the topic the students are asked to devise a solution to the dilemma. Bridges (1992), a pioneer in the use of educator training methods, argued that administrative skills, problem solving skills and the build up of a knowledge base are all outcomes of this approach. The incorporation of computer simulations into this approach has been developed at Peabody College, Vanderbilt University (Hallinger and McCary 1992).

Initiative such as those described above provide useful alternatives to the familiar didactic approach. Since the most promising professional development seems to emerge from methods which engage learners with genuine questions and issues it is likely that they represent the way forward for effective methodologies.

GOALS AND CONTENT

In seeking to cope with what Buckley (1985) has called 'a frantic succession of disconnected activities' in the role of the principal all authorities seem to agree that commitment, dedication, flair and panache, whilst admirable qualities in themselves, are insufficient to the task of school leadership. There is a consistent consensus in the educational management rhetoric on both sides of the Atlantic that training is crucial and, indeed, that such training should be planned as a continuous process throughout the professional 'life cycle' of the principal. Not only should principals be given training prior to, or very quickly after, their appointment but they will also require follow up learning after their early years in post as well as continuous updating at regular intervals throughout their career. This unanimity about career-long training for principals, however, masks an inability or unwillingness to define in detail the nature of such training, to agree the list of stakeholders who might collaboratively construct such a definition and to express overtly and coherently the rationale upon which such training ought to be based. In North America Stout (1989) describes a lack of agreement about the mix of theoretical, research based course content with content drawn from workplace practice. He points to the side by side existence of courses which are heavily academic with no direct connection to practice with those which are extensively technical, mechanical with little or no underpinning by theory and conceptual frameworks. Scrutiny of the content of many EdD and PhD programmes, for example, reveals very little difference in some universities. Stout's overall criticism of the rationale and content of many American educational management courses is focused on their lack of agreement about what educational management is, what school principals do, what they should do and how what happens to them in their university courses is related to their working lives.

For the UK, Glatter (1972) was equally critical in urging that principal training needed to be closely related to the actual functioning of a school. More recently, the School Management Task Force (DES, 1990) urged a move away from provider-determined syllabi and an increase in the use of individual and school determined course content. Training initiatives should be less concerned with knowledge acquisition and should place an increased emphasis on performance enhancement with more active, interactive learning replacing the traditional learning of many courses.

Surveying the scene in Western Europe Buckley (1985) argued that the development of training programmes for headteachers seems to have been sharper in those countries where a national initiative accompanied by national funding has led to the establishment of a central organising body (e.g. Denmark). These central bodies have often provided national guidelines for the development of training. Amongst other things, they have drawn up national sets of aims and guidelines, developed documentation and training materials, trained trainers, carried out research and made clear recommendations about course content, methods, follow-up activity and evaluation.

Tomlinson (1994) speculated on the case for a General Teaching Council as a promoter and guardian of professional standards. Such a body, he argued, would have a care for, and would scrutinise, the qualifications and professional standards of teachers throughout their careers. Not only would the council promote and provide in-service training but it would require teachers at all levels to re-register periodically, registration being dependent upon holding appropriate qualifications for the professional task being performed.

The notion of standards, standardisation and certification as goals for headship training were discussed by Cooper and Shute (1988) a long way ahead of the new NPQH initiative. The American authors took as their starting point the fact that in the UK a licence to teach is the only formal requirement for becoming a head teacher. They contrasted this with the situation in North America where a school principal will usually have a Masters degree in Educational Administration and is legally required to have an administrative certificate issued by the state education department. The authors argued a case for change in the UK suggesting that separate certification for head teachers was essential. The obligatory certification requirement in the USA, Canada and Australia was compared to the situation in the UK where preparation for headship ranged from no formal training whatsoever, through brief, intermittent short courses with LEAs and Colleges to full scale, full-time residential graduate programmes leading to masters degrees. Until national requirements were set down UK head teachers would continue to receive piecemeal training (if any) and Britain would remain about the only major Western European nation to have educators appointed to leadership positions without systematic training and certification.

The authors did not suggest the simple importing into the UK of the American system. Indeed they criticised the weaknesses of the system in the USA for what they regarded as its over-reliance on the 'management sciences', the neglect of social, ethical and moral issues, the unfocused and low quality teaching and the unresolved theory–practice debate in the monopoly holding universities.

Despite a consensus about the need for training, and even where such training has become a legal requirement, the vexed questions remain unresolved – what are the training needs of principals and how are they to be recognised? Buckley (1985) outlines one such framework which incorporates managing oneself, managing people, managing the curriculum and so on. Similar taxonomies are endemic in the literature. Useful as they are these frameworks are essentially 'lists' with little validation of their comprehensiveness or taxonomic accuracy. A more objective, systematic and 'scientific' approach to the identification of training needs, however, is offered in the 'competence' movement on both sides of the Atlantic.

Chown (1994) explains how the competence approach is derived from behaviourist views of human learning and experience. Discrete elements of competence, derived from functional analysis procedures, are combined into free standing units which are claimed to provide a complete picture of competent performance at work. Its proponents claim that it can inform training, selection, appraisal, accreditation of performance, and promotion (cf. the POST project findings). Certainly competences have become firmly established as a framework for staff selection and development in a wide range of organisations and occupations. Esp (1993) defines competence as 'the ability and willingness to perform a task' and sees it as an attractive and useful concept for management training because it concerns *actions* and not simply the possession of knowledge. Everard (1990) describes the identification of such characteristics amongst 2,000 managers in 41 occupational groups from 12 public and private organisations. This same approach was adopted by the NASSP (National Association for Secondary School Principals) who researched and established a set of generic competences for the development and selection of school principals in assessment centres. The NASSP competences were:

- *Administrative competences* – problem analysis, judgement, organisational ability and decisiveness.
- *Interpersonal competences* – Leadership, sensitivity, stress tolerance.
- *Communicative competences* – oral communication, written communication.
- *Personal Breadth competences* – range of interests, personal motivation, educational values.

The success of this approach has led to its widespread use in Canada, Australia and the UK. The National Educational Assessment Centre project (NEAC) in the UK was founded in 1990 using the NASSP model, suitably culturised, and is currently very active nationally and regionally in both the selection and development dimensions of competence based assessment for educational leaders.

The Consortium for Management Development, (SMTF funded originally) in north west England was similarly ground breaking (Bowles 1992). The aim was to establish a programme of development and training for senior teachers in schools which incorporated in its goals an attempt to put together a coherent, career-long development programme. If completed, this programme would ensure that a teacher had adequate practical and theoretical training before taking up a senior management post in school and would have subsequent opportunities for further development of their management skills. Extending over 2 years the programme would involve action learning, visiting other organisations, discussions with colleagues and some teaching on other elements of the course. Similarly the ACP (Management) qualification of the College of Preceptors was trialed in 1991–92 in Kent and Norfolk and was formally linked to NVQ Level 4. It enables teachers to collect evidence of their competences in a portfolio which, augmented by personal study of materials provided by the Bristol Management Centre, is eventually authenticated by the teacher's head teacher and assessed by the College.

These and other similar competence based initiatives would appear to go some way in meeting the need for training courses to move away from the tutor-directed, off site approaches so much criticised in both countries and go some considerable way in meeting the recommendations in the UK of the SMTF with its plea for management development to be seen essentially as a school based activity, supported elsewhere. Only in this way, it was argued, would management development deal realistically with the long called-for shift away from academic, off site, course driven training.

NPQH AND THE WAY AHEAD

The preceding analysis shows some congruence between the North American and UK experiences. In both cultures, the central core of award-bearing (Masters) provision has dominated. In both cases the alternatives to this academic provision have had a patchy track record. The North Americans have gone a long way towards formalising the preparation and accreditation of school principals, yet even where competence based approaches and their affiliates are dominant in particular states or provinces the academic qualification still carries prestige and acts as a threshold. Even within the arena of Masters provision there are important debates about focus, content and audience as between M.Ed., MA, M.Sc., MBA etc.

However, the very recent developments in the UK promise a quantum leap in addressing Buckley's earlier critique. Following a long period of dalliance and position taking the UK is about to embrace a model for the accreditation of headship which will dominate all aspects of the CPD debate for the foreseeable future.

The National Professional Qualification for Headteachers (NPQH) began its pilot phase in England and Wales in January 1997. The fundamental features of this initiative can be summarised as follows:

1. A voluntary qualification, awarded by the Teacher Training Agency (TTA), and available to aspiring headteachers (usually deputies).

2. An expectation that this NPQH rapidly becomes the threshold qualification for headship.
3. A regional structure of NPQH provision where training and preparation are separated from assessment and the award itself.
4. A combination of more or less formal training elements, related to the core tasks of headship, with provision for the demonstration of 'fit' via profiling and portfolio building.
5. The availability of distance learning modes of study and preparation.
6. The funding of individuals to undertake the qualification on suitable recommendation and via regional quotas.
7. An important emphasis on achievement within NPQH related tasks and abilities as demonstrated in the work place.

The whole is wrapped up in a comprehensive rationale, set of standards and predetermined features.

There is not space here to give full justice to the detail of NPQH but the very comprehensiveness of the initiative addresses most or all of the premisses which have dominated the debate on school leader preparation as identified in this paper. NPQH offers in its rationale (TTA, 1996d) a working definition of the tasks, abilities and standards of achievement which characterise successful headship. It leads very firmly to a view of headship which is about creating and sustaining the vision and mission of a school. It locates heads as people who consistently drive educational standards upwards and who can plan, monitor, lead, evaluate and deploy within this context of permanent improvement.

Thus we now have in the NPQH a curriculum for the preparation of new generations of headteachers. This curriculum will now dominate the actions, intentions and vision of all the players in the arena of CPD for school leaders. From a consumer perspective, aspiring heads – who account for a good proportion of the consumers of teacher CPD – will now wish to concentrate their scarce resources of time and money on those CPD activities which will contribute to the eventual attainment of the NPQH whether they are currently registered for it or not. From a provider perspective, universities, LEAs, private sector trainers and others who mount CPD for school leaders or generally in educational management must now take serious cognisance of the NPQH curriculum and methodology in determining and marketing CPD products for the leadership audience. From an end-user perspective, the governors who appoint heads will presumably guarantee the dominance of NPQH over other evidence of suitability by the simple act of specifying it as a selection criterion.

THEMATIC REFLECTIONS

The scope for radical initiatives of the order of NPQH is limited in North America where the policy apex is regional rather than national. Accreditation which combines academic credibility with professional certification is *de facto* in most jurisdictions and has evolved organically and incrementally. In the UK, the leap from smorgasbord to table d'hôte has been rapid and comprehensive. Thus the trajectory of

CPD for school leaders in the two cultures now begins to converge further in terms of the accreditation dimension but to diverge in terms of the spectrum of methodologies.

Despite the voluntary nature of the NPQH, it nevertheless represents a shift towards compulsion (or at least 'high expectation') for most aspiring heads. This compulsion will impact early on their CPD experiences and is congruent with trends identified in parallel professions (Tomlinson and Holmes, 1996).

A concomitant of this formalising of the CPD arena is that it will be accompanied by a particular emphasis on initiating, recording, evaluating, monitoring and evidencing work based action which is cognate with the demands of NPQH. Thus, while the formal off-site (or distance learning) elements of NPQH restate the contribution which the universities and other CPD providers will make, headship preparation now contains a formalised and pre-eminent work based focus. In terms of Sparks' (1993) model all three questions of *locus, method* and *goals* have been answered comprehensively in the NPQH.

One question which remains is the perennial theory/practice issue. The dimensions of that issue raised in this paper are not, and could not be, finally resolved by one initiative. Comprehensive accreditation schemes such as NPQH attempt to define the academic content of leadership preparation and may indeed succeed in specifying relevant areas of study. However, they do not address the individual's aspiration for knowledge or their discernment in selecting knowledge and learning which makes particular contributions to individual growth. Thus, aspiring leaders will still seek combinations of learning and experience which transcend accreditation processes.

Debates about effective leadership tend to the cyclical. We are perhaps at the apex of a technological evolution in our view of what counts as the effective leader. Thus the most recent developments in CPD for school leaders discussed here are driven by the desire to taxonomise, task-relate and otherwise dissect the mysterious business of leadership into addressable chunks. The logical evolution may be to a more holistic, person-centred model in which the fundamental fitness of the individual for the business of leadership is dominant. In this vein, the next century may see a fundamental reshaping of the CPD arena. Glatter (1996), reminds us that 'the can-do culture of the present day tends to dismiss the dilemmas and ambiguities that are the stuff of leadership activity and are pervasive in organisational life'. Thus the challenge for CPD remains: it must deliver the purposes of its audiences, but if it does not also deliver better school leaders then it has failed.

Questions for discussion

How has the preparation and training for headship changed?

What similarities and differences are there between the UK and North American experiences?

How can headteachers best learn to improve their performance and that of their schools?

12

Continuing Professional Development: the European Experience

JOANNA LE MÉTAIS

Although the informal tradition of continuing professional development (CPD) goes back to the beginning of the century in a number of countries (e.g. Austria, Finland, Germany and Sweden), educational reforms and other social changes have provided a stimulus for change in both policy and practice throughout Europe. This chapter will outline the general framework and provision of CPD in the European Union and European Economic Area countries and then focus on two contrasting forms of provision, namely France, where a framework has been developed to meet grass roots demand, and the Netherlands, where compulsory CPD is part of a coherent staff management policy.[1]

CONTEXT

Economic competition between the developed countries places pressure on education systems in these countries to 'deliver the goods'. The effectiveness of schools comes under ever greater scrutiny by governments (seeking value for money), parents (seeking optimum opportunities for their children) and employers (seeking young people able and willing to take their place in working life). Where there are perceived deficiencies in the service, there are calls for generalised changes in initial training or large scale 'retraining' of teachers through CPD.

The extent to which teachers fulfil society's expectations of them is influenced principally by the social context, the educational context and the match between their initial training and the requirements of their current post.

Social context

The perception of education as the golden road to individual achievement has resulted in massive investment by individual families and by society and a corresponding pressure on schools and teachers. At the same time, 'changes in society and family life have contributed to altering greatly the role and conception of the school' (Coolahan, 1991, p. 4) and the rapid changes in employment patterns require schools to prepare children not for a single occupation, but for a career of constant change and development. Finally, increasing unemployment has thrown into relief a culture clash between those who are prepared to work for a number of years in anticipation of long-term rewards (occupational satisfaction and salary) and those who require short-term gratification, and have made it more difficult to retain the motivation even of the former group.

Educational context and changes

The past two decades have seen major changes in educational policy, including:

- the raising of the school leaving age in many countries, and an increase in the staying on rates as employment opportunities have fallen. This involves teachers in relationships with young people who are older, and who have different concepts of authority. 'The mystique of the teacher has gone, and pupils' genuine openness may be perceived as insubordination' (Swan 1991b, p. 20);
- structural changes, resulting in more heterogeneous teaching groups as regards 'ability, application, aspiration, motivation, social class background and attitudes to authority' (Coolahan 1991, p. 4). Examples include the move to non-selective education in France and Spain, the amalgamation of different school-types in the Netherlands and the integration of special needs pupils in Italy and elsewhere;
- greater involvement of, and accountability to, parents and other members of the community (for example, through schools councils in Spain and co-decision making bodies in the Netherlands) which require headteachers and other senior staff to develop both management and public relations skills;
- curricular changes, involving new subjects or new output-led models. These have been introduced in several countries e.g. the Netherlands and Spain; and
- different teaching styles e.g. direct method foreign language teaching and the use of calculators and computers in the classroom.

Perceived match between initial training and current roles

As Table 12.1 shows, most countries make clear distinctions between teachers according to the age of pupils whom they teach. Nevertheless, there has been a converging trend in initial training. On the one hand, greater emphasis on the academic training of primary and lower secondary school teachers has led to graduate status for many more teachers. On the other hand, there is an increasing recognition that academic training alone is not sufficient preparation, even for the teaching of secondary age pupils, and professional training is therefore a requirement throughout the countries studied. The sole exception

Table 12.1 Teachers' status and qualifications[1]

	Status; Security of Tenure[2]	Separate teacher Corps[3]	Graduate Status	Duration (years)
Austria	Tenured civil servant	Primary	No	3
		Lower Secondary	No	3
		Upper Secondary	Yes	4.5 + 1
Belgium	Civil/Public servant	Primary	No	3
		Secondary	Yes	4–5
Denmark	Contract	Compulsory	No	4
		Upper Secondary	Yes	5
Finland	Tenured civil servant	Primary[4]	Yes	4–5
		Secondary	Yes	5–6
France	Tenured civil servant	Compulsory	Yes	3+1+1
		Upper Secondary	Yes	–
Germany	Tenured civil servant	Primary	Yes	4.5 to 6
		Secondary[5]	Yes	4.5 to 6.5
Greece	Tenured civil servant	Primary	Yes	4
		Secondary	Yes	4–5
Iceland	Tenured civil servant	Compulsory	Yes	3–5
		Upper Secondary	Yes	3–4 + 1
Ireland	Tenured public servant	Primary	Yes	3
		Secondary	Yes	3+1
Italy	Tenured civil servant	Primary	No	4
		Secondary	Yes	4–6
Luxembourg	Tenured civil servant	Primary	No	3
		Secondary	Yes	4–5 + 3
Netherlands	School employee	Primary	No	4
		Lower Secondary	Yes	4
		Upper Secondary	Yes	4+1
Norway	Tenured civil servant	Compulsory	No	4
		Upper Secondary	Yes	4–6
Portugal	Tenured civil servant	Primary	No	3
		Lower Secondary	Yes	4
		Upper Secondary	Yes	5–6
Spain	Tenured civil servant	Primary	No	3
		Secondary	Yes	4–5 + 1
Sweden	Civil servant	Compulsory	Yes	3.5–4.5
		Upper Secondary	Yes	4–5.5

NOTES

1. This table refers only to teachers in mainstream, general education.
2. Civil or public servants may be employed by the state, the province or *Land,* or the municipality.
3. All other European countries have separate teacher *corps*, which differ in initial training, qualification, salary and conditions of employment. The most common division is according to the age of pupils taught, but in Germany there are three different categories of secondary school teacher, see note 5 below. The Nordic countries (Denmark, Finland, Iceland, Norway, Sweden) have a two-tier education structure, comprising a single all-through school for pupils of compulsory school age (age 6/7 to 16) and a post-compulsory or upper secondary school.
4. Primary teachers in Finland are qualified to teach pupils aged 7–13; secondary teachers may teach those aged 14–16 in the 'all through' school referred to in note 3, as well as those aged 16–19 in post-compulsory schools. Both courses include academic and professional studies.
5. German secondary teachers may train to teach in *Hauptschule, Realschule* or *Gymnasium.*

to both of these trends is Italy, where primary school teachers are still trained in upper secondary institutions (age 14–18) and secondary teachers require only a university degree in the subject to be taught.

The second important characteristic of teachers in most European countries is their civil service status, which entails rigorous competition at entry, but confers a status and security of tenure throughout their professional life. This has tended to limit the demand for continuing professional development. However, this situation is changing, not least because of the shift in the age profile of teachers. Demographic changes in most European countries mean that some two-thirds of teachers are now over 40 years of age (Commission of the European Communities, 1996, p. 107) and the potential for transfer to posts outside the classroom is limited. Given the social and educational changes referred to above, training undertaken up to 30 years ago may not enable teachers effectively to meet the needs of today's pupils. 'We cannot live the afternoon of life according to the programme of life's morning, for what was great in the morning will be little at evening and what in the morning was true, will at evening have become a lie' (Jung, cited by Swan, 1991b, p. 21).

PROVISION

Social and educational changes, and the perceived mismatch between initial training and current requirements, have resulted in a formalisation of CPD requirements and provision (see Table 12.2). In most countries, CPD is described as a professional right and duty, without the extent of the obligation being defined. Compulsory attendance applies, in given circumstances, in eight countries, although much of this takes place during school hours. A particular circumstance arises in Greece; because up to ten years may elapse between qualification and first appointment, CPD is compulsory for all newly appointed teachers.

The extent to which teachers voluntarily participate in CPD depends on their perceptions of the adequacy of their initial training in the context of social and educational changes, their status, and the culture of performance appraisal (self appraisal or external appraisal). In some cases, CPD directly or indirectly leads to enhanced salary and status. Broadly speaking, therefore, CPD is provided, and undertaken, for one of four reasons.

Improving individual performance

The motivation to improve individual performance may come from the teacher as a result of personal reflection, or it may result from a performance appraisal.

Teachers in many European countries have civil or public servant status and security of tenure (see Table 12.1). In several countries (e.g. France, Greece, Italy and Spain) they are recruited by national competition and deployed according to the needs of the service, without reference to teachers' preferences or to the characteristics of individual schools. Systematic staff appraisal is

Table 12.2   Continuing professional development

	CPD	Purpose (see text)	Salary Promotion	Current Priority Themes
Austria	Undefined duty, compulsory for major innovations	a b c d	No By new diplomas	Foreign languages; IT; interdisciplinary teaching; European dimension; multicultural education; SEN and migrants; school management
Belgium (Francophone Community)	Right to 10 days p.a.	a b c d	No	Cross curricular/interdisciplinary learning; attainment targets; IT; European dimension; staff time management and communication; admin/financial management for headteachers
Belgium (Flemish Community)	Right – no obligation	a b c d	No By new diploma	IT; SEN; sciences; behavioural problems; immigrant children in multicultural perspective; methodology; teamwork for management
Denmark	Voluntary, sabbatical possible	a b c	No	Individual teaching; IT; improving written and oral presentation; bilingual (immigrant) children; peer observation/appraisal
Finland	Duty 3–5 days p.a.	a b c	No Diploma credits	Curricular development; foreign languages; immigrants; vocational guidance and counselling; internationalism
France	Right, especially summer schools; sabbatical possible	a b c d	No Diploma credits	Reading skills; individual teaching in maths/ science; SEN; civics
Germany	Undefined right and duty.	b c	By diploma	Nature conservancy and environmental protection; intercultural learning; health education; IT and career counselling
Greece	Compulsory induction, then 3 months every 5–6 years	a b c d	No	Theory and practice of education; child development; practical exercises; SEN
Iceland	Duty 2 weeks every 2 years	a b	Yes; salary credit	Subject knowledge and skills; IT; European dimension; school management
Ireland	Unspecified right and duty	a b c d	No By diploma	Updating knowledge/skills/curriculum; careers guidance and counselling; special intervention techniques; management skills
Italy	Duty 40 hours p.a.	a b c d	No	Primary foreign language and creative subjects; new curriculum and assessment in secondary; monitoring and assessment
Luxembourg	Right 40 hrs p.a.	a b c	Primary only	IT and communication; diversification of teaching methods; assessment; needs of SEN and immigrant children; moral and social
Netherlands	Duty 171 hours p.a.	a b c d	No By diploma	Demand-led by schools: IT; Dutch and arithmetic for underprivileged children; SEN; intercultural; management (esp. for women)
Norway	Duty 1 week p.a.	a b c d	Yes credits By diploma	Internationalisation; the environment; IT (forthcoming reforms will affect priorities)
Portugal	Right up to 8 days p.a. (only for teachers)	a b c d	Yes, credits	Themes must be approved. subject knowledge and skills; management training
Spain	Unspecified right and duty.	a b c d	Yes credits By diploma	Knowledge/skills updating; foreign languages; international courses; educational guidance; school review; school administration
Sweden	Duty 5 days p.a., right up to 17 days	a b c d	No	SEN; general subjects; foreign languages; media and environmental studies; internationalisation; pupils' rights/duties; leadership and management

relatively rare, and where it does occur, it tends to be a formality and only exceptionally has financial or disciplinary outcomes. Teachers progress as a result of years of service.

However, despite the apparent lack of incentive for self-improvement, (other than that required by employers or in pursuit of promotion), significant numbers of teachers are taking advantage of opportunities for voluntary participation, and in some countries (e.g. Iceland) demand exceeds supply.

Enhancing teachers' ability to meet changing needs

Changes in structure, curriculum or assessment are currently a feature in many European countries. CPD is a key means of informing staff, enhancing their ability to implement reforms, and changing attitudes and behaviours which are no longer considered to be appropriate. For this reason, CPD often forms part of policies for reform. In the case of Spain, teachers have been actively involved in consultation on the reforms, as well as in training to support their implementation. Some countries make such staff development compulsory (e.g. Austria), others rely on the individual's professional desire to update his/her knowledge and skills.

Training for diversity or promotion

A third category of CPD applies to cross-training or additional training. Such training may enhance a teacher's employability (by qualifying them to teach additional subjects, in Germany, Austria or Denmark) or meet a national shortage (such as that in mathematics and IT in England during the 1980s) without entailing a change in status or salary. Alternatively, as in Spain and Portugal, it may contribute to enhanced status and salary because the teacher benefits from promotion credits 'earned' through participation in approved CPD activities (see Table 12.2, Salary).

In those countries which have several distinct *corps* of teachers (e.g. Denmark, the Netherlands, France), qualified teachers in one *corps* may progressively work their way up the scale by undertaking the relevant training and passing the examinations (see Table 12.2, Promotion). In Denmark, teachers in the *Folkeskole* (age 7–16) who have the necessary academic qualifications, may seek employment in the *gymnasium* and qualify by part-time study. Similarly, a *2e graads* (lower secondary) teacher in the Netherlands may, by obtaining the *1e graads* qualification, achieve the salary and status of an upper secondary teacher (Le Métais, 1992).

Preparation for management

Teachers in England and Wales have traditionally developed their management skills (and their professional status) by means of professional development and promotion through a hierarchy of posts of responsibility. Most other countries have a flatter hierarchy and, as has been shown, derive their status from initial qualifications rather than from position. In fact, primary head-teachers in France and in Luxembourg have virtually no enhanced status. In contrast, it is interesting that, as long ago as the 1960s, prospective primary school teachers in the Netherlands had the option to extend their (non-university) training by one year to obtain a headteachers' qualification (*hoofd-akte*), in preparation for the day, presumably some years later, when they might be appointed to such a post.

However, the more explicit accountability of schools to their local com-munity and the trend towards devolution of financial and management respon-sibilities to schools are two factors which underline the need for headteachers to develop management as well as teaching skills. For example, Sweden has provided CPD specifically for headteachers since 1976 and introduced a head-teachers' qualification in 1992.

As Table 12.2 shows, all four areas are catered for in virtually all countries, although the major emphasis is still on subject knowledge and teaching skills for classroom teachers, followed by training for teaching special groups such as pupils with special educational needs or immigrants.

CPD traditionally favoured off-site courses provided by institutions of initial teacher training, but a trend towards decentralisation means that there is competition from individual consultants and other providers. Greater em-phasis is also being placed on whole-school and school-based training, and peer observation of and reflection on teaching. Networks of specialist teacher advice and support centres have been set up in many countries, to provide on-site and off-site support e.g. regional centres for the continuing training of education staff (*Mission Académique à la Formation des Personnels de l'Edu-cation Nationale* or MAFPEN) in France, regional centres for continuing pro-fessional development (PEK) in Greece, regional centres for information, research, innovation and continuing teacher education (*Istituto Regionale di Ricerca Sperimentazione Aggiornamento Educativi* – IRRSAE) in Italy and pedagogic centres (*Landelijke Pedagogische Centra*) in the Netherlands.

The remainder of this chapter will focus on two countries: France and the Netherlands. The first case study looks at the way in which the centralised system in France is attempting to meet its legal duty to provide professional development for teachers (and other education professionals), whose particip-ation is voluntary. The Netherlands is of interest because it has sought to manage staff redundancies, stress and premature retirements by means of a cohesive policy of staff management within a framework of devolved financial and management responsibility.

FRANCE

France is one of the countries which has only recently developed a systematic framework for the CPD of teachers (Altet, 1993). This is partly accounted for by the particular characteristics of teachers' civil servants status, as detailed in

Nicholas Beattie's (1996) analytical comparison of recruitment in France and England and Wales.

First, like all French civil servants, teachers are recruited, by means of competitive examinations (*concours*), to a professional *corps*, within which they have guaranteed tenure, although they may be redeployed in accordance with the needs of the service. Promotion to the most prestigious category of teachers (*agrégés*), or to posts as headteacher, administrator or inspector is treated as recruitment and requires successful participation in the relevant *concours*. The right to participate in a *concours* depends on qualifications and length of service.

Second, once admitted to the *corps*, staff are deemed competent to fulfil their function effectively in *any* school in the country *throughout* their professional life. The English concept of matching teachers to particular posts in particular schools does not exist in the French recruitment process.

Third, in contrast to English teachers, who derive professional status from their position (e.g. promotion) or external honours (e.g. a higher degree), the status of French teachers, as well as their salary and conditions, is determined at the outset of their career and derives from their corps, e.g. *agrégés*. It should be noted that the separation of teachers into superior and inferior *corps* continues into the headteacher, inspection and administrative posts.

> *Jurys* [i.e. recruitment panels] are conscious of seeking a quality of mind that will carry a candidate through a lifetime's teaching: 'The *jury* has indeed attempted to identify, in a candidate who is perhaps only two months removed from walking into his/her first class, the ability to project his/her thought, in however superficial a way, into the condition of being a teacher . . . and to look at documents and situations originating outside him/herself in the style which throughout his/her life he/she will need to bring to bear on his/her own professional behaviour'
>
> Beattie, (1996, p. 19)

The French system of recruitment and promotion is highly competitive and its clearly defined criteria governing procedures and participation are perceived as objective and egalitarian. Failure is seen as relative and unsuccessful applicants are willing to present themselves on numerous occasions in order to attain a coveted grade or post.

Secondary teachers, as all other civil servants, are subject to annual appraisal (see Le Métais, 1994). Forty per cent of the grade is awarded by the principal in accordance with guidelines intended to ensure parity of treatment across the country. These guidelines indicate the appropriate grade for teachers on different incremental points and recommend that no teacher be graded below 30 points. The remaining 60 per cent relates to teaching performance and is awarded by inspectors, who are deemed to require no guidance. Given the limited number of inspectors, teachers are not inspected more than once every three years and 'satisfactory' teachers may be inspected even less frequently. Between inspections, the inspectors' gradings are annually adjusted upwards, on the assumption that additional service always results in improved performance. CPD plays no part in the grade achieved, and even if it contributes to a better performance, this may not be formally observed for several years.

Provision

Minister Alain Savary called for each university district or *académie* to survey its needs and available resources and to develop a regional training plan (*Plan Académique de Formation*) which 'meets general training objectives linked to the renewal of the education system as well as to the permanent CPD of all staff' (Savary, 1982). The survey revealed a multiplicity of demands and of supply and was followed by the creation of a *Mission Académique à la Formation des Personnels de l'Education Nationale* (MAFPEN) in each *académie* (Ministerial order dated 24 May 1984). Decree 85–607 of 14 June 1985 defines three types of CPD:

- centrally organised courses open to all staff, including summer schools and courses which form part of the national or regional training plans;
- courses to prepare staff for competitive examinations leading to promotion; and,
- courses and other activities chosen by individual teachers for their own development.

Centralised training focuses on structural and curricular changes such as those introduced in the *New Contract for Schools* (*Ministère de l'Education Nationale*, 1995), on provision for students with special needs, and on the development of teachers' ability to take on new responsibilities such as an enhanced pastoral and guidance role (see Table 12.2). Within the national plans, there are also courses to train trainers.

Staff are entitled to paid leave (at 85 per cent of salary) to undertake personal or professional training. This may be to prepare for competitive examinations within or outside the teaching profession, or to undertake other long-term studies leading to university credits or diplomas.

Preliminary outcomes

In analysing CPD in France, Altet (1993) discerned three clear phases, which show the extent to which the system has been able to adapt and adjust to demand.

1982–84 The *information–learning–acquisition–updating* model. Most courses were dedicated to specific subject areas and focused on content rather than on the teaching of the discipline.

1984–88 The *reflective practitioner* model. This responded to the demands of teachers who analyse their practice and situation. The reform of secondary education stimulated demand from schools for CPD and resulted in more effective tailoring of courses to meet school needs. Courses dealt less with subject content, but focused on teaching and learning and on professional collaboration (e.g. differentiated teaching; formative evaluation; needs analysis; reading; team work). However, the absence of a coordinating plan meant that schools might engage in a number of CPD activities and thus use their resources and teachers' time in ways which would not necessarily result in the desired improvements.

1988 onwards   The *teacher-as-researcher model*. This phase saw the introduction of school (development) plans and greater negotiation between providers on the one hand and schools and teachers on the other. There was greater emphasis on the analysis of institutional effectiveness and problem solving (including the identification of CPD needs), which contributed to the development of a school plan and, in some cases, a short-, medium- and long-term staff development plan. MAFPENs therefore needed different types of trainers: consultants (giving targeted advice and training), subject-specific trainers, and cross-disciplinary, general education trainers.

CPD/research groups have emerged in all MAFPENs and teachers are producing action research based on their experience, to step back from practice; seek a theoretical basis for their practice; and transfer this through collective work. These groups seek to resolve a real problem, experienced in the classroom, by means of cooperative work, drawing on the experience and knowledge of all members of the group and of *ad hoc* external researchers, who provide a theoretical perspective or methodological help at the request of the group. Teacher-researchers want to improve their methodology but only a few groups have the necessary resources and organise regular methods seminars. Some of their research papers are published by MAFPENs, others in national journals. Several teachers register for further academic study, e.g. for a higher (research) degree.

It is expected that these practitioner–researchers will form the basis of future CPD providers because the effects of this form of training are visible.

* in terms of the production of formalised knowledge;
* in terms of attitudes and interpretations, accompanying a change in professional identity; and
* in terms of psychological and social effects in the institution.

The teachers' unions support the entitlement to CPD, but their support is theoretical rather than practical and career development remains largely dependent on individual initiative and commitment (Altet, 1993). This is not surprising since career progress is achieved in strict competition against other aspirants and the unions seek to maintain a system which offers maximum opportunities for all to reach the highest salary levels within their *corps* before retirement.

THE NETHERLANDS

Educational policy and provision in the Netherlands are influenced by two major forces. The first is the constitutional right of any individual or group to establish a school and, subject to meeting certain conditions, to obtain state funding at the same level as public-sector schools. This results in the division of educational institutions, from nursery to university level, into four groupings (known as 'pillars') which represent the municipal (public) sector and the three private sectors (Catholic, Protestant and non-denominational). The second is the legal right of representatives of the four 'pillars' to be consulted on all educational policies and legislation.

The education system in the Netherlands, like that of England and Wales, has undergone widespread change during the past decade. This includes: lowering of the school starting age; devolution of funding and management to local authorities and schools; school amalgamations to reduce surplus places; and reformed curricula for both phases of secondary education. During the same period, university level training for upper secondary teachers has been reformed and new (regionally negotiated) conditions of service have been introduced for teachers. These include a specified annual work load (1,710 hours) and criteria for appraisal on transfer to a new post or new salary scale. The amalgamation of secondary schools which had traditionally catered for pupils of different academic abilities and aspirations, has created larger, more heterogeneous communities than ever before. This initiative has resulted in a pool of redundant and 'displaced' staff who, although without a post, are paid 'waiting' salaries.

As in England and Wales, Dutch teachers have been criticised for deficient subject knowledge, old-fashioned teaching styles, general rather than differentiated teaching and an inability to deal effectively with ethnic minorities whose mother tongue is not Dutch (*Trouw*, 1996). There is general recognition that, within a per capita funding system, the reduction in initial teacher training (ITT) numbers threatens the viability of the providers and therefore the quality of both ITT and CPD. In response, the Government has decided to transfer the funding of the 'waiting' pool into 'quality' staff management policies (OCW, 1996b).

Provision

First, the recognised professional status of teachers in the Netherlands brings with it a requirement that 10 per cent of the working year (171 hours) must be devoted to the individual's CPD. Up to 50 hours per year may be prescribed, on the basis of negotiation, to meet school needs (e.g. whole school development or activities outlined in the school development plan or the school CPD plan). The remainder is at the discretion of the individual teacher who must, however, account for the way in which the time is spent. Since 1993, schools have received an allowance for CPD as part of the total devolved budgets for recurrent expenditure. Until 1 August 1997, they are obliged to spend at least 80 per cent of this budget on services from existing providers, principally the initial teacher training establishments. Unspent funds may be saved up to a maximum of the total CPD budget for the previous three years; any surplus must be repaid to the government (OCW, 1996a).

Second, the Government has taken steps to address the needs of specific groups of teachers. Newly qualified teachers require appropriate induction and support, much of which can be provided by experienced teachers. The Government is introducing a 'package' of shorter hours and less demanding, non-contact duties, to retain 'seniors' who are retiring prematurely due to the demands of the job and the lack of salary increases. The reduction in class contact time is linked to the needs of newly qualified teachers by giving 'seniors' mentoring and induction duties.

Similarly, the Government feels that middle aged teachers, who have reached the top of their salary scale after 24–26 years and may have little prospect of career advancement, would benefit from a lighter working load, time for retraining, or opportunities to save for leave or flexible retirement. This is the target group for sabbatical leave. From 1997, 0.5 per cent of the education budget will be set aside for sabbatical leave and to offset the reduced workload of older staff. This sum will be doubled for 1998, and increase annually until it constitutes 3 per cent of the budget (OCW, 1996b).

Thirdly, and separately from sabbatical leave, the Government recognises the importance of time away from the workplace for 'refreshment' and re-orientation to the teaching profession. It has introduced a scheme which enables teachers in primary schools and special schools (heads, deputies, teachers, full or part-time) to 'save' for paid leave which they can use for CPD, for retraining or for other paid or unpaid activities. The 1996 regulations entitle teachers to 'bank' up to 5 per cent of their salary for a period of their choice, between four and eight years. The government contributes 1.27 hours for every two hours saved, which means that at the end of four years the teacher is entitled to 13.78 weeks' leave, in addition to the normal school holidays. Those who save the maximum number of hours, for the maximum period of eight years, have an entitlement of 27.55 weeks' leave. 'Refreshment leave' must be taken immediately following the end of the 'saving' period (OCW, 1996c).

Fourth, in June 1994, the Ministry of Education commissioned a project *(Project Kwaliteit Nascholing)* to develop a manual for schools and providers jointly to control and improve CPD. The project is built on the assumptions that:

- quality depends on the clear definition of objectives and the commitment of both provider and recipient;
- outcomes can only be fully assessed by observing teacher behaviour, in the classroom, after a period of time;
- the effectiveness of CPD can be enhanced or hindered by the extent to which schools provide a supportive environment for the implementation of new knowledge and skills.

The project provides checklists for self evaluation; models and instruments for an inventory of needs, intake, contract negotiation and evaluation (Van Riessen and Schoor, 1995).

Preliminary outcomes

Many of the above initiatives are too recent for evaluation. However, a research project was commissioned to report on the way in which schools managed their delegated CPD funds. Karstanje *et al.* (1995) reported that 15 million out of a total of 111 million guilders remained unspent. This was due to the fact that many schools are unwilling to use resources until they have defined their own policy and the development of a policy is time consuming. However, they found a distinct difference between primary and secondary schools. The former had become more responsible in their use of CPD and there was a better match between demand and provision at this level. Karstanje *et al.* (1995) postulated that this might be because primary schools have small teams working within an established structural and curricular framework. These findings are endorsed by Van Riessen and Schoor (1995) who found primary schools much more careful in choosing between providers and even taking management training to help them establish a good CPD plan. In contrast, many secondary schools had not developed CPD plans, nor spent their budgets and there was, overall, less evidence of effective match between demand/supply. This was attributed, in part, to the demands on secondary schools of school amalgamations, a new foundation curriculum and the reform of the 15+ curricula, and to the larger numbers of staff involved.

The higher education council (representing many ITT/CPD providers) expressed concern in January 1995 that schools' tendency to hoard their CPD funds undermined the forward planning, and therefore the viability, of the traditional CPD providers. Moreover, the fact that municipalities received block funding to provide school support services was seen as giving these services an unfair advantage over traditional providers (a) because they could plan more securely, and (b) because their regular contacts with schools for SEN support made them the 'familiar face'. It was feared that this advantage would work against traditional providers if the current ring-fencing of 80 per cent of CPD funding were to be lifted. However, in some areas ITT institutions are overcoming this problem through close networking with schools and the development of computer programmes to help schools develop a CPD plan, select from the courses on offer, and calculate the budget remaining. In other areas, the municipal school support services have been drawn into the partnership, making a broader range of services available to schools and providing better continuity between the normal work of the school, CPD and the implementation of student support (Van Riessen and Schoor, 1995).

Teachers' early reactions vary. Most acknowledge that competence diminishes without adequate CPD. However, whilst some appreciate the scope for teacher-suggested initiatives within the CPD plan and the opportunities to stand back, to reflect, alone and with colleagues, about one's subject and one's teaching, others argue that the providers do not always meet their needs for practically-oriented training (Kleis Jager, 1995b). In their defence, providers claim that many schools still do not know what they want and, due to inadequate care, some teachers enrol for inappropriate courses (Van Riessen and Schoor, 1995).

Although school CPD plans are no longer compulsory, experience has shown that they make a positive contribution to effective staff development because they involve staff in review, planning and decision making and explicitly relate the expressed wishes of individual teachers to the overall needs of the school (Kleis Jager, 1995a; Van Riessen and Schoor, 1995; Van der Mee, 1996). Other initiatives which have proved successful are mentoring (Van Riessen, 1995), CPD networks bringing schools and ITT providers together (Kleis Jager, 1995b) and self-directed collegial groups, where participants are actively involved in sharing, and validating, their own expertise and knowledge (Kleis Jager, 1995c).

CONCLUSION

This brief summary of CPD provision in sixteen European countries reveals, despite the diversity, some commonality with developments in England and Wales, namely, the linking of CPD provision more directly to school and system needs, the emergence of development plans, the involvement of agencies other than traditional training establishments in the provision, the devolution of CPD funding to schools and the creation of a market (in the Netherlands) and the promotion of teacher-researchers (in France). Unfortunately, the integration of initial training, induction and CPD into a continuous, coherent process still seems to be some way off.

ACKNOWLEDGEMENT

I am grateful to Barbara Dickinson and Sharon O'Donnell for their comments on the draft of this paper.

NOTES

1.   The EU Member States are: Austria, Belgium, Denmark, Finland, France, Germany, Greece, Ireland, Italy, Luxembourg, the Netherlands, Portugal, Spain, Sweden, the United Kingdom. The EEA members are: Iceland, Liechtenstein, Norway and Switzerland. Comparable details on Liechtenstein and Switzerland were not available for inclusion in this chapter.

Questions for discussion

What are the significant characteristics of the French model?

What are the significant characteristics of the Netherlands model?

What can be learned from developments in Europe?

13

Building on Success: Professional Development in the Future

BRIAN FIDLER

The development of professionals is a long term process. Such development should be progressive and go on over the working lifetime of a professional. As such it needs to be planned but other, possibly conflicting, priorities, such as the needs of the organisation, also have to be considered. This is at the heart of the challenge of continuing professional development.

This final chapter has two components: (1) some personal views on CPD incorporating references to some features from earlier chapters and (2) a perspective on management development from the work of BEMAS Committees and documents they have produced.

CONTEXT

Whilst it has often been noted that the quality of leadership in schools is a vital element in their performance, it should also be noted that the quality of teachers makes an equally vital contribution.

The present time is very formative for the teaching profession in England and Wales. Its development is receiving detailed consideration from the Teacher Training Agency in a more comprehensive way than ever before. Unfortunately this is being carried out in great haste moving from very general principles to detailed proposals without taking adequate account of previous developments. Indeed there almost seems a wish to ignore what has happened in the past and to start afresh.

An important element of the context in which these proposals are being developed concerns teacher recruitment. Increasingly in the 1980s it became difficult to recruit subject specialists in shortage areas and then progressively more difficult to recruit teachers in general, especially in inner city areas. Expectations that this would be a continuing theme in the 1990s were overtaken by the depth, severity and length of the economic recession in the UK in the early 1990s. As has happened in previous recessions teacher recruitment became buoyant, however now, the first signs of depleted intakes to initial teacher training in shortage subjects are beginning to show and there are selective reports of difficulties in recruitment to teaching posts. After the recession in the early 1980s these signs were the indicators of the start of a long period when teacher recruitment was increasingly challenging (Fidler 1993).

This has implications for the continuing professional development of teachers. Research in the 1980s showed that the initial monetary rewards for beginning teachers were comparable with other professions but rewards after six years of teaching were relatively poor. Teachers' salaries have increased in absolute terms since then and there have been larger rises for more senior posts but it is doubtful if the basic monetary comparisons of the 1980s have been overturned. This leaves the non-monetary rewards of teaching.

There are two contributions to job satisfaction. Firstly, there is the actual task of teaching to be considered and its rewards. Over the last few years the following changes may be noted: a reduction in the scope of professional decisions; increasing challenges in controlling pupils; and an increasing pressure to improve the quality of schooling. These do not appear to offer much scope for easing recruitment difficulties. Secondly, and more hopefully, there is the prospect of joining a profession which offers both rewarding development and also clearer career paths.

It is perhaps worth differentiating the importance of professional development as a means of increasing the attractiveness of teaching as a career option from its potential for directly developing teachers. Whilst it may be unpalatable, it should be recognised that there are limits to what can be expected from professional development in terms of increasing performance. It should not be considered as a panacea for remediating the results of an inadequately prepared and poorly qualified intake into teaching. Just as the outcomes of schooling for pupils are conditioned to a substantial extent by the ability of the intake so what can be achieved by the development of teachers will be conditioned to a large degree by the quality of recruits. As Stewart and Stewart (1983, p. 72) remarked on the remediating potential of training, 'Some people benefit from training; some are unscathed; and some come back worse than they went.' A well-thought out and well-resourced plan for developing the professional teaching force offers an unparalleled opportunity to improve recruitment and also to prepare teachers to meet the continuing challenges ahead.

DEFINING TERMS

There are a number of terms which do not have a common usage in the literature. I should like to differentiate some of them here to clarify different contributions to the development of professionals:

- professional development: involves developments which increase the personal professional skills of a teacher;
- staff development: involves the development of the staff to meet the needs of the institution in which they work;
- career development: involves the development of individuals so that their careers can progress.

These differences in terms indicate a difference in function. For the success of the educational system, professionals need to develop, schools need to develop and careers need to develop. Career development means not only that individuals can develop their careers but also that schools can recruit experienced and developed individuals to take on more senior posts.

The transfer of much of the responsibility and resources for professional development to schools in the late 1980s and early 1990s has led to professional and career development for individuals being accorded rather lower priority than staff development which served schools' interests. The teaching profession has been the loser from this atomisation of responsibility to nearly 25,000 schools. A sense of coherence, and particularly the longer term development of the teaching force, has not been evident. There have been particular difficulties in funding forms of preparation for more senior posts in other schools, particularly preparation for headship.

To leave professional and career development entirely to individuals and their assessment of the market for more developed professionals is to endanger a vital national service. Clearer expectations as regards qualifications, types of experience and professional learning for different career paths are necessary if individuals are to make informed choices about the kinds of professional development which will lead to future career opportunities. Too many individuals, in the past, have missed out on career opportunities because they were simply unaware of what was possible or did not receive advice about what were realistic possibilities in their case. A combination of staff appraisal and clearer career paths in the profession, should enable individuals, in the future, to make more informed career choices at an earlier stage in their career. As Sue Law suggests, individuals alone cannot engineer positive situations for development.

IS TEACHING A PROFESSION?

Teaching is unusual as a profession in a number of ways. A few are worth noting here. It is an almost wholly employed workforce rather than being self-employed and it shares with those in the health service a responsibility for providing an essential national service. Imposed national reforms in education have led a number of commentators to draw attention to what they regard as the deskilling of professional practice by the removal of many professional choices of subject content from teachers. Most professions also have control, through a representative body, of entry and development within the profession.

Teaching shares a number of the attributes of a craft, a science, an art and a profession (Fidler 1994) although the strongest correspondence is with a profession. One of the areas of difficulty as regards acceptance as a profession concerns the professional knowledge base on which a teacher operates. The need to possess subject knowledge is clear, whilst the acceptance of a need for some underlying theory of pedagogy is more contested.

Teachers are required to make decisions about appropriate learning strategies for individuals. In other professions there would be a clear underlying theoretical base for such decisions. Although an underlying base of social science knowledge particularly in psychology, sociology and pedagogy can be identified as relevant, recent trends in teacher training have tended to reduce this base and replace it with greater craft knowledge gained from practice in schools.

I believe that there is a problem with the initial training of the teaching profession although it is not primarily the one which has been the cause of the current preoccupation with a national curriculum for initial teacher training. Whilst there has been criticism of the practical skill base of beginning teachers, this has been allowed to mask their lack of theoretical knowledge, particularly in the one-year PGCE. Teachers need a sound base of theoretical knowledge as well as practical skills. For all professions the ability to translate theoretical knowledge into practical actions in unique situations represents a challenge to conceptual understanding. Schon (1983) has proposed the process of reflective practice for this developing ability to set up personal mental schema to organise and process learning from experience in order to provide an expert diagnosis of individual client needs. In the case of a teacher this would mean responding to the needs of a learner by providing appropriate teaching and learning support. However, as McIntyre (1993) has pointed out, teachers need appropriate theoretical knowledge upon which to theorise their actions. The successful training of teachers involves more than a demonstrated set of competences in action.

The aim of making teaching a research based profession though laudable is, as presently envisaged, unlikely to be attainable because of this lack of an underlying base of social sciences and pedagogical knowledge upon which to carry out informed research. The initial training of teachers is important because it provides the base upon which continuing professional development can be built. The James Report of 1972 recognised that initial teacher preparation should take at least two years.

As the chapter by Harry Tomlinson demonstrates, most professions are currently planning to enhance the professional development expected of their members. Increasingly demonstrated professional development will be a condition for continued professional registration.

HOW PROFESSIONALS LEARN

If the learning of professionals is to be facilitated, a valid model which conceptualises the process is needed in order to plan development. The learning cycle of Kolb (1974), based on the work of Kurt Lewin, has been proposed as a means of conceptualising the learning stages of professionals. This has four elements (see Figure 13.1). Whilst such learning involves activity, the process also requires much more. This is the distinction between experience and learning from experience. Activity needs to be reviewed and this mental activity

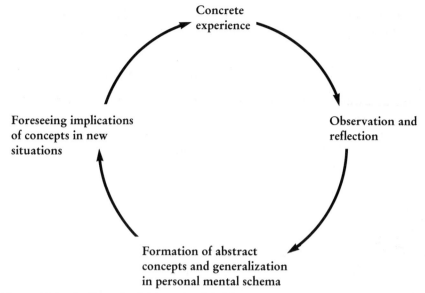

Figure 13.1   An Experiential Learning Model

should lead to theorising or trying to translate the experience into some more abstract framework in a form that will be useful in planning subsequent actions. Although these processes could go on unaided and unplanned, they are likely to be greatly facilitated by the provision of theoretical frameworks to help accommodate the results of practical learning and by the planning of learning experiences. External courses can provide exposure to appropriate theoretical and conceptual frameworks and help individuals to make sense of and learn from their experiences. The interplay between theoretical ideas derived from attending external courses and related practical activity in schools is most likely to lead to the development of mental schema to inform future practice.

The Kolb cycle also suggests the need for help in planning experience and reviewing and theorising afterwards. This is a role which a mentor could perform. Some characteristics of a mentor are suggested by this analysis. The person should understand the process of reflective practice and be able to facilitate it. Facilitation involves an understanding of the relationship between types of experience and suitable theoretical underpinnings which can enhance the processes of reflection and theorising. A mentor also needs appropriate behavioural skills to work successfully with other adults.

Professionals can learn from any activity, but, in a crowded and hectic work schedule, there will be pressure on time to reflect. Also the lack of a suitable theoretical stimulus to provide fertile ground for the development of mental frameworks of understanding is likely to mean that planned opportunities for learning will be more productive. Further, the opportunity of discussing learning experiences with other professionals from varied backgrounds helps to form more valid generalisations. It is mainly this planned activity which will be the subject of comment in the remainder of this chapter.

STAGES OF PROFESSIONAL DEVELOPMENT

For any post which an individual occupies there can be expected to be preparatory activities, induction and development activities whilst in the post. This cycle can be expected to be repeated as an individual takes up each new post in his or her career from beginning teacher through to headteacher. Professional development activities for each post involves the following stages:

- preparation for the post;
- induction;
- development in the post.

This framework can include adding new activities to an existing school post although, in such a case, preparation and induction may be much more cursory than for more major changes of post.

Each of these activities may involve school based activities and off-site activities. The location is rather less important than whether teachers from other schools are involved, and can share experiences, and whether there is a substantial theoretical content.

An analysis of each stage of the framework indicates that there are different beneficiaries, as is summarised in Figure 13.2

1. *Preparation for a future post* is largely aimed at the professional and career development of the teacher although it will have benefits for the profession in providing a supply of qualified personnel for more senior posts. However, for the school which the promoted person is likely to leave there will be few immediate benefits. The school will have the opportunity of appointing a new member of staff (or not as the school chooses) who may bring in new expertise, a fresh perspective and new personal characteristics (in favourable recruitment conditions). Further, the school may acquire a reputation as a training ground for staff who go on to more senior posts and thus find it easier to recruit staff in the future.
2. *Induction into a new post* has benefits for the professional development of the teacher and the school. The teacher has the opportunity of settling in to their new post, and a new school, with support. The school has, in addition to the more structural aspects of induction, an opportunity of assimilating the new teacher into the organisational culture that the school wishes to adopt (Fidler *et al.* 1996). The career of a teacher will be enhanced by the teacher being able to perform more effectively and more quickly by being given guidance about the expectations of the school.
3. *Development in post* is likely to be the most substantial and the most rewarding activity from the individual's, the school's and the profession's

points of view. It is also likely to be the most varied since it will depend on the needs of the school and the needs of the individual teacher.

This formulation helps to differentiate development in post from preparations for the next post. The current post is taken as the focus for activity. In this way, as Jeff Jones and Fergus O'Sullivan suggest, the development of, for example, middle managers can be viewed as an activity in its own right rather than as merely part of the preparation of headteachers.

	Individual Development		School Development	National Professional Development
	Professional	Career		
Preparation	+++	+++	+	+++
Induction	+++	++	+++	+
Development	+++	++	+++	++

Figure 13.2 Summary table of beneficiaries of the three stages of professional development (the number of pluses gives an indication of the strength of the benefit)

BEGINNING TEACHER

Preparation for an initial teaching post will, for most candidates, have involved initial teacher training. They will have demonstrated an array of competences during training. Thus induction is the first professional development activity. In this case induction involves

- induction to the post;
- induction to the school;
- induction to the profession.

Inevitably in the first year of teaching new recruits will be experiencing the full range of activities expected of a teacher – teaching, pastoral activities, parental meetings and contributions to whole staff activities. Many of these may be new to beginning teachers and will certainly involve differences from previous teaching practice. The beginning teacher will need briefing for these events and support through them. Some support may be subject specific and should come from specialists inside or outside the school but much support will be personal and, more generally, professional and could come from a wider group of people. It may be that from among this wider group induction to the school can also be organised. Induction to the school provides an opportunity for the school's expectations of staff to be made clear. The beginning teacher is being inducted into the organisational culture. This provides a chance to influence the existing organisational culture and thus represents a very formative period particularly in a small school where one member of staff can make an appreciable difference.

Both the former two aspects of induction apply to any teacher new to a school. Both the post and the school will be new to the teacher and expectations need to be clarified on both sides since more experienced teachers will bring with them expectations based on their previous experience. Experienced teachers who are new to a school provide an opportunity to gain insights into the assumptions which underpin actions in that school. Such teachers should be well placed to observe differences of priority which indicate different underlying assumptions of staff in the new school (Fidler 1997b). This may help bring out cultural differences which established teachers in the school are unaware of. Clarifying the organisational culture is an important precursor to major organisational change or strategy formulation (Fidler *et al.* 1996).

Completing the induction of beginning teachers, as the chapter by Ken Jones and Peter Stammers suggests, is induction to the profession. This involves meeting with beginning teachers from other schools and an overview of the profession from a wider perspective than an individual school and is best carried out off-site and probably by an LEA.

The initial professional development of beginning teachers can be expected to be a further development of competences in their career entry profile. They will also be expected to play their part along with other staff in school development activities which will involve learning to work in new ways and to develop new skills. The prioritisation of professional and career development and staff development for each teacher should be carried out during an appraisal interview and follow-up interview every year (Fidler and Cooper 1992).

CAREER DEVELOPMENT

It is an irony of career development in teaching as presently constituted that advancement means spending less time teaching and more time managing. One inevitable consequence is that this leads to a diminished status of teaching as an activity. A second consequence is that good teachers leave the classroom and may, or may not, become good managers. Thus there is an urgent need to raise the status of teaching. In the USA the concept of master teacher has been developed to reward and give status and provide a career for those whose expertise is in the classroom. Such a concept with a less sexist name is required here.

There is a further role of mentor which could remain close to teachers and classrooms which could have teaching and the development of teaching expertise as its distinctive function. Not all good teachers would be suitable for this role. Those who have abilities to work with and develop other adults in addition to being good teachers would be the group from which mentors could be drawn. Although Pauline Smith identifies this role with heads of department, it could be separated (although close liaison would be required). There are two advantages to recognising this as a separate role. It recognises a role for teachers with this potential who do not wish to become managers and it also provides a mentor function which does not also have a hierarchical relationship with teachers who are being mentored.

Both these two groups and also potential managers will need to develop their practical teaching skills and also their theoretical knowledge of

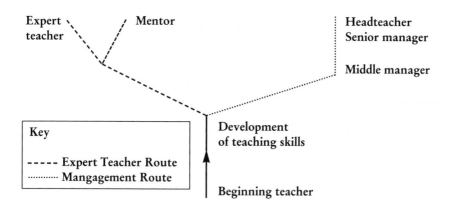

Figure 13.3 A model of two career paths in teaching

developments in teaching. Managers in schools are responsible for children's learning; thus they need to understand that which they are managing. Schools are unusual in having a degree of freedom in setting their own goals in circumstances where these are value-based. Whilst schools are required to deliver the National Curriculum they have some freedom over how the remaining 20 per cent of curricular time is spent and further freedom over how the school's priorities for non-cognitive development are exercised. Such choices, even if made by governors, need expert advice.

The third avenue for career development is by entering management. Here there are differences between primary and secondary schools. In primary schools most teachers are subject coordinators. As the name implies this role is more one of coordination rather than management (although development before and in the post is still needed). There are fewer middle manager posts in primary schools which involve the management of staff. Then there are the senior posts of deputy head and headteacher. In secondary schools there are academic middle managers and pastoral middle managers and senior managers including deputy heads and headteachers.

A possible schematic career structure within schools with two routes – expert teacher and management – is shown in Figure 13.3. It should be recognised that such a career structure for the teaching profession also has implications for the organisational structure of each school (Fidler 1992, 1997a). If the expert teacher (and mentor) is to be a career route, to whom should such teachers be accountable? The positioning of posts on Figure 13.3 has implications for status and salary within schools.

MANAGEMENT OF CONTINUING PROFESSIONAL DEVELOPMENT

There are two aspects to this – what and who? What activities are to be managed and who is involved in managing them?

What activities?

There are three sets of activities – staff, professional and career development.

Staff development and school improvement

The main determinants of staff development will be the need to develop staff to implement externally imposed changes and to implement internal school improvement initiatives chosen by the school. Some suggest that there are some prerequisites for school development and that some staff development may also be necessary to develop a school culture in a way which is conducive to school improvement.

These requirements should emerge from a strategic or school development plan. Initiatives will be proposed which have staff development implications. Some prior training before a new initiative is begun may be required. However, the findings from many change projects have pointed out the need for on-going training and support whilst a new initiative is being implemented rather than all the training being provided at the start. Detailed plans for particular aspects of school development should have included the requirements and resources needed for staff development.

Professional development

Professional development for each individual should be going on continuously. Some staff development will also provide professional development but there should be thought given to developments in skills and theoretical knowledge of each individual year by year. Some of this will be professional subject updating, some will be improving individual elements of performance, some will be conceptual development of understanding and some will be learning from new experiences.

Career development

Those who have career aspirations should have the opportunity by study and experience to prepare for career advancement.

Need for a policy

Schools need a policy which deals with professional, career and staff development. The policy will need to deal with priorities and resourcing and set general expectations for staff. Detailed plans will be needed to implement the policy.

Who is involved?

A large number of people will be involved in these activities in some way. There will be those who are managing the policy and those who are carrying it out. Unless one person manages the whole policy, there will need to be coordination between those who manage – student teachers, induction programmes, INSET days, staff and professional development, appraisal. Viv Garrett and

Colin Bowles report the difficulties of this when senior posts have been reduced in number. In addition there will be many more managers who are carrying out the policy by appraising and facilitating the development of their staff.

The implementation of a policy for development will need to be treated as a major change in the school. As such there will be a need for awareness raising, training and familiarisation and supported implementation.

MANAGEMENT DEVELOPMENT

Since its inception in 1971 BEMAS has been concerned to promote management development in education. The survey of professional development provision in 1980 (Hughes *et al.* 1982) had its origin in a BEMAS conference devoted to management development. The survey report recognised the variety of provision and called for coordination, expansion and geographical coverage. At that stage it was estimated that some 2,000 people each year were obtaining qualifications which included a substantial study of education management. As Gary Holmes and Austin Harding describe there were a number of subsequent developments which increased funding and exposure to management courses.

In a paper produced by the BEMAS Education Management Teachers Committee in 1988 there was a call for

- career-long management development;
- a substantial study of education management before headship;
- the integration of training and experience;
- the development of attitudes by managers which took account of the philosophical and ethical bases of schooling

The paper noted the value of management ideas from outside the world of education and was aware of much translating of such ideas which had already appeared in the education management literature.

When the School Management Task Force was appointed in 1988 there was an expectation of substantial further developments. However, there was little expectation of further resources. After an interim report from the Task Force in 1989, BEMAS suggested that management development in education was in danger of being considered in isolation from more general management development. It was worried by the lack of importance accorded to qualifications in school management. In 1989 BEMAS warned that substantial research and development work would be needed to identify in a detailed and systematic way the skills needed by varying groups of managers, to arrange these needs in training frameworks and to relate them to qualifications. This is being done by the TTA at breakneck speed in the mid 1990s without the accumulated expertise that could have been available had the work been well-planned rather than driven by a seemingly political imperative.

The Task Force reported in 1990 and proposed moving the major emphasis of management development to school based work. The BEMAS response warned that such a move was premature and that other organisations which had made this move had preceded it with a wide-spread, long-term use of training courses to prepare the culture and develop organisational capability.

BEMAS regretted the low profile which management development achieved following the disbanding of the Task Force and pressed DES/DFE to set up another initiative. However, it was not until 1993 that a Teacher Training Agency was proposed which was to have further professional development of teachers as one of its remits. Despite the suspicions of many regarding the political motivation for setting up a quango TTA rather than a widely representative General Teaching Council BEMAS recognised TTA as a possible focus for further professional development. However, it made clear that a GTC would be needed if the TTA did not merit the confidence of the education profession. When the TTA was set up its members were personal appointments of the Secretary of State or what Peter Newsam called FOM (Friends of the Minister). What was needed BEMAS had argued in its submission to the National Commission on Education was a planning, coordinating and advisory group representing a broad range of professional interests including providers of management training and headteachers and other managers in education.

Ideas from outside education

It is rather sad to see TTA documents in 1996 indicating a lack of knowledge of the work, referred to earlier, of taking ideas from outside the educational world and translating them for use in schools. Expectations that the commercial world has ideas to contribute to education management which have not already been exploited is to ignore all that has happened in the past, particularly since 1983. The Circular 3/83 initiatives supported by the National Development Centre at Bristol introduced further ideas from the non-educational world to education management. Not that such ideas had been neglected, as any glance at Open University readers from the 1970s demonstrates (Houghton *et al.* 1975; Dobson *et al.* 1975). Successive editions of textbooks like Everard and Morris (1996) have been enormously influential. The CNAA Educational Organisation and Management Board which approved award bearing courses in the former non-university sector had representatives from outside education to ensure that courses made use of appropriate ideas from outside education. However, such use of practices from outside education needs some critical reflection (Glatter 1996). Appropriateness and effectiveness are not referred to in TTA documentation but are vital criteria to apply before importing ideas from the commercial world as the figure below demonstrates. This is not the occasion to discuss the ways in which schools are different to other non-profit making and commercial organisations since these are covered elsewhere (Fidler *et al.* 1996) but it is important to recognise that there are differences and they may be crucial. Only ideas from outside education which work effectively (and recognise this as a value-laden concept) and which deal with issues which are relevant to schools have

	Relevance	
	Appropriate	*Inappropriate*
Effective	Worth while	Irrelevant
Ineffective	Poor	Worthless

Effectiveness is shown on the left spanning the Effective/Ineffective rows.

Figure 13.4 Effectiveness and Relevance of General Management Ideas to Education

anything to offer. Thus it really is disingenuous to imply that many new management ideas from outside education have the power to change schools. Particularly so, when informed commentators on the management scene bemoan the demise of so many failed management nostrums in the commercial world (Caulkin 1996). In government quangos the ritualistic denigration of education still goes on. To paraphrase Pauline Smith, where's the respect in that?

PROPOSALS FOR THE FUTURE

What then is in prospect and how does it match up to the views of professionals in the field?

An education in management?

At least two qualifications – one for middle managers and one for prospective headteachers are proposed. Since they are being developed piecemeal it is not clear whether these will amount to an education in management over the career of a headteacher or whether a masters degree in education management will also be needed to give rigour and depth. Such courses may also be needed because the qualifications based upon post will involve courses for people at only one level in the organisation – deputy head or middle managers. One great strength of many award-bearing courses is that they involve a mix of personnel from different management levels in different schools. These different perspectives add greatly to the prospects of learning from experience.

The proposals do involve qualifications before appointment and thus some level of preparation should be in place for appointees. The NPQH qualification will attempt to combine study with work in school. In this way it should go beyond an ability to write about management. How valid this will be as a measure of ability to perform as a headteacher in another school is more problematic.

High quality?

The lack of a commitment to rigourous, independent, open evaluation of the provision, as opposed to each provider, is a major concern. This is yet another experiment with the whole educational system which does not represent a development based on successful existing provision but an attempt to replace it. Commercial managers would recognise this as a high risk strategy.

Development in school?
To be successful, continuing professional development must be a reality in schools. A major shortcoming of the recent proposals from TTA is the lack of consideration of how they are to be organised in schools. How are schools to organise CPD by combining planned experience and off-site education and training for professional and career development whilst also organising staff development to implement the school development plan? This process has not been modelled in a variety of schools to examine its cost and impact. This is the rational problem. There may also be attitudinal and conceptual problems involved in many schools.

The School Management Task Force were right to focus on schools as the essential units for the organisation and facilitation of CPD but they underestimated the difficulties of doing so. Research and development work is urgently needed to offer working models for doing this successfully in a variety of school types and sizes. When there are demonstrated models of good practice OFSTED inspections of schools then have a valid basis for comparing individual school practices with good practice and recommending this area as a key point for action if necessary (Ouston *et al.* 1996; Earley *et al.* 1996).

What remains to be done?
HEADLAMP for newly appointed first headships is the sole provision for headteachers in the TTA framework. As Busher and Paxton remind us, heads are often the last ones to consider their own training needs. BEMAS has long argued that management development starts at the top. The management development of headteachers is both a necessary symbol to other staff of the worth of continuing professional development and is also functionally necessary so that heads can manage better. Any provision for headteachers will need to be more flexible than NPQH and related to school improvement in a holistic way.

Resourcing
The various initiatives which have been announced so far have only redistributed existing resources rather than involved additional resources. If continuing professional development is to add to the attractiveness of teaching as a profession then provision will need to be at least adequately resourced. CPD should be regarded as a right and an entitlement. This should include professional development, staff development and career development. As we have seen earlier, for each of these there are gains for schools and for the educational system. A target of 5 per cent of the salary budget to be spent on CPD (excluding release costs) is the level of resources which other organisations would consider appropriate.

Education is a long term business. There is a need to consider investment for the longer term rather than the short term 'quick-fixes' which keep being attempted. Teachers need continuous education rather than only short term training.

What's it all for?

Finally, it is salutary to remind ourselves why a well-developed teaching force is necessary. Improved management and continuing professional development are both means to the same end: better education of children and young people in schools. Well-directed learning of teachers can lead to well-directed learning of children and young people. As the challenges of improving schools grow, so does the need for high quality and appropriate continuing professional development.

Questions for discussion

Is teaching a profession?

What do the developments in CPD imply for the teacher's career?

How do you understand the differences between staff development, professional development, career development and management development?

Bibliography

Advisory Committee on the Supply and Education of Teachers (1984) *The In-service Education, Training and Professional Development of School Teachers*, London: DES.

Advisory Committee on the Supply and Training of Teachers, (1974) *In-service Education and Training: some considerations*, London : DES.

Advisory Committee on the Supply and Training of Teachers (1978) *Making INSET Work*, London: DES.

Altet, M. (1993) France, *European Journal of Teacher Education*, Vol. 16, no. 1, pp. 21–22.

Argyris, C. and Schon, D. (1974) *Theory in Practice : Increasing Professional Effectiveness*, New York: Jossey-Bass.

Audit Commission, (1989) *Losing an Empire, Finding a Role: The LEA of the Future*, London: The Audit Commission.

Baker K. (1986), *LEA Responses to the New INSET Arrangements*, Slough: NFER.

Baker, L. (1996) *The Professional Development of Headteachers: LFA Provision for Management development and Training of Headteachers Beyond Induction*. Slough: EMIE/NFER.

Ball, S.J. (1987) *The Micropolitics of the School*, London: Methuen.

Ball, S. (1990) *Politics and Policy Making in Education: Explorations in political sociology*, London: Routledge.

Ball, S. and Goodson, I. (1985) *Teachers' Lives and Careers*, Lewes: Falmer.

Barber, B. (1963) Some Problems in the Sociology of the Professions in *Daedalus*, no. 92, pp. 669–688.

Barber, B. (1978) Control and Responsibility in the Powerful Professions in *Political Science Quarterly*, Vol. 93, pp. 599–615.

Barber, M., (1994), Entering the unknown universe: reconstructing the teaching profession. Paper presented to British Educational Management and Administration Society, Annual Conference, September 1994.

Barber, M. (1995) Reconstructing the teaching profession, *Journal of Education for Teaching*, Vol. 21, no. 1, pp. 75–85.

Barker, S., Brooks, V., March, K. and Swatton, D. (1996) *Initial Teacher Education in Secondary Schools*, Institute of Education, University of Warwick.

Barth, R. (1990) *Improving Schools from Within: Teachers, Parents and Principals can make the Difference*, San Fransciso CA: Jossey Bass

Barton, L., Furlong, J., Miles, S., Whiting, C. and Whitty, G. (1996) *Partnership in Initial Teacher Education: A Topography*, MOTE Project, Institute of Education, London.

Beare, H., Caldwell, B., and Millikan, R. (1989) *Creating an Excellent School: some new management techniques*, London: Routledge.

Beare, H. and Slaughter, R. (1993) *Education for the Twenty-First Century*, London: Routledge.

Beattie, N. (1996) Interview and concours: teacher appointment procedures in England and Wales and France, and what they mean, *Assessment in Education*, Vol. 3, no. 1, pp. 9–28.

Benner, P. (1984) *From Novice to Expert*, Addison-Wesley, Menlo Park.

Bennett, N. (1995) *Managing Professional Teachers*, London: Paul Chapman.

Blanchard, K., Carew, D. and Parisi-Carew, E. (1992) *The One Minute Manager Builds High Performing Teams*, London: Harper Collins.

Blase, J. and Blase, J.R. (1994) *Empowering Teachers: What successful principals do*, London: Sage.

Bolam, R. (ed) (1982) *School-focused In-Service Training*, London: Heinemann Educational Books.

Bolam, R. (1987) What is effective INSET? Paper addressed to the Annual Members Conference of the National Foundation for Educational Research.

Bolam, R. (1990) Recent developments in England and Wales, in Joyce, B. (ed) *Changing School Culture through Staff Development*, Yearbook of the ASCD, Alexandria, Va.

Bolam, R. (1993) *The Continuing Professional Development of Teachers. Recent Developments and Emerging Issues*, General Teaching Council, London.

Bolam, R., Clark, J., Harper-Jones, G., Jones, K., Jones, R., Thorpe, R. and Timbrell, T. (1994) *The Induction of Newly Qualified Teachers in Wales: a report for the Welsh Office*, Cardiff: School of Education, University of Wales.

Bolam, R., Clark, J., Jones, K., Harper-Jones, G., Timbrell, T., Jones, R., and Thorpe, R. (1995) The Induction of Newly-Qualified Teachers in Schools: where next? *British Journal of In-service Education*, Vol. 21, no. 3.

Bolam, R., McMahon, A., Pocklington, K., and Weindling, D. (1993) *Effective Management in Schools: a report for the Department for Education via the School Management Task Force professional working party*, London: HMSO.

Bollington, R., Hopkins, D. and West, M. (1990) *An Introduction to Teacher Appraisal*, London: Cassell.

Bowles, G. (1992) *Educational Management Project: Final Report*, Consortium for Management Development in North West England.

Boyatzis, R. (1982) *The Competent Manager*, New York: Wiley.

Bradley, H., Connor, C. and Southworth, G. (eds) (1994) *Developing Teachers Developing Schools: Making INSET effective for the school*, London: David Fulton.

Briault, E.(1976) A distributed system of educational administration, *International Review of Education*, London: Dent and Sons.

Bridges, E.M. (1977) *The Nature of Leadership. Educational Administration*. L.L. Cunningham et al. Berkeley CA: McCutcheon.

Bridges, E.M. (1992) *Problem Based Learning for Administrators*, Eugene, Oregon, Eric Clearinghouse on Education Management, University of Oregon.

Brighouse, T. (1995) Teachers Professional Development: a British innovation, *Journal of Education for Teaching*. Vol. 21, no. 1, pp. 69–73.

Brown, S. and Earley, P. (1990) *Enabling Teachers to Undertake In-service Education and Training: A Report for the DES*, Windsor: NFER.

Buckley, J. (1985) *The Training of Secondary School Heads in Western Europe*, Windsor: NFER.

Buckley, J. and Styan, D. (1988) *Managing for Learning*, London: Macmillan.

Bullock, K., James, C. and Jamieson, I. (1994) The Process of Educational Management Learning, Paper to BEMAS Annual Conference, Oxford.

Burford, C. (1995) A Transformative Reflective Model of Leadership: Theoretical Foundations and Developmental Processes. Paper presented at BEMAS Annual Conference, Oxford.

Burgess, R. (1993) The Context of In-Service Education and Training, in Burgess *et al.*, *Implementing In-Service Education and Training*, Lewes: Falmer.

Burgess, R., Connor, J., Galloway, S., Morrison, M. and Newton, M. (1993) *Implementing In-service Education and Training*, London: Falmer.

Bush, T. (1995) *Theories of Educational Management*, 2nd ed, London: Paul Chapman.

Busher, H. and Hodgkinson, K. (1996) Cooperation and Tension between Autonomous Schools: a study of inter-school networking, *Educational Review* , Vol. 48, no. 1 pp. 55–64.

Butt, N. (1989) In-service training for the new era, *Support for Learning*, no. 4, pp. 67–74.

Caulkin, S. (1996) Business fashion: whats in and out, *Observer*, 19 May.

Chown, D. (1994) Beyond Competence, *British Journal of In Service Education*, Vol. 20, no 2.

Clark, J., Harper-Jones, G., Jones, R., Bolam, R. and Timbrell, T. (eds) (1994) *Primary Schools Handbook: the induction of newly qualified teachers in Wales*, Cardiff: School of Education, University of Wales.

Commission of the European Communities (1996) *Key Data on Education in the European Union 95*, Luxembourg: Office for Official Publications of the European Communities.

Cooper, B.S. and Shute, R.W. (1988) Training for School Management: Lessons from the American Experience, *Bedford Way papers 35*, Institute of Education, University of London.

Coolahan, J. (1991). Foreword, In: Swan, D. (ed) (1991a).

Coopers and Lybrand (1995) Teacher Training Agency, Allocations and Funding Study Report.

Coulson, A. (1986) The Managerial Work of Primary Headteachers, *Sheffield Papers in Education Management, 48*, Sheffield Hallam University.

Crewe, I. and Searing, D. (1996) All Quiet on the Civics Front, Research findings reported in *Times Educational Supplement* N Pyke, TES 7/6/96.

Davies, B. and Ellison, L. (1997) *Educational Leadership for the Twenty-first Century: a competency and knowledge approach*, London: Routledge.

Day, C. (1989) INSET: the marginalising of higher education, *British Journal of Inservice Education*, Vol. 15, pp. 195–196.

Day, C. (1993) Research and the Continuing Professional Development of Teachers, Inaugural Lecture, University of Nottingham, 19 November.

Deal, T. (1988) The symbolism of effective schools in Westoby, A., (ed.) *Culture and Power in Educational Organisations*, Milton Keynes, Open University Press.

Dempster, N. (1991) University agencies for in-service education: survival in an educational market economy, *British Journal of Inservice Education*, 11, pp. 181–189.

Dent, H.C. (1977) *The Training of Teachers in England and Wales 1800–1975*, Hodder and Stoughton, London.

Department for Education (1992) Circular 9/92 *Initial Teacher Training Secondary Phase*, London: DfE.

Department for Education (1992a) Grants for Education Support and Training Circular, July 1992.

Department for Education (1992b) *Choice and Diversity: a new Framework for Schools*, London, HMSO, White Paper.

Department for Education (1993a) *The Initial Training of Primary School Teachers: New Criteria for Courses*, (Circular 14/93), London: DfE.

Department for Education (1993b) *The Government's Proposals for the Reform of Initial Teacher Training*, London: DfE.

Department for Education (1995) *Developing Senior Managers in Schools* London: HMSO.

Department for Education and Employment (1996) Press Release, *Shephard sets agenda for quality and standards in schools*, 12 June 1996.

Department for Education and Employment (1996) Press Notice 141/96, *Teachers in Service: provisional January 1996 statistics*, DFEE, London.

Department of Education and Science (1972a) *Teacher Education and Training* (The James Report), HMSO, London.

Department of Education and Science (1972b) *Education: a Framework for Expansion* (Cmnd 5174), London: HMSO.

Department of Education and Science (1977), *Ten Good Schools: A Secondary School Enquiry, HMI series: Matters for Discussion 1*, London: HMSO.

Department of Education and Science (1979) *Aspects of Secondary Education in England*, London: HMSO.

Department of Education and Science (1983) Circular 3/83, *The In-service Teacher Training Grants Scheme*, London: DES.

Department of Education and Science (1984) Circular 4/84, *The In-service Teacher Training Grants Scheme*, London: DES.

Department of Education and Science (1985) *Better Schools* (Cmnd 9469), HMSO, London.

Department of Education and Science (1986) Circular 6/86 *Local Education Authority Training Grants Scheme: Financial Year 1987–88*, London: DES.

Department of Education and Science/HM Inspectors (1989) *The Implementation of the Local Education Authority Training Grants Scheme (LEATGS): Report on the First Year of the Scheme 1987–88*, London: DES.

Department of Education and Science (1989) *The New Teacher in School: A Survey by H.M. Inspectors in England and Wales*, London: HMSO.

Department of Education and Science (1990) Report of the School Management Task Force *Developing School Management: The Way Forward*, London: HMSO.

Department of Education and Science (1991) *School Teachers Review Body: Written Evidence from the Department of Education and Science*, London: HMSO.

Department of Education and Science (1992) *The Induction and Probation of New Teachers*, London: HMSO.

Dobson, L., Gear, T. and Westoby, A. (eds) (1975) *Management in Education: Some Techniques and Systems*, London: Ward Locke Educational.

Doyle, W. (1988) Classroom Organisation and Management, in Wittrock, M.C. (ed) *Handbook of Research on Teaching* (Third Edition), New York: Macmillan.

Dreyfus, S. and Dreyfus, H. (1979) The scope, limits and training implications of three models of air-craft pilot emergency response behavior. Unpublished report supported by the Air Force Office of Scientific Research, USAF, University of California at Berkley.

Drucker, P.F. (1979) *Management*, Pan Books: London.

Earley, P. (1992a) *The School Management Competencies*, Crawley: School Management South.

Earley, P. (1992b) *Beyond Initial Teacher Training: Induction and the Role of the LEA*, Slough: NFER.

Earley, P. (1993) Using competencies for School Management Development in Busher, H. and Smith, M. (eds) *Managing Educational Institutions: Reviewing Development and Learning*, Sheffield Papers in Education Management 95, BEMAS/Sheffield Hallam University, Sheffield.

Earley, P. (1995) *Managing our Greatest Resource: The Evaluation of the Continuous Professional Development in Schools Project*, London: NFER/UBI.

Earley, P., Fidler, B. and Ouston, J. (eds) (1996) *Improvement through Inspection? Complementary Approaches to School Development*, London: David Fulton.

Earley, P. and Fletcher-Campbell, F. (1989), *Time to Manage*, Berkshire: NFER.

Earley, P. and Kinder, K. (1994) *Initiation Rights. Effective induction practices for new teachers*, Slough: NFER.

Earthman, G. (1989) A Regional On-Site Administrator Programme from the USA., in Ribbins *et al.* op. cit.

East Midlands 9 / School Management Task Force (1993) *Personal Development Planning*, School of Education, University of Nottingham.

Education (1996) Fundraising is becoming harder, *Education*, p. 2, 5 January.

Education (1996) Advisory posts have fallen by a third, *Education*, p. 3, 5 January.

Education Digest (1983), *Selecting Heads; the POST Project*, Education Journal Digest, 8 July.

Education Digest (1984), *School Management Training*, Education Journal Digest, 12 October.

Eraut, M. (1994) *Developing Professional Knowledge and Competence*, London: Falmer.

Esp, D.(1993) *Competences for School Managers*, London: Kogan Page.

EURYDICE (1995) *In-service Training of Teachers in the European Union and the EFTA/EEA Countries*, Brussels: EURYDICE European Unit.

Everard, B. (1990) The Competency Approach to Management Development, *Management in Education*, Vol. 4, no. 2.

Everard, B. (1995) Values as central to competent professional practice in Busher, H. and Saran, R. (eds) *Managing Teachers as Professionals in Schools*, London: Kogan Page.

Everard, K.B. and Morris, G. (1996) *Effective School Management (3rd Edn.)*, London: Paul Chapman Publishing.

Evetts, J. (1994) *Becoming a Secondary Headteacher*, London: Cassell.

Feinman-Nemser, S., and Floden, R. (1986). The Cultures of Teaching, in M.C. Wittrock (ed) *Handbook of Research on Teaching*, New York: Macmillan.

Fidler, B. (1992) Job Descriptions and Organisational Structure, in Fidler, B. and Cooper, R. (eds) *Staff Appraisal and Staff Management in Schools and Colleges: A Guide to Implementation*, Harlow: Longman.

Fidler, B. (1993) Balancing the Supply and Demand for School Teachers in Fidler, B., Fugl, B. and Esp, D. (eds) *The Supply and Recruitment of School Teachers*, Harlow: Longman.

Fidler, B. (1994) Partnership in Teacher Education: Partnership, Integration and Funding Implications in McCulloch, M. and Fidler, B. (eds) *Improving Initial Teacher Training? New Roles for Teachers, Schools and Higher Education*, Harlow: Longman.

Fidler, B. (1997a) Organisational Structure and Organisational Effectiveness in Harris, A., Bennett, N. and Preedy, M. (eds) *Organisational Effectiveness and Improvement*, Buckingham: Open University Press.

Fidler, B. (1997b) Addressing the Tensions: Culture and Values in Fidler, B., Russell, S. and Simkins, T. (eds) *Choices for Self-Managing Schools: Autonomy and Accountability*, London: Paul Chapman Publishing.

Fidler, B. and Cooper, R. (eds) (1992) *Staff Management and Staff Appraisal in Schools and Colleges: A Guide to Implementation*, Harlow: Longman.

Fidler, B. with Edwards, M., Evans, B., Mann, P. and Thomas, P. (1996) *Strategic Planning for School Improvement*, London: Pitman.

Fullan, M. (1985) Change processes and strategies at the local level, *Elementary School Journal*, Vol. 85, no. 3, pp. 391–421.

Fullan, M. (1993) *Change Forces: Probing the Depths of Educational Reform*, Lewes: Falmer Press.

Further Education Unit (1982) *Teaching Skills*, FEU, London.

Garrett, B. (1987) *The Learning Organization*, London: Fontana/Collins.

Garrett, V., Aspinwall, K., Cupitt, P., Hall, S., Holland, M. and Munsey, A. (1992) *Managing Staff Development in Schools: an Open Learning Pack*, Sheffield, Sheffield Hallam University School of Education.

Garrett, V. (1996) Principals and headteachers as leading professionals in Ribbins, P. (ed) (forthcoming) *Leaders and Leadership in the School, College and University*, London: Cassell.

Garrett, V. (1997) Managing Change in Davies, B. and Ellison, L. *School Leadership for the 21st Century*, London: Routledge.

Gaunt, D. (1995) Supporting Continuing Professional Development, in H. Bines and J. Welton (eds.) *Managing Partnership in Teacher Training and Development,* London: Routledge.

Gilroy, P. and Day, C. (1993) The erosion of INSET in England and Wales: Analysis and proposals for a redefinition, *Journal of Education for Teaching,* 19 February.

Glatter, R. (1972) *Management Development for the Education Profession,* London: Harrap.

Glatter, R. (1996) Leadership, markets and values: Educational change in context. Paper presented at the BEMAS annual conference, Coventry, September 1996.

Glatter, R. (1996) Context and Capability in Educational Management. Keynote Paper, BEMAS conference.

Glickman, B. D. and Dale, H. C. (1990) *A Scrutiny of Education Support Grants and the Local Education Authority Training Grants Scheme,* London: DES.

Glover, D. and Law, S. (1993) *Changing Partners: Professional development in transition,* Keele University: Keele Professional Development Papers.

Glover, D. and Law, S. (1995) Meeting Needs . . . and Developing Processes, *Management in Education,* Vol. 9, no. 5.

Glover, D. and Law, S. (1996) *The Management of Professional Development in Education: Issues in Policy and Practice,* London: Kogan Page.

Goddard, D. (1989) GRIST: the development of the design in R. McBride (ed.) *The Inservice Training of Teachers,* Falmer, Lewes.

Goode, W. (1960) Encroachment, Charlatanism and the Emerging Professions: Psychology, Sociology and Medicine, in *American Sociological Review, 25,* pp. 902–913.

Graham, J. (1996) The Teacher Training Agency, Continuing Professional Development Policy and the Definition of Competences for Serving Teachers, *British Journal of Inservice Education,* Vol. 22, no. 22, pp. 121–132.

Greenfield, T. (1989) Organisations as social inventions in T. Bush (ed.) *Managing Education: Theory and Practice,* Milton Keynes, Open University Press.

Griffiths, D. (1988) *Leaders for American Schools,* Berkeley, CA: McCutcheon.

Hallinger, J. and McCary, J. (1992) *Developing the Strategic Thinking of Instructional Leaders,* Occasional Papers 13, Harvard Graduate School of Education, Cambridge, Massachussetts.

Hargreaves, A. and Fullan, M. (eds) (1992) *Understanding Teacher Development,* London: Cassell.

Hargreaves, D. (1996) A Cosy World of Trivial Pursuits, *Times Educational Supplement,* 28 June 1996 p. 14.

Hargreaves, D. H. (1996) Teaching as a research-based profession: possibilities and prospects. *Teacher Training Agency annual lecture,* 16 April.

Harland, J. (1987) The new INSET: a transformation scene, *Journal of Education Policy,* Vol. 2, no. 3, pp. 235–244.

Harland, J., Kinder, K., and Keys, W. (1993) *Restructuring INSET: privatisation and its alternatives,* Slough: National Foundation for Educational Research.

Harris, A., Jameson, I.M. and Russ, J. (1995) A study of accelerating departments, *School Organisation,* Vol. 15, no. 3.

HEFCE (1995) Circular 27/95: *Redistribution of HEFCE Funding for Teaching for the Academic Year 1995–6,* Bristol: HEFCE.

Hellawell, D. (1988) OTTO Revisited: Management Training and Management Performance: some perceptions of headteachers and key subordinates, in *Educational Studies,* Vol. 14, no. 2.

Henderson, E.S. (1978) *The Evaluation of In-service Teacher Training,* Croom Helm, Beckenham.

Her Majesty's Chief Inspector (HMCI) (1995) Annual Report 1994/95. London: HMSO.

Hewton, E. (1988), *School-focused Staff Development: Guidelines for Policy Makers*, Lewes: Falmer Press.

Hewton, E. and Jolley, M. (1991) *Making Time for Staff Development: a report for the DES*, Sussex: Institute of Continuing and Professional Education, University of Sussex.

Hickcox, E.S. and House, J. (1991) Educational Administration: Internship Programmes in Canada, in Ribbins, P. *et al.* op. cit.

HMI (1993) *The Management and Provision of Inservice Training funded by the Grant for Education and Support (GEST): A Report from the Office of Her Majesty's Chief Inspector of Schools*, London: OFSTED.

Holmes, G. and Neilson, A. (1988) Headteachers or Managers, Implications for Training, in *Journal of European Industrial Training*, Vol. 12, no. 8.

Houghton, V., McHugh, R. and Morgan, C. (eds) (1975) *Management in Education: The Management of Organizations and Individuals*, London: Ward Locke Educational.

How, W. and Rees, R. (1977). The Bureaucratic Socialisation of Student teachers, in *Journal of Teacher Education*, Vol. 28, no. 1.

Hoyle, E. (1981) The Process of Management, in *Management and the School E323 Block 3* Milton Keynes: Buckingham, Open University Press.

Hughes, M.G. (1975) The innovating school head: autocratic initiator or catalyst of co-operation, *Educational Administration*, Vol. 4, no. 1, pp. 29–41.

Hughes, M.G. (1981) *Professional Development Provision for Staff in Schools and Colleges*, Birmingham: University of Birmingham.

Hughes, M. (1985) Leadership in Professionally Staffed Organisations, in Hughes, M., Ribbins, P. and Thomas, H. (eds) *Managing Education: The System and the Institution*, Eastbourne: Holt, Rinehart and Winston.

Hughes, M., Carter, J. and Fidler, B. (1981) *Professional Development Provision for Senior Staff in Schools and Colleges: A DES-Funded Research Project: The Final Report*, Birmingham: University of Birmingham.

Institute of Management (1995) *C.P.D. The I.M. Guide*, Institute of Management.

Issacs, J. (1992) The Florida Approach to Competenece Based Training for School Managers. Paper given at the British Educational Management and Administration Society Annual Conference, Bristol University.

Jenkins, H.O. (1991) *Getting it right: a Handbook for Successful School Leadership*, Oxford, Basil Blackwell.

Jirasinghe, D. and Lyons, G. (1995) Management Competencies in Action: a practical framework in *School Organisation*, Vol. 13, no. 3, pp. 267–281.

Jirasinghe, D. and Lyons, G. (1996) *The Competent Head*, London: Falmer Press.

Jones, K., O'Sullivan, F. and Reid, K. (1987) The challenge of the New INSET, *Educational Review*, Vol. 39, no. 3, pp. 191–202.

Jones, K., Thomas, P., Thorpe, R., Bolam, R. and Timbrell, T. (eds) (1994) *Secondary Schools Handbook: the induction of newly qualified teachers in Wales*, Cardiff: School of Education, University of Wales.

Joyce, B.R. and Showers, B. (1980) Improving in-service training: the messages of research, *Educational Leadership*, 37, pp. 379–385.

Joyce, B. and Showers, B. (1980) *The Impact of In-service Training: the messages from research 1980*, New York: Longmans.

Joyce, B.R. and Weil, M. (1996) *Models of Teaching* (5th edition), Englewood Cliffs, NJ: Prentice-Hall.

Karstanje, P.N., Bosma, K.Y.G.C., Van de Venne, L.H.J. with Jongmans, C.T. (1993) *Afstemming van nascholingvraag en -aanbod. Deel I: Beginsituatie en verwachte gevolgen*, [Match between CPD demand and supply. Part 1: Starting point and expected outcomes.] (SCO Rapport nr. 357.) Amsterdam: SCO-Kohnstamm Instituut voor Onderzoek van Opvoeding en Onderwijs, Universiteit van Amsterdam. (Research Report Series).

Karstanje, P.N., Bosma, K.Y.G.C., Van de Venne, L.H.J. with Jongmans, C.T.(1995). *Afstemming van nascholingvraag en -aanbod. Deel II*, [Match between CPD demand and supply. Part 2.] (SCO Rapport 400.) Amsterdam: SCO-Kohnstamm Instituut voor Onderzoek van Opvoeding en Onderwijs, Universiteit van Amsterdam. (Research Report Series).

Kemp, R. and Nathan, M. (1989) *Middle Management in Schools: a survival guide*, Oxford: Blackwell.

Kleis Jager, P. (1995a). Nascholingsplan hoort by zelfbewuste school. [A confident school needs a CPD plan.] *Didaktief*, May, p. 7.

Kleis Jager, P. (1995b). De tijd van het incidentele sectie-uitstapje is voorbij. [The time of the day trip has gone.] *Didaktief*, May, pp. 12–13.

Kleis Jager, P. (1995c). In collegiaal netwerk tellen eigen kennis en ervaring. [Collegial networks validate personal knowledge and experience.] *Didaktief*, May, p. 13.

Knoop, M. (1996). CAO-VO rond, *NLG Blad*, 2 March.

Knowles, M. (1980) *The Modern Practice of Adult Education*, Chicago: Follett Publishing.

Kolb, D.A. (1974) Learning and Problem Solving: On Management and the Learning Process in Kolb, D.A., Rubin, I.M. and McIntyre, J.M. (eds) *Organizational Psychology: A Book of Readings* (2nd edn), Englewood Cliffs, NJ: Prentice-Hall.

Law, S. and Glover, D. (1993) *Changing Partners: Professional Development in Transition*, Keele University: Keele Professional Development Papers.

Law, S. and Glover, D. (1995) The Professional Development Business: school evaluations of LEA and higher education INSET provision, *British Journal of Inservice Education*, Vol. 21, no. 2, pp. 181–192.

Lawlor, S. (1990) *Teachers Mistaught: Training in Theories or Education in Subjects?* Policy Study no. 116, Centre for Policy Studies, London.

Lawson, H.A. (1992) Beyond the New Conception of Teacher Induction, *Journal of Teacher Education*, Vol. 43 no. 3.

Leithwood, K.A. (1991) The principal's role in teacher development in Fullan, M. and Hargreaves, A. *Teacher Development and Educational Change*, Philadelphia: Falmer Press.

Leithwood, K.A. and Avery, C. (1987) In-Service Education for Principals in Canada, in Leithwood, K.A. *et al.* op. cit.

Leithwood, K.A., Rutherford, W. and Van Der Vegt, T. (1987) *Preparing School Leaders for Educational Improvement*, London: Croom Helm.

Le Métais, J. (1992) Teachers salaries, in Tomlinson, H. (ed) *Performance-related Pay in Education*, London: Routledge.

Le Métais, J. (1994) *Teachers Salaries in France, Germany and Scotland. A Report for the School Teachers Review Body*, Slough: NFER.

Locke, M. (1992) The application of 'trust' in the management of institutions. Paper given at the *British Educational Management and Administration Society* Annual Conference, Bristol University.

Lomax, P. (1987) The political implications of defining relevant INSET, *European Journal of Teacher Education*, Vol. 10, no. 2.

Lortie, D.C. (1975) *Schoolteacher: A Sociological Study*, Chicago, The University of Chicago Press.

Louis, K.S. (1994) Beyond Managed Change: Rethinking how Schools Improve, *School Effectiveness and School Improvement*, Vol. 5, no. 1, pp. 2–24.

Louis, K.S. and Kruse, S.D. and Associates (1995) Professionalism and Community: Perspectives on Restructuring Schools (mimeo), Minneapolis, MN: Center on Organisation and Restructuring of Schools, University of Minnesota, in Stoll, L. and Fink, D. (1996) *Changing Our Schools*, Buckingham: Open University Press.

Low, G. (1995) The Self Refreshing Teacher, *Education*, July, p. 14–15.

Lyons, G. (1976) *Heads Tasks*, Slough, NFER.

Lyons, G (1993) The development of a Headteachers Assessment Centre, in Busher, H. and Smith, M. (eds) *Managing Educational Institutions: Reviewing Development and Learning Sheffield Papers in Education Management 95* Sheffield, BEMAS/Centre for Education Management, Sheffield Hallam University.

Lyons, G. and Jirasinghe, D. (1992) Headteachers' assessment and development centres in *Educational Change and Development*, Vol. 13, no. 1, pp. 3–5.

Macpherson, R.J.S. (1996) Accountability: Towards Reconstructing a Politically Incorrect Policy Issue, *Educational Management and Administration*, Vol. 24, no. 2, pp. 139–150.

Madden, C. and Mitchell, V. (1993) *Professions, Standards and Competence: A Survey of Continuing Education for the Professions*, Bristol: Department for Continuing Education, University of Bristol.

Maguire, M. and Ball, S.J. (1994) Discourses of Educational Reform in the UK and USA, *British Journal of In Service Education*, Vol. 20, no 1.

Main, A. (1985) *Educational Staff Development*, London: Croom Helm.

Management Charter Initiative (MCI) (1994) *Draft Overview of Senior Management Standards*, London: MCI.

Mann, P. (1995) *Third Survey of LEA Advisory and Inspection Services*, Slough: NFER.

Martin, J. and Meyerson, D. (1988) Organizational Culture and the Denial, Channelling and Acknowledgement of Ambiguity, in L.R. Pondy, R.J. Bolam and H. Thomas (eds.) *Managing Ambiguity and Change*, New York: Wiley.

Maw, J. (1984) Education plc? Headteachers and the New Training Initiative, in *Training for Headship, Bedford Way Papers, Number 20*, University of London Institute of Education.

McCulloch, M. and Fidler, B. (eds) (1994) *Improving Initial Teacher Training*, Harlow: Longman.

McHugh, M. and McMullan, L. (1995) Headteacher or manager? Implications for training and development in *School Organisation*, Vol. 15, no. 1, pp. 23–34, March 1995.

McIntyre, D. (1993) Theory, Theorizing and Reflection, in Calderhead, J. and Gates, P. (eds) *Conceptualizing Reflection of Teacher Development*, London: Falmer Press.

McIntyre, D. (1994) Classrooms as Learning Environments for Beginning Teachers, in Wilkin, M. (ed) *Collaboration and Transition in Initial Teacher Training*, Kogan Page.

McMahon, A. (1994) *Supporting Professional Growth through a Mentoring Programme for New Headteachers.* Paper no. 21, British Educational Management and Administration Society Annual Conference, Manchester.

Ministère De L'education Nationale (1995) *Le Nouveau Contrat pour l'École; 150 décisions*, Paris: Ministère de l'Education Nationale.

Ministerie Van Onderwijs, Cultuur En Wetenschappen (1996a). *Regeling vaststelling nascholing 1995–1996.* [CPD regulations 1995–6.] [OC en W Regelingen] Zoetermeer: OC en W. (Administrative Memorandum).

Ministerie Van Onderwijs, Cultuur En Wetenschappen (1996b). *CAO-BOD Ritzen staat in teken van onderwijskwaliteit.* [Minister Ritzen in support of quality.] Persbericht 71, 15 May. Zoetermeer: OC en W. (Press Release).

Ministerie Van Onderwijs, Cultuur En Wetenschappen (1996c). *Opfrisverlof Onderwijsgevend Personeel 1996* [Refreshment leave for teaching staff.] [Uitleg OC en W Regelingen] Zoetermeer: OC en W. (Administrative Memorandum).

Mintzberg, H. (1979) *The Structuring of Organisations: A Synthesis of the Research*, Englewood Cliffs, NJ: Prentice Hall.

Morant, R.W. (1981) *In-service Education Within the School*, London: Unwin Education.

Morgan, C., Hall, V. and Mackay, H. (1983) *The Selection of Secondary School Head Teachers*, Milton Keynes, Open University Press.

Morgan, G. (1986) *Images of Organisation*, London: Sage.

MORI (1995) *Survey of Continuing Professional Development*, MORI, London.

Morris, G. (1990) Towards the millennium, *Education*, 5 January, pp. 9–10.

Morris, R. (1995) *The TTA on CPD*, Centre for Educational Policy and Management, The Open University, Milton Keynes.

Murphy, J. and Hallinger J. (1992) The Principalship in an era of Transformation, *Journal of Educational Administration*, Vol. 30, no 3.

NASSP (1985) *Performance Based Preparation for Principals: A Framework for Improvement*, Reston, Virginia USA NASSP.

NASSP (1992) *Developing School Leaders: A Call for Preparation*, Reston, Virginia USA NASSP.

National Commission on Education (1993) *Learning to Succeed*, Report of the Paul Hamlyn Foundation, London: Heinemann.

Nias, J. (1989) *Primary Teachers Talking*, London: Routledge.

Nias J., Southworth, G. and Yeomans, R. (1989) *Staff Relationships in the Primary School* London: Cassell.

OFSTED (1993) *Framework for the Inspection of Schools*, London: OFSTED.

OFSTED (1994) *Improving Schools*, London: HMSO.

OFSTED (1995) *Partnership: Schools and Higher Education in Partnership in Secondary Initial Teacher Training*, London: HMSO.

OHMCI (1993) *The New Teacher in School*, London: HMSO.

O'Neill, J. (1994) Managing professional development in Bush, T. and West-Burnham, J. (eds) *The Principles of Education Management*, Harlow: Longman.

O'Sullivan, F., Jones, K. and Reid, K. (1988) *Staff Development in Secondary Schools*, London: Hodder and Stoughton.

Ouston, J., Earley, P. and Fidler, B. (eds) (1996) *OFSTED Inspections: The Early Experience*, London: David Fulton.

Owens, R. (1987) *Organisational Behaviours in Education*, London: Prentice Hall.

Page, B. and Fisher-Jones, L. (1995) *Survey of Continuing Professional Development: Research conducted for the Teacher Training Agency*, London: MORI.

Peters, T. and Waterman, R. (1982) *In Search of Excellence*, London: Harper Row.

Pfeffer, N. and Coote, A. (1991) *Is Quality good for you? A critical review of quality assurance in the welfare services*, London: Institute of Public Policy Research.

Plant, R. (1987) *Managing Change and Making it Stick*, London: Fontana.

Poster, C. (1987) School Management Training in the UK., in Leithwood, A.K. *et al.* op. cit.

Quinn, R., Faerman, S., Thompson, M. and McGrath, M. (1996) *Becoming a Master Manager: a competency framework*, New York: Wiley.

Ribbens, P. Glatter, R., Simkins, T. and Watson, D., (eds) (1991) *Developing Educational Leaders*, London: Longman and BEMAS.

Rogers, G. and Badham, L. (1994) Evaluation in the Management Cycle in Bennett, N., Glatter, R. and Levacic, R. (eds) *Improving Educational Management through Research and consultancy*, London: Paul Chapman.

Santinelli, P. (1985) Surprise ACSET decision provokes anger, *Times Higher Education Supplement*, 8 February, p. 1.

Savary, A. (1982) Letter from Minister Savary to *Recteurs* and *Inspecteurs d'Académie*, La formation continue des personnels, dated 24 May 1982, No 82.215 B.O. of 17 June 1982.

Schein, E. (1991) The Role of the Founder in the Creation of Organisation Culture, in Frost, P.J., Moore, L.F., Louis, M.F., Lundberg, C.C. and Martin, J. (eds) *Reframing Organisational Culture*, Newbury Park: Sage.

Schemp, P.G. and Graber, K.C. (1992) Teacher socialisation from a dialectical perspective: Pretraining through induction, *Journal of Teaching in Physical Education*, 11(4).

Schemp, P.G., Sparkes, A.C. and Templin, T.J. (1993) The Micropolitics of Teacher Induction, *American Educational Research Journal* Vol. 30, no. 3.

Schon, D.A. (1983) *The Reflective Practitioner: How Professionals Think in Action*, London: Maurice Temple Smith.

Schon, D. (1987) *Educating the Reflective Practitioner: How Professionals think in Action*, New York: Basic Books.

Schoor, C. (1995) In basisonderwijs komt nascholingsbeleid voorzichtig van de grond. [CPD developing gently in the primary sector.] *Didaktief*, May, pp. 5–6.

Schroder, H.M. (1989) *Managerial Competence, the Key to Excellence*, Iowa, Kendall/Hunt.

Senge,. P. M. (1990) *The Fifth Discipline: The Art and Practice of the Learning Organisation*, New York: Doubleday.

Shephard G. (1995a) Speech at the Launch of Teacher Training Agency's Corporate Plan, March 1995.

Shephard, G (1995b) The Continuing Professional Development of Teachers. Letter to the Teacher Training Agency, 31 October.

Smith, P. and West-Burnham, J. (ed) (1993) *Mentoring in the Effective School*, Harlow: Longman.

Smith, P. (1995) *Evaluating the Implementation of Appraisal in Oldham Schools*, Manchester Metropolitan University Quality Development Service, Oldham LEA.

Smith, P. (1996) *Evaluating the Implementation of Appraisal in Manchester Schools*, Manchester Metropolitan University Inspection and Advisory Service, Oldham LEA.

Sparks (1993) A Synthesis of Research on Staff Development for Effective Teaching. *Educational Leadership*, November, pp. 65–72.

Stenhouse, L. (1975) *An Introduction to Curriculum Research and Development*, Heinemann, London.

Stewart, V. and Stewart, A. (1983) *Managing the Poor Performer*, Aldershot: Gower Press.

Stoll, L. and Fink, D. (1996) *Changing Our Schools*, Buckingham, Open University Press.

Stout, T. (1989) A Review of Criticisms of Educational Administration: The State of the Art, in J.L. Burdin (ed.) *School Leadership: A Contemporary Reader*, London: Sage Publications.

Swan, D. (1991a) Teachers as Learners. Inservice Education for the 1990s. Proceedings of a Seminar of the Standing Committee of Teacher Unions and University Departments of Education, Dublin.

Swan, D. (1991b) Reorganising in-service education as the key to educational reform and teacher renewal. In: Swan, D. (ed) (1991a).

Taylor, W. (1993) Why Government Should Think Again On Teacher Reform, *THES* 22 October.

Teacher Training Agency (1994) *The Headteacher Leadership and Management Training Programme: Consultation Document*. London: HMSO.

Teacher Training Agency (1995a) *Initial Advice to the Secretary of State on the Continuing Professional Development of Teachers*, London: TTA.

Teacher Training Agency (1995b) *HEADLAMP – Leadership and Management Programme for New Headteachers*, London: TTA.

Teacher Training Agency (1995c) *Headlamp 3/95 TETR J02437ONE Headlamp Programme Document Appendix 2*, London: TTA.

Teacher Training Agency (1995d) *Corporate Plan. Promoting high quality Teaching and Teacher Education*, London: TTA.

Teacher Training Agency (1996a) *Corporate Plan. Promoting Excellence in Teaching*, London: TTA.

Teacher Training Agency (1996b) *Report on National Consultation on the National Professional Qualification for Headship*, July 1996, London: TTA.

Teacher Training Agency (1996c, d, f) *Consultation Paper on the National Professional Qualification for Headteachers*, London: TTA.

Teacher Training Agency (1996e) *Effective Training Through Partnership: Working Papers on Secondary Partnership*, London: TTA.

Teacher Training Agency (1996g) *Report on the outcomes of Consultation. Principles and Options for a New Funding and Student Allocations Methodology for ITT*, London: TTA.

Teacher Training Agency (1996h) *Summary of New funding and Student Allocation Arrangements for 1997/98*, London: TTA.

Teacher Training Agency (1996i) *Review of Headteacher and Teacher Appraisal*, June 1996, London: TTA.

Teacher Training Agency (1996j) *Teachers make a difference*, London: TTA.

Teacher Training Agency (1996k) *Teaching as a Research-Based Profession*, London: TTA.

Thomas, H. (1985) Perspectives in Evaluation in Hughes, M., Ribbins, P. and Thomas, H. (eds) (1986) *Managing Education*, New York: Holt Rinehart Winston.

Thomas, R. (1982) The Training and Certification of Principals and Supervising Officers in Ontario: A perspective for the future, *Review and Evaluation*, Vol. 3, no. 4.

Thompson, M. (1991). Induction: A view from the Teachers Organisations, in *British Journal of In-service Education*. Vol. 17, no. 3.

Times Educational Supplement (1996) Heads back Training Reform, TES 13.9.96.

Times Educational Supplement (1996) Projects funded by the Teacher Training Agency. TES 13.9.96.

Times Higher Education Supplement (1995) Hybrid Ripe for Change, Anthea Millett, THES 1.12.95.

Times Higher Education Supplement (1996) Teaching: Just another Subject? Anthea Millett, THES 5.7.96

Tischer, R.P. (1984) Teacher Induction: an international perspective, in Katz, L.G. and Raths, J.D. (eds) *Advances in Teacher Education*, Vol. 1, Norwood, New Jersey.

Tolley, H., Biddulph, M. and Fisher, T. (1996) *Beginning Teaching Workbook 5: The First Year of Teaching*, Cambridge: Chris Kington Publishing.

Tomlinson, H. and Holmes, G. (1996) CPD in Five Professions, Research report commissioned by TTA.

Tomlinson, J. (1994) Inset and the General Teaching Council, *British Journal of In Service Education*, Vol. 20, no. 1.

Tomlinson, J. (1995) Professional development and control: the role of the General Teaching Councils, *Journal of Education for Teaching*, Vol. 21, no. 1, pp. 59–68.

Tomlinson, P. (1995) *Understanding Mentoring*, Buckingham, Open University Press.

Trafford, J. (1996) *Learning to Teach: Aspects of Initial Teacher Education*, Papers in Education, University of Sheffield. Division of Education.

Trotter, A. (1994) Considering Competence and Competency, paper for MBA Cohort, Leeds Metropolitan University.

TROUW (1996) Betere kwaliteit leraren afdwingen met centraal examen. [Improving teacher quality by means of centralised examinations.], unattributed article in *TROUW*, 21 March, p. 4. (Newspaper article).

Turner, M. (1995) Profiling Induction, *British Journal of In-service Education*, Vol. 21, no. 2.

Van der Mee, G. (1996). Kamervragen en reacties op enquête naar besteding budget, [Parliamentary questions and reactions to the enquiry on budget spending.] *NLG Blad*, 2 March. (Newspaper article).

Van Hoewijk, R. (1993) Integrated Management Development: Does that solve the problem? in Bolam, R. and Van Wieringen, F. (eds), *Educational Management across Europe*, De Lier: Academisch Boeken Centrum.

Van Riessen, M. (1995). Supervisie zou eigenlijk onderdeel van personeelsbeleid moeten zijn. [Peer review should constitute part of staff management.] *Didaktief*, May, p. 11. (Educational Journal article).

Van Riessen, M. and Schoor, C. (1995). Kwaliteitszorg nascholing is zaak van instelling en scholen samen. [Quality assurance of CPD is a joint task for providers and schools.] *Didaktief*, May, pp. 8–10.

Veeneman, S. (1984) Perceived problems with beginning teachers, *Review of Educational Research*, Vol. 54, no. 2.

Waller, W. (1932) *The Sociology of Teaching*, New York: Russell & Russell.

Warnock, M. (1979) *Education: a way ahead*, Oxford: Basil Blackwell.

Warwick, D. (1975) *School-based In-Service Education*, London: Oliver and Boyd.

Watkins, J. and Drury, L. (1994) *Positioning for the Unknown: Career Development for Professionals in the 1990s*, University of Bristol Department of Continuing Education.

Watkins, J., Drury, L. and Bray, S. (1994) *The Future of the UK Professional Associations*, University of Bristol Department of Continuing Education.

Watson, B. and Ashton, E. (1995) *Education, Assumptions and Values*, London: David Fulton.

Webb, G. (1996) *Understanding Staff Development*, Buckingham: SRHE and Open University Press.

White, P. (1982) Democratic perspectives on the training of headteachers, in *Oxford Review of Education*, Vol. 8, no. 1, pp. 69–82.

Whitty, G. and Willmot, E. (1991) Competence-based teacher education: approaches and issues, *Cambridge Journal of Education*, Vol. 21, no. 3, pp. 309–318.

Williams, M. (1991) *In-Service Education and Training*, London: Cassell.

Williams, M. (1993) *The Continuing Professional Development of Teachers. Changing Policies and Practices*, General Teaching Council, London.

Wilkin, M. (1996) *Initial Teacher Training. The Dialogue of Ideology and Culture*, London: Falmer Press.

Wilson, K. and MacIntosh, A. (1991) The Preparation of Educational Administrators: Is a Division of Labour the answer? in Ribbins, P. *et al*. op. cit.

Woodhead, C. (1995) Regarding Headship: a view from OFSTED, Keynote address to the British Educational Management and Administration Society Annual Conference, Oxford.

Young, K. (1983) Introduction: Beyond Centralism, in Young, K. (ed) *National Interests and Local Government*, London: Heinemann.

Zeichner, K. and Gore, J. (1990) Teacher Socialisation, in R. Houston (ed) *Handbook of Research on Teacher Education*, New York: Macmillan.

Index

access, NPQH 115, 117
activities
  CPD, management 169–71
  professional development 166–7
Advisory Committee on the Supply and
  Education of Teachers (ACSET) 3
Advisory Committee on the Supply and
  Training of Teachers (ACSTT) 2–3,
  8
appointments
  contractual changes, NQTs 86–7
  headteachers 112, 114
appraisals
  France 154
  professional development 32
  respect 45–9
architects, CPD 14–16
assessments 104, 113–14, 116
Assuring the quality of partnerships 77
authority, establishing, NQTs 83
Average Units of Council Funding 72

BEMAS 171–2
benchmarks 49–51
beneficiaries, professional development
  166–7
Better schools 3, 54
Blessed Edward Oldcorne, CPD
  programme 101–6

career development 13, 162, 168–9,
  170
centralisation, education system 52–3
classroom situations, NQTs 82
collaboration 40–1, 44–5

competence
  models 94–5, 97f
  movement 123, 143
competences
  headteachers 113–14
  NQTs 49–51
Competences of teaching 49
competency
  assessments 104, 113
  France 154
  middle managers 94–6
  profiles 85
Consortium for Management
  Development 144
consultancies 57–8
continuing professional development
  (CPD)
  Europe 147–60
  five professions 13–26
  government intervention 1–12
  management of 169–71
  resources 174–5
  school leadership 111–12
  school-based programme 101–6
  UK and North America 135–46
  values and ethical issues 40–51
  see also professional development
*Continuing professional development in
  five professions* 13
contractual changes, appointments 86–7
Coopers & Lybrand Report 70–1
Corporate Plan, TTA 68
costs, disparity of, ITT 72
culture
  headteachers 110

organisational, CPD 44–5
professional development 59–60
Rawlins 34–5, 39

delegation, leadership 63–5
diversity
    teachers, Europe 152
    training 69

ecological change, teacher development
    31–2
Education: a framework for expansion 2
education
    management development 171–3
    social context, Europe 147–8
Education Reform Act (1988) 52
Education Support Grants 4
educational policy
    Europe 148
    Netherlands 156–7
Effective training through partnership
    73, 77
engineers, CPD 18–20
enthusiasm 44
ethics, CPD 40–51
Europe, CPD 147–60
expertise, professional 9, 41–2

fairness 43–4
France, CPD 153–6
funding
    INSET changes 1–5
    ITT 70–1, 72–3

general practitioners, CPD 16–18
General Teaching Council (GTC) 11, 142
Grants for Education Support and
    Training (GEST) 5
group development, stages of 99f

HEADLAMP 111, 113
    basis for programme 122–6
    creation 120–2
    early outcomes 131–3
    future 174
    programme development 127–9
    structure of 129–31
headteachers
    HEADLAMP 120–34
    NPQH 108–19

training programmes, Western Europe 142
higher education, changing role of 6–7
Higher Education Funding Council for
    England (HEFCE) 10
higher education institutions, changes in
    56–7
Hughes Report 138

*In-service education and training: some
    considerations* 2–3
*In-service education, training and
    professional development of school
    teachers* 3
induction 167–8
    dimensions of 81–3
    professional development 87–90
    Welsh Office Project 84–7
information trends, management
    development 92
initial teacher training (ITT) 66–78
    Europe 148–50
INSET (in-service education and training)
    changing policy 53–5
    funding 1–5
    partnerships 6–7
Institution of Mechanical Engineers 19
integrity 42–3
Investors in People (IIP) 32, 33–4, 38
isolation, NQTs 82

James Report 2–3

Keele Effective Educators Project (KEEP)
    59–60, 63, 64
knowledge development 28–30
Kolb learning cycle 164–6

Law Society 23–4
leadership 46
    delegated 63–5
    styles 98–100
    teacher development 31–2
    see also National Professional
        Qualification for Headship
learning, professionals 164–6
Local Education Authorities (LEAs)
    advisory services 6
    changes 56
Local Education Authority Training
    Grants Scheme (LEATGS) 3–5

Local Management of Schools (LMS) 4, 6, 111

Making INSET work 3
management
    career development 169
    of CPD 169–71
    defined 96
    development 92–4, 171–3
    education in 173
    preparation for, Europe 152–3
Managing professional teachers 45
Manpower Services Commission 3–4
marketisation 56–8
mentoring 38, 50, 76, 85, 119, 130, 168
middle management 91–107
Modes of Teacher Education (MOTE) 69, 72, 76
MORI survey 7
motivation 30–1

National Development Centre for School Management, Bristol 138–9, 172
National Educational Assessment Centre 95–6
National Professional Qualification for Headship 9, 108–19, 144–5
Netherlands, CPD 156–60
newly qualified teachers (NQTs) 167–8
    competences 49–51
    induction 79–90
North America, CPD 135–46
nurses, CPD 20–2

observation 47–8
OFSTED
    grading of quality 71–2
    inspections 32, 33, 34, 91
One-Term Training Opportunities (OTTO) 111–12, 138
Open University, ITT 70
openness 42
organisations
    culture, CPD 44–5
    excellence in 94

    partnerships 69, 73–7
    HEADLAMP 120–34
    INSET 6–7
performance

competence based standards 123–5
    indicators 49–51
    teachers, Europe 150–2
policy statements
    architects 15–16
    engineers 20
    general practitioners 17–18
    nurses 22
    solicitors 24–5
POST project 112
potential, measuring, headteachers 110–11
Prep Report 20–1
primary schools, NQTs 87
profession, defined 13
professional, defined 27
professional development
    culture 59–60
    defined 162
    induction 87–90
    management of 170
    profiles 85
    role of 27–39
    stages of 166–7
Professional Development Co-ordinators, role of 60–3, 63–4
Professional enrichment for school improvement 129
professionals, learning methods 164–6
profiles, professional development 85
promotion, teachers, Europe 152

quality assurance 70–1, 77
Quinn's competency model 97f

Rawlins Community College, case study 33–9
recruitment
    France 154
    teachers 161–2
relationships, headteachers and governing bodies 115
Report on the outcomes of consultation 70
research
    professional development 29
    Rawlins 35–7
    teaching profession 10–11
resourcing, CPD 174–5
respect
    appraisals 45–9

rigour 49–51
value of 42–4
Review of headteacher and teacher appraisal 45
rigour, appraisals 49–51

sabbaticals, Netherlands 158
School Centred ITT schemes 69
school improvement
  CPD management 170
  success factors 39
School Management Task Force 100, 171–2, 174
schools
  CPD policy 170
  middle management 96–100
  new roles and responsibilities 58–9
  professional development in 28–32, 174
secondary schools, NQTs 87
selection, headteachers 112, 114
self-understanding, teacher development 30–1
skills development 28–30
social trends, management development 92
solicitors, CPD 23–5
staff development 170
  continuous 111
  defined 162
  training programme 126
standards 8–9
  headship training 142
  request for views on 115–17
support networks, NQTs 84–5

teacher development 28–32
  delegating leadership 63–5

Teacher education and training 2
Teacher Training Agency 7–10, 11–12, 52
  HEADLAMP 120, 121, 123
  ITT 66–78
  NPQH 108, 110, 115
teachers *see* headteachers; newly qualified teachers
Teacher's Pay and Conditions Act (1987) 4
teaching
  induction 81–90
  professional development 27–39
  routes into 80–1
  status of 168
  uniqueness of profession 163–4
Ten good schools 108
terminology 162–3
training
  approaches to 28–32
  Blessed Edward Oldcorne, CPD programme 101–6
  diversity, Europe 152
  France 155
  mentoring programmes 76
  senior management, schools 111–12
  UK and North America
    context of 137–9
    goals and content 141–4
    process 139–41
  see also HEADLAMP; initial teacher training
Trotter, competence model 94–5
TVEI Related Training Grants Scheme (TRIST) 3–4

values, CPD 40–51
Welsh Office Project, induction 84–7
workshop learning 29